Self-Conscious Realism
Metafiction and the Nineteenth-Century Russian Novel

LEGENDA

LEGENDA is the Modern Humanities Research Association's book imprint for new research in the Humanities. Founded in 1995 by Malcolm Bowie and others within the University of Oxford, Legenda has always been a collaborative publishing enterprise, directly governed by scholars. The Modern Humanities Research Association (MHRA) joined this collaboration in 1998, became half-owner in 2004, in partnership with Maney Publishing and then Routledge, and has since 2016 been sole owner. Titles range from medieval texts to contemporary cinema and form a widely comparative view of the modern humanities, including works on Arabic, Catalan, English, French, German, Greek, Italian, Portuguese, Russian, Spanish, and Yiddish literature. Editorial boards and committees of more than 60 leading academic specialists work in collaboration with bodies such as the Society for French Studies, the British Comparative Literature Association and the Association of Hispanists of Great Britain & Ireland.

The MHRA encourages and promotes advanced study and research in the field of the modern humanities, especially modern European languages and literature, including English, and also cinema. It aims to break down the barriers between scholars working in different disciplines and to maintain the unity of humanistic scholarship. The Association fulfils this purpose through the publication of journals, bibliographies, monographs, critical editions, and the MHRA Style Guide, and by making grants in support of research. Membership is open to all who work in the Humanities, whether independent or in a University post, and the participation of younger colleagues entering the field is especially welcomed.

ALSO PUBLISHED BY THE ASSOCIATION

Critical Texts
Tudor and Stuart Translations • New Translations • European Translations
MHRA Library of Medieval Welsh Literature

MHRA Bibliographies
Publications of the Modern Humanities Research Association

The Annual Bibliography of English Language & Literature
Austrian Studies
Modern Language Review
Portuguese Studies
The Slavonic and East European Review
Working Papers in the Humanities
The Yearbook of English Studies

www.mhra.org.uk
www.legendabooks.com

EDITORIAL BOARD

Chair: Professor Jonathan Long (University of Durham)
For *Germanic Literatures*: Ritchie Robertson (University of Oxford)
For *Italian Perspectives*: Simon Gilson (University of Warwick)
For *Moving Image*: Emma Wilson (University of Cambridge)
For *Research Monographs in French Studies*:
Diana Knight (University of Nottingham)
For *Selected Essays*: Susan Harrow (University of Bristol)
For *Studies in Comparative Literature*:
Dr Emily Finer, University of St Andrews, and
Professor Wen-chin Ouyang, SOAS, London
For *Studies in Hispanic and Lusophone Cultures*:
Trevor Dadson (Queen Mary University of London)
For *Studies in Yiddish*: Gennady Estraikh (New York University)
For *Transcript*: Matthew Reynolds (University of Oxford)

Managing Editor
Dr Graham Nelson
41 Wellington Square, Oxford OX1 2JF, UK

www.legendabooks.com

Self-Conscious Realism

Metafiction and the Nineteenth-Century Russian Novel

Margarita Vaysman

LEGENDA
Modern Humanities Research Association
2021

Published by Legenda
an imprint of the Modern Humanities Research Association
Salisbury House, Station Road, Cambridge CB1 2LA

ISBN 978-1-78188-383-9 (HB)
ISBN 978-1-78188-386-0 (PB)

First published 2021

All rights reserved. No part of this publication may be reproduced or disseminated or transmitted in any form or by any means, electronic, mechanical, photocopying, recording or otherwise, or stored in any retrieval system, or otherwise used in any manner whatsoever without written permission of the copyright owner, except in accordance with the provisions of the Copyright, Designs and Patents Act 1988, or under the terms of a licence permitting restricted copying issued in the UK by the Copyright Licensing Agency Ltd, Saffron House, 6–10 Kirby Street, London EC1N 8TS, England, or in the USA by the Copyright Clearance Center, 222 Rosewood Drive, Danvers MA 01923. Application for the written permission of the copyright owner to reproduce any part of this publication must be made by email to legenda@mhra.org.uk.

Disclaimer: Statements of fact and opinion contained in this book are those of the author and not of the editors or the Modern Humanities Research Association. The publisher makes no representation, express or implied, in respect of the accuracy of the material in this book and cannot accept any legal responsibility or liability for any errors or omissions that may be made.

Trademark notice: Product or corporate names may be trademarks or registered trademarks, and are used only for identification and explanation without intent to infringe.

© Modern Humanities Research Association 2021

Copy-Editor: Dr Nigel Hope

CONTENTS

	Acknowledgements	ix
	Notes on the Text	xi
	Introduction: Blindspots of a Theory, or the Curious Case of Russian Nineteenth-Century Metafiction	1
1	The Political Self-Conscious: The Russian Novel in the 1860s	19
2	A Matter for Debate	31
3	An Author of a Different Kind	79
4	A Woman's Answer	111
	Conclusion	143
	Bibliography	147
	Index	159

*This book is for my grandfather, Yakov Vaysman,
the most inspiring academic I have ever had a chance to meet.*

ACKNOWLEDGEMENTS

The first work of metafiction that I have read consciously was John Fowles's *The French Lieutenant's Woman* (1969), which had somehow found its way onto my Russian high school reading list. This monograph, and a lot of my work that precedes it, is a result of an early fascination with this peculiar style of prose and a determination to find out what exactly makes texts like Fowles' so uniquely pleasurable to read. And so, my first debt of gratitude is to the inspirational people who taught me about literature's hidden mechanics throughout the years, from evening classes on Victorian literature in Perm to seminars on the Russian novel in Oxford: Andrei Zorin, Andrew Kahn, Anna Arustamova, Philip Bullock, Julie Curtis, Pamela Clemit, Catriona Kelly, Boris Kondakov, Robin Feuer Miller, Rita and Monika Spivak, Galin Tihanov, and Mikhail Odessky.

My family, in Russia and in the UK, have been a constant source of support through the years that it took to transform essays into dissertations, into articles, into books. From parents and grandparents making sure I always had enough money for bread, butter and jam in between sparsely funded academic positions, to countless rounds of proofreading (including this paragraph) undertaken by my long-suffering partner Angus, none of these texts would have been finished without you. Thank you. I am endlessly inspired by my mother's bravery, love and open-mindedness – here is to more adventures together as a clan of two.

My friends, frighteningly talented people within and outside academia, lived with this book for almost as long as I have. Svetlana Shteba, my indefatigable comrade-in-reading-arms and an accidental connoisseur of Pisemskii's novels, is a constant source of encouragement and intellectual curiosity. Vladimir Drozd provided much-needed moral and physical support, celebrating my achievements as if they were his own and making sure I knew there was always a sofa ready for me on my travels. Katia Bowers, Connor Doak, Kirill Zubkov, Rob Daly and Philip Chadwick graciously read through more drafts of these chapters than any copy-editor or reviewer ever would. I will be returning these favours for years to come.

My colleagues at St Andrews have been instrumental in making sure this manuscript ended up on the publisher's desk, first extending an offer to join the Russian department and then patiently reading through book proposals and funding applications. Svetlana Booth, Victoria Donovan, Emily Finer, Jesse Gardiner, Claire Whitehead and Mikhail Vodopyanov, thank you for all your help with this and other projects. I am also grateful to the School of Modern Languages for its generous research leave policy, which allowed me to finish working on this manuscript on sabbatical in 2019.

Finally, many thanks to the hardworking editors at Legenda, and to Maria Erokhina for the beautiful cover of this book.

M.V., February 2021

NOTES ON THE TEXT

The Library of Congress transliteration system is used throughout. Exceptions are made for titles of and quotations from primary and secondary works where the authors themselves use other systems. The names of Russian scholars are cited including abbreviated forms of first names and patronymics unless the authors themselves have omitted them. The names of Russian scholars who have published in English are transliterated in accordance with their preferred forms. Continuing periodicals, such as *N. G. Chernyshevskii: Stat'i, issledovaniia i materialy*, are cited variously as journals or edited volumes, according to how a particular volume was catalogued in Russian GOST bibliographies.

Quotations from Russian-language sources are given in Russian for fiction, and English for non-fiction and correspondence. Orthography has been modernised where necessary. Short quotations from Russian sources, with a length of less than a sentence, are translated into English. All such translations are my own, unless otherwise indicated. Where the original Russian wording is essential for the clarity of the argument, the original Russian is supplied immediately afterwards in square brackets. References are given in footnotes and in accordance with the conventions of the MHRA Style Guide, 2nd edn (London: Modern Humanities Research Association, 2008). Full references are given for the first citation of the work and abbreviated forms are used thereafter.

The following abbreviations are used:

GIKHL	Gosudarstvennoe izdatel'stvo khudozhestvennoi literatury
IRLI RAN	Institut russkoi literatury Rossiiskoi akademii nauk
KGU	Kasakhskii gosudarstvennyi universitet
LGU	Leningradskii gosudarstvennyi universitet
MGU	Moskovskii gosudarstvenyi universitet
OGIZ	Ob''edinenie gosudarstvennykh knizhno-zhurnal'nykh izdatel'stv
RKhGA	Russkaia khristianskaia gumanitarnaia akademiia
RSFSR	Rossiiskaia sovetskaia federativnaia sotsialisticheskaia resbuplika
SPbGU	Sankt-Peterburgskii gosudarstvennyi universitet

All these games, by the intensity of their effects, demonstrate the importance of the boundary they tax their ingenuity to overstep, in defiance of verisimilitude — a boundary that is precisely the narrating (or the performance) itself: a shifting but sacred frontier between two worlds, the world in which one tells, the world of which one tells.

GÉRARD GENETTE, *Narrative Discourse: An Essay in Method*

INTRODUCTION

Blindspots of a Theory, or the Curious Case of Russian Nineteenth-Century Metafiction

> И вот уже трещат морозы
> И серебрятся средь полей...
> (Читатель ждет уж рифмы розы;
> На, вот возьми ее скорей!)¹

> [Already crisp hoar frosts impose
> O'er all a sheet of silvery dust
> (Readers expect the rhyme of rose,
> There! take it quickly, if ye must).]²

When Aleksandr Pushkin teased the readers of his novel in verse, *Evgenii Onegin* [*Eugene Onegin*] (1833), suggesting they supply the missing rhyme in a couplet quoted above ('frost' [морозы] in the Russian original offers a meteorologically unlikely pair to 'rose' [роза]), this was not seen as a revolutionary development of the poetic language. If anything, this passage firmly situated Pushkin's otherwise inventive poetic endeavours in the long tradition of Romantic texts that freely made use of irony to address their readers directly. The passage also demonstrates, without a doubt, that throughout the nineteenth century the Russian reading public encountered acutely self-conscious metaliterary observations in the most popular, and now canonical, texts of the period.

In the history of this passage's interpretation, however, this rhyming *rose* was for a long time given many other names, from a contemporary reviewer's perhaps a touch too evocative 'Sternian wart',³ through 'parody', to Vladimir Nabokov's almost dismissive definition of a Russian example of Pope's 'sure returns of still-expected rhymes'.⁴ Eventually, its 'meta' character was identified by Iurii Lotman, who described this couplet as a 'metatextual reflection on the problems of poetic technique'.⁵

As these definitions testify, it was not so much that this type of playful advance to the reader went unnoticed for centuries. Rather, they show, Sternian warts and all, that there was, until a certain point, no single term to describe something so deeply rooted in the Russian poetic tradition. To use Viktor Shklovskii's words, it has taken more than fifty years of numerous 'merry acts of destruction'⁶ of the critical canon to make the discussion of this curious phenomenon — nineteenth-century Russian metafiction — possible.

Metafiction, also known as self-conscious fiction, is a narrative technique that forces readers to be aware that they are reading a work of fiction. First fully conceptually explored in landmark studies such as Linda Hutcheon's *Narcissistic Narrative: The Metafictional Paradox* (1980) and Patricia Waugh's *Metafiction: The Theory and Practice of Self-Conscious Fiction* (1984), it was initially considered to be an almost exclusively twentieth-century and specifically postmodernist phenomenon. As the theory developed over the last forty years, it expanded the geographical and chronological scope of the texts it aimed to describe, prompting a series of questions about metafiction's hidden pasts and locations.

The chapters that follow focus on the specific time and place — the 1860s in Russia — in metafiction's long history. It is not the intent of this book to offer a comprehensive history of metafiction in Russia; neither is this feasible in an intensely analytical study as this one aims to be. Rather, by close reading and examining critical trends, I explore the persistence of metafictional narrative strategies in nineteenth-century Russian novels, focusing on examples of 'self-conscious realism' from the 1860s — a decade particularly conducive to literary metanarrative. Rightly remembered as a period of intense public debates on the relationship between aesthetics and social change,[7] the 1860s were a time when the ideas of literary and political self-consciousness fused in a way that was uniquely revealing about the state of contemporary culture as a whole. Not entirely coincidentally, Russian literature's most recognised genre, the classic realist novel, came to maturity in the same period. To chart and describe metafiction's complex correlation with the history of the Russian novelistic tradition is the principal aim of this study.

To this end, I begin by considering the role that narrative self-consciousness played in the development of the Russian novel; and devote the rest of my study to a narratological analysis of three literary texts that feature prominent metanarrative strategies: Nikolai Chernyshevskii's *Chto delat'?* [What Is to Be Done?] (1863), Aleksei Pisemskii's *Vzbalamuchennoe more* [Troubled Seas] (1863) and Avdot'ia Panaeva's *Zhenskaia dolia* [A Woman's Lot] (1862). Published within a year of each other and written, respectively, by a famous political radical, an almost forgotten reactionary novelist, and a female writer struggling for professional recognition, these three representative texts showcase various uses of the same narrative strategy — metafiction. I read these novels alongside private and public historical sources (diaries, letters, memoirs and publishing business records, etc.), aiming to prove that the rise of self-conscious elements in nineteenth-century Russian fiction, mainly in the novel, coincided with the rise of ideological self-consciousness in readers and writers.

Undermining the authority of 'grand' historical and social narratives is a functional characteristic of metafiction, and, through questioning the ontological status of literature, politically engaged novelists of the 1860s forced their audience to re-examine its ideological assumptions. In the second half of the nineteenth century, metafiction remained present in Russian fiction even when realism became the dominant literary aesthetic — a time when such narrative practices were rare in the French and English novels. Moreover, I argue that, even though it flourished particularly in this period, self-consciousness is also an inherent trait of the entire Russian novelistic tradition, and can be traced from the earliest examples of the genre in the late eighteenth century to recent postmodernist experiments.

The Rise of Metafiction

Metafiction is a type of self-conscious fiction,[8] defined as 'fictional writing which self-consciously and systematically draws attention to its status as an artifact in order to pose questions about the relationship between fiction and reality'.[9] This type of narrative, often referred to as 'fiction with self-consciousness, self-awareness, self-knowledge [or] ironic self-distance',[10] has long been present in the Russian literary tradition. Even a cursory knowledge of nineteenth-century Russian literature is enough to enable a reader to spot instances of highly self-conscious narration in Pushkin, Lermontov, Gogol', Dostoevskii and Tolstoi,[11] among others.

And yet, for reasons accounted for in this study, remarkably few theoretical studies of metafiction examine this phenomenon in the context of the Russian literary tradition, even though the general theory of metanarrative has developed rapidly in the last fifty years. From early critical approaches to metanarrative in literature to more recent enquiries into meta-descriptive strategies in historiography, metafiction has enjoyed significant critical attention. The term has been enthusiastically adopted in various fields, such as history, philosophy, linguistics, psychology, film and digital culture studies, and by disciplines as diverse as semiotics, poetics, narratology, studies of ideology and rhetoric, and genre theory.[12] Following the publication and enthusiastic reception of the landmark studies in the 1980–90s, slowly but surely there emerged a single vocabulary to describe the research methods and findings across these varied fields — and yet, with few exceptions, it bypassed the Russian novel as one of the forms in which metanarrative was present in nineteenth-century fiction.

The initial surge of interest in metapractices in the 1970s and 1980s was conditioned by developments in both literary fiction and critical theory. Self-consciousness, though found in fictional narratives of every historical period, became a characteristic feature of early twentieth-century modernist literature. Later, it turned into an almost obligatory component of late twentieth-century postmodernist narratives, manifesting their own ironic awareness of their inescapable cultural and literary context. Naturally, an analytical apparatus needed to be developed to deal with these complex narrative issues. Considering how intertwined the notions of literary practice and literary criticism are in metafiction, it is not surprising that the term itself is generally thought to have been coined by American writer William H. Gass in the late 1960s.[13] Soon afterwards, in a series of essays, John Barth, also a writer, discussed the problem of metafiction as a critical and theoretical construct.[14] The idea was then taken up by critics and historians of literature, who were interested in the broader implications of the technique. A general understanding was eventually reached within the field: any narrative explicitly conscious of its own ontological status can be considered metafictional.

Considering the trajectory of general critical theory in the post-war period, this 1970s–1980s focus on metafiction could be seen as almost inevitable. It followed, first, Roman Jakobson's application of Saussurean linguistics to literary analysis, then Roland Barthes's preoccupation with linguistic self-consciousness and, ultimately, Jacques Derrida's ideas on metalanguage and Paul de Man's deconstruction of rhetorical reflexivity.[15] In other words, as Patricia Waugh pointed out, the occurrence of such terms as 'metapolitics, metarhetoric and metatheatre' was 'a reminder of what has been, since the 1960s, a more general cultural interest in the problem of how human beings reflect, construct and mediate their experience of the world'.[16] Critics single out different reasons for the rise of this interest, from its socio-economic and historical context to the crisis of realism and the crisis of the novel. Nonetheless, most agree that the problematisation of language, represented by the concept of metalinguistics and the ideas of analytical philosophy, lies at the core of the modernist interest in and the postmodernist obsession with metafiction.[17]

Another point of consensus in the gradually developed understanding of metafiction is that it is by no means a recent phenomenon. One must therefore be wary of historicising the development of metafiction solely in the context of the twentieth century and its intellectual achievements. Rather, we should assume that metafiction as *practice* existed for as long as fictional narratives themselves, but that it was only in the second half of the twentieth century that a *theory* of it could avail itself of the terminology developed in the philosophy of language and in linguistics. Theorists were finally able to describe in conceptual terms the narrative strategies that have always stood out as playful and subversive; an applied methodology was also formulated. The surge of interest in and widespread use of meta-analysis over the last forty years thus represented both the development and the culmination of a long tradition of self-consciousness in literature and criticism. Of course, Pushkin's readers have always been able to make sense of his playful 'rose rhyme', but, before the 1970s, theorists, both in Russia and abroad, lacked a unified methodological apparatus with which to describe and analyse it.

Over the years, as the study of metafiction matured as a field, its scope widened, both conceptually (critics have identified types of feminist, Black, moral, ethical, historiographical, etc., metafiction) and geographically. Recently, the theory has been applied to a wide variety of literatures outside the Anglo-American canon and has made a significant contribution to the literary criticism of various national traditions and to comparative literary studies. Tracing metafiction back to ancient Chinese manuscripts[18] and early Greek and Roman texts,[19] these studies demonstrate that it is also not unique to Western literary culture. In a way, it is as old as literary fiction itself.

Since the theory of metafiction was developed largely by Anglo-American critics, it is easy to see how a popular view of metafiction as a mode of narration practised mostly in mid- or late twentieth-century literature, primarily written in English, has come into being. The major theoretical studies of metafiction tended to limit their corpus of texts to a small selection of American and British writers: John Barth, William H. Gass, Saul Bellow, Donald Barthelme, Vladimir Nabokov, Kurt Vonnegut, John Fowles, Martin Amis, Malcolm Bradbury, Anthony Burgess, and Iris Murdoch, with an occasional foray into French (nouveau roman and anti-novel) and Latin American fiction, mostly Jorge Luis Borges and Julio Cortázar.[20]

In the majority of early studies, far more British and American novels were examined as examples of metafiction than Latin American and European novels.

With the exception of Günter Grass and Vladimir Nabokov's Russian novels, very few other German or Russian writers were mentioned (even though Russian literary theory almost always gets an honorary citation).[21] Even historical accounts of the development of metafiction — which are, by their very nature, broader in their geographical and historical scope — tended to draw on the same rather limited pool of authors: Laurence Sterne, Cervantes, Diderot, André Gide, and Samuel Beckett.[22] Considering the often privileged position assigned to Russian nineteenth-century writers in comparative studies of the history of the novel, I have found this oversight extremely intriguing — and worth a separate investigation.

Russian Novels and the Debate on the Nineteenth-Century Metafiction

Slavic studies integrated the theory of metafiction in the 1990s, when trail-blazing investigations by David Shepherd, Mark Lipovetskii, Nina Kolesnikoff, and others adapted Linda Hutcheon's and Patricia Waugh's methodology to the study of the poetics of twentieth-century literature in Russia and the Soviet Union.[23] This both chronologically and methodologically specific focus was so insistent during the early period of Russian metafiction studies that the two iconoclastic exceptions from the general rule deserve to be specially mentioned here.

Dmitrii M. Segal's 1981 articles 'Literatura kak okhrannaia gramota' [Literature as a laissez-passer] and 'Literatura kak vtorichnaia modeliruiushchaia sistema' [Literature as a secondary modelling system] emerged as products of an important scholarly approach to metafiction that originated in Russia.[24] Instead of using the term 'metafiction', Segal talked about 'metapoetics' [metapoetika] as a characteristic feature of modernist Russian texts by Konstantin Vaginov, Osip Mandel'shtam, Vasilii Rozanov, Vladimir Nabokov, Mikhail Bulgakov, Boris Pasternak and Anna Akhmatova. Even though Segal saw literary self-consciousness [samosoznanie literatury] as an inherent characteristic of Russian literature in general, he considered it 'a reaction on the part of literature towards an outside intrusion, a response to the removal of the realist tradition'[25] at the beginning of the twentieth century. Even though such texts as Pushkin's *Evgenii Onegin* (1833), Gogol''s *Mertvye dushi* [Dead Souls] (1842) and, later, Dostoevskii's *Dnevnik pisatelia* [Diary of a Writer] (1873–81) were obviously metafictional, according to Segal, this quality was nevertheless not manifested strongly enough to challenge the traditional perception of Russian classical texts as 'primary modelling systems' (i.e. unmediated models of reality). Segal explored the possibility of this 'secondary modelling' as a uniquely modernist phenomenon, thus firmly situating the concept of Russian metapoetics in the twentieth century. To this day, Segal's study remains an exceptional example of an original approach to Russian metafiction that relies on its own methodological apparatus.[26]

Another striking exception was Michael C. Finke's 1995 study *Metapoesis: The Russian Tradition from Pushkin to Chekhov*. Finke used Jakobson's theory of metalanguage as an overarching theoretical framework to describe what he called a 'metapoetic' Russian literary tradition. Finke charted this 'Russian tradition' from

Pushkin's poetry, through Gogol''s plays, to the prose of Tolstoi, Dostoevskii and Chekhov. Finke's selection of texts, including Chernyshevskii's novel that I will discuss in one of this book's chapters, was tailored to 'suggest that with the rise of realism the metapoetic tradition becomes esoteric, goes underground'.[27] Providing an overview of 'metapoetic' techniques in the nineteenth-century, Finke shared the established theoretical assumption that realism, in Russia or elsewhere, was incompatible with metafiction. My own focus on the Russian realist novel offers an approach to the Russian meta-tradition that contradicts but also expands Finke's model, introducing the issue of Russian realism's metafictional potential to this already complex theoretical equation.

After the collapse in the 1990s of the aesthetic hierarchy of Soviet literary studies that took the primacy of realism for granted, investigations of this literary phenomenon sank to the very bottom of the list of urgent scholarly concerns. However, once the yoke of Marxist-Leninist interpretations had been lifted from the readings of the 'Tolstoyevskii' stalwarts of the realist canon, a new wave of scholarship emerged both in Russia and abroad. Building on the existing non-Soviet readings of nineteenth-century Russian novels, it aims to make use of the most recent advances in the transnational theories of realism to re-evaluate its manifestations in Russia. From interdisciplinary studies such as Molly Brunson's *Russian Realisms: Literature and Painting, 1840–1890* (2016) to Katherine Bowers's, Ani Kokobobo's and Alexei Vdovin's, Kirill Zubkov's and Andrei Fedotov's edited volumes on the 'realisms' of the 1850s and the *fin de siècle* published in 2015, these investigations have highlighted the need to include the Russian examples in the more general, transnational theoretical frameworks of realism.[28] In this study, I am guided by the spirit of this recent reappraisal and aim to contribute to it by introducing the theory of metafiction to this ongoing discussion.

If Finke's study broached the subject of self-conscious narration in nineteenth-century Russian prose, drama and verse, my aim is to focus specifically on the practice of metafiction in the nineteenth-century Russian novel. Considering the doubly 'incriminating circumstances' of, first, the novel's precedence as the most common genre of metafictional writing, and, second, recent scholarly interest in early metafiction, it might be interesting to explore, at this juncture, why it has, so far, escaped sustained scrutiny. It would be easy to explain this omission as natural for a theory devised to deal with modernist and postmodernist texts, and yet I would argue that there is a more serious methodological issue at stake here.

In her foundational theoretical study of metafiction, Patricia Waugh discusses what she defines as a significant difference in how metafiction works in a nineteenth- and a twentieth-century English novel. Noting that 'metafiction is a tendency or function inherent in all novels', she argues that that there is an 'intuitive sense that although Fielding, Trollope and George Eliot, for example, often "break the frame" of their novels they are by no means self-conscious novelists'.[29] Waugh compares narrative techniques used in George Eliot's *Adam Bede* (1859) and in John Fowles's *The French Lieutenant's Woman* (1969) and maintains that in the nineteenth century, metalinguistic commentary in novels reaffirmed the ontological statuses of the narrator and the reader, reinforcing the mimetic illusion. In a functioning metafiction, on the contrary, the illusion should be broken by the narrator's intrusion, drawing the reader's attention to the need to suspend disbelief. If, in Eliot, introducing the figure of the self-conscious narrator barely manages to break the frame of mimetic narration, in Fowles, 'it is not just the mimetic function of the traditional novel that is attacked [...] in metafiction, it is the language of the realistic novel which has sustained and endorsed such a view of reality'.[30]

Robert Alter makes a similar argument in his *Partial Magic: The Novel as a Self-Conscious Genre* (1975), where he maintains that in nineteenth-century novels self-conscious narrative techniques were sidelined by more frequent mimetic representations of reality. The nineteenth-century European novel, in Alter's view, was characterised by 'fits and starts' of self-consciousness since around the 1830s when realism became 'the central impulse of the novel'; as a result, in these novels the detailed documentation of historical change became more urgent than the exploration of the medium through which these changes were recorded. Thus, Alter discards any instances of self-consciousness in nineteenth-century novels (for example, in Thackeray's *Vanity Fair* (1847–48) or Melville's *Confidence Man* (1857)) as 'discontinuous, incomplete'.[31]

Considered alongside metafiction's acknowledged long lineage that reaches, for the novel, at least as far back as Cervantes's *Don Quixote* (1605) and Laurence Sterne's *The Life and Opinions of Tristram Shandy, Gentleman* (1759),[32] this argument exposes a revealing presupposition shared by the early theorists of metafiction. Essentially, both Waugh and Alter maintain that the strong mimetic impulse of the nineteenth-century realist novel undermined narrative self-consciousness to such a degree that it had all but disappeared during that period. My own study works both with and against this presupposition, using it as a starting point for a discussion of the place of the Russian realist novel in the theory and history of metafiction. In this book, I seek to correct the — admittedly, often contradictory — existing historical accounts of metafiction as a literary phenomenon that skim over the nineteenth-century Russian novel. Considering the important role that the Russian realist novel played in the transnational history of the genre, I argue that its continuous omission from this type of theoretical models misrepresents European realism in general and misinterprets Russian realism specifically. One of the aims of this book is to explore the surprising consequence of the popularity of this genre outside of Russia — a gap between what a Russian realist novel is considered to be and what it actually was, a phenomenon that I call an 'invented tradition of the Russian realist novel'.

An Invented Tradition of the Russian Realist Novel

The knock-on effects of the way the theory of metafiction had recast the history of European realism had been felt across the studies of various literary traditions. In my exploration of the metafictional potential of the Russian realist novel, I am guided by Ann Jefferson's approach to a similar issue in her study *Reading Realism in Stendhal* (1988). An assumption that the nineteenth-century realist novel was incompatible with narrative self-consciousness, implicit in the foundational theories of metafiction, methodologically leads to a clear binary opposition: a novel can be either metafictional or realist.

Jefferson suggests that the dichotomy of realistic/metafictional has not only been artificially imposed by twentieth-century literary theorists, but has also been counterproductive in terms of its implications for the study of realism. Stendhal, as Jefferson maintains, was 'as metafictional and as self-conscious a writer as any twentieth-century novelist', but his aesthetic aim, nonetheless, was to reproduce reality as faithfully as possible. His focus on the reader as an object of emotional manipulation through mimesis ('reading for effect') and at the same time his preoccupation with reality 'in its representational form' proves that 'realism is not incompatible with literary self-consciousness, and that mimesis is a vital counterpart to metafiction'.[33] Jefferson's counterargument primarily concerns Stendhal, but it sheds light on the general assumptions that metafictional literary criticism makes about nineteenth-century literature.

Jefferson's well-argued understanding of realism as a 'more self-conscious and sophisticated phenomenon than it has hitherto been conceived as being'[34] is one I have adopted in my own study. Russian realism tends to be defined even more narrowly than its European counterparts, since, for the best part of the twentieth century, the basic assumption of Soviet and much Marxist literary criticism was that realism is the ultimate aesthetic goal of the literary process. It was therefore as easy to find 'certain features' of realism in the work of 'pre-realist writers such as Pushkin [and] Gogol'"[35] as it was to overlook the metafictional elements in texts by the same authors. The existence of a self-conscious literary tradition in Russia hardly needs to be argued. But, for many years, Soviet critics' insistence on the importance of realism[36] hindered the development of a theoretical approach to the tradition in Russia, whereas, in Slavic studies in the West, it was the reputation of nineteenth-century Russian novels as the ultimate realist fiction that stood in its way.

Indeed, the Russian literary tradition, especially that of the second half of the nineteenth century, is perceived as a string of realist masterpieces. From Henry James's definition of the 'large, loose, baggy monsters'[37] to the generally accepted view of Tolstoi's influence on the novelistic genre, Russian literature is most lauded for its realist novels. This trend is understandable: there is nothing more compelling than a well-crafted mimetic narrative that completely immerses the reader in the events is describes. It takes a degree of literary sophistication, though, to notice the different kinds of realist narrative techniques practised in the period. For example, Lidiia Ginzburg pointed out a qualitative connection between Tolstoi's psychological introspection and self-referential representation of 'pure psychological processes' in the French *nouveau roman* of the 1950s–1960s.[38] In Tolstoi, running authorial commentary and shifts in narrative focalisation should, in theory, compromise the idea of narrative verisimilitude. And yet, his texts are exemplarily mimetic.[39]

In fact, Russian realism has always followed a path of its own. As a literary movement, Realism reached Russia later than Germany and England, approximately twenty years after it had originated in France in the 1830s. It was, arguably, all the more intensive for having arrived late.[40] The difference between 'the use of the term "realism" in reporting French developments and the adoption of the term as a slogan for a local school of realistic writing'[41] was more prominent in Russia than anywhere else. Vissarion Belinskii's conceptualisation of Russian realist trends as the 'naturalist' and, later, 'Gogolian' school of writing was illuminating in this respect. Gogol', hailed by Belinskii as a 'poet of reality' and the 'absolute truth of life',[42] was a good example of the gap between the general contemporary understanding of realism and what Russian critics of the period took it to be. Extremely self-conscious, often relying on the ultimate metafictional device of parody,[43] Gogol' was also, according to Belinskii, a realist, but a Russian one. It is precisely this specific understanding of realism in Russia that explains why self-consciousness did not go into eclipse in nineteenth-century Russian literature: Russian realism did not insist on abandoning self-consciousness. If anything, it promoted it.

Belinskii's idea of realism, which adapted the critical apparatus of German aesthetics to the contemporary Russian literary process, showcased, among other things, a tendency in Russian realism, more prominent than in its Western counterparts, to rely on the narrative legacy of Romanticism, particularly — and this is of specific interest to the argument made here — on Romantic irony. Certain 'Romantic' qualities of Russian realism have long been noted, and Donald Fanger's argument about the 'Romantic realism' of Gogol' and Dostoevskii was based on the assumption that 'a whole stage in [the novel's] nineteenth-century development, which up to now has been uneasily called romanticism or realism, is really marked by a fusion of the two'.[44] Due to this overlap, Realism and Romanticism had multiple points of convergence in the Russian prose of the period. Even though the start and end dates of literary movements are never as chronologically precise as the histories of literature would have us believe, in nineteenth-century Russia, the contemporary literary canon included a surprisingly wide array of texts from different literary epochs. In *Evgenii Onegin* (1823–31), an encyclopaedia of educated Russians' literary tastes, Tat'iana reads the English sentimental novels of her mother's youth, whereas Lenskii prefers German Romantic poetry and Onegin favours Byronic poetry and French prose. Lermontov's Pechorin, in his turn, is under the spell of late Byronism of the 1830s and 1840s, just as *Geroi nashego vremeni* [A Hero of Our Time] (1838–40) is a product of Lermontov's fascination with the prose of Alfred de Musset and Benjamin Constant.[45]

By the 1840s, Russian writers were fully immersed in post-Romantic literary endeavours, such as the further development of psychological prose. Simultaneously, a different type of realist narrative was gaining momentum, also aiming to reach the heights of realistic representation by different means and with a different motivation. The French naturalist school of writing, inspired by the use of photography and the descriptive narratives of the nascent social sciences such as anthropology and experimental psychology, was becoming more and more influential in Russia. Journalistic and literary pieces were presented to the public side by side through the all-encompassing medium of 'thick journals', blurring the line between fact and fiction and popularising examples of the truthful representation of contemporary reality, written 'dispassionately, impersonally, objectively'.[46]

The basic paradox of realist writing in general — the attempt to depict reality faithfully through a process that itself transforms it — brings about a heightened self-reflexivity in its practitioners. If Romantic narratives were concerned about the emotional effect they were producing on their readers, realist narratives often made reference to their own ontological status, the degree of verisimilitude achieved and the relative similarity of the story to a reader's own circumstances. I would like to offer here a contention that in Russia this heightened literary self-consciousness reached its peak in the 1860s, when literature, alongside other forms of public debate, became a forum for discussing political and social issues. The chapters that follow offer three case studies of intensely metafictional nineteenth-century novels, which nonetheless play by the rules of literary realism as it was understood in Russia in the 1860s — a particular time in the history of both realism and metafiction, when the convergence of these two phenomena on the Russian literary scene produced fascinating examples of narrative self-consciousness.

The structure of this book reflects this focus on a particular decade in the history of nineteenth-century Russian metafiction. In chapter 1, I focus on the period of the 1860s as especially important in the history of Russian nineteenth-century metafiction. Adapting the Horatian ideal of the Poet Citizen to the contemporary political situation, Russian novelists followed the battle cry of the leading literary critics of the era, who demanded that literature should have a clear, practical purpose. Vissarion Belinskii's ideas of realism as a 'poetry of reality' gave way to Dmitrii Pisarev's demand for literature to perform 'feats of denunciation'. How did this focus on literature's direct effect on society fit into the contemporary debates on aesthetics? How did it square with Russian realism's avowed distrust for didactics? And how did metafictional texts fit in with the popular naturalistic sketches of peasant life and urban poverty?

Chapter 2 examines the fluid boundaries of reality as represented in Nikolai Chernyshevskii's novel *Chto delat'?* (1863). Chernyshevskii, the critic and editor responsible for the formation of the new radical editorial board of the literary journal *Sovremennik* [Contemporary] in the late 1850s, wrote his novel while imprisoned in the Peter and Paul Fortress. Chernyshevskii's philosophical concern with the ontology of literary fiction directed his choice of metafiction as the main narrative mode of the novel. Generations of Russian scholars have debated whether the novel was based on true events, or if Chernyshevskii was painting a utopian picture of the future. Building on this rich critical heritage, this chapter redirects this by now habitual vector of enquiry, arguing that precisely this unresolved ontological ambiguity was essential for expressing Chernyshevskii's political and aesthetic argument.

In the third chapter, I investigate Alexei Pisemskii's theory of meta-realism, an important but under-studied contribution to the polemic around aesthetic principles of literary realism in the 1860s. A master of detailed, almost forensic, descriptions, Pisemskii won his place in the Russian literary canon because of his naturalist sketches of contemporary life. And yet, in 1863, he published a novel in which the polemic thrust of an anti-nihilist argument was interspersed with reflections on the nature of fiction and even featured a narrator entering his own story and conversing with his fictional characters. What does its publication in 1863 say about the realist fiction of the period? And, perhaps more importantly, how does the novel's almost complete disappearance from the modern Russian canon reflect our commonly held assumptions about what the Russian realist novel should and should not do?

Chapter 4 explores the issue of narrative transvestism in Avdot'ia Panaeva's metafictional novel *Zhenskaia dolia* (1862), which had first appeared in *Sovremennik* under her usual pen-name 'N. Stanitskii'. Constrained by the social conventions that did not encourage women's participation in public debates, Panaeva put forward her thoughts on female emancipation, the power of imaginative literature, and the privileged point of view of traditional realist narratives, in a series of meta-observations. Through these observations, Panaeva revealed to her readers a common but usually concealed literary mechanism by which authentic first-hand accounts of female suffering were legitimised by providing a male perspective on the issue. How did the novel's transgressive narrative voice relate a story composed by a woman but narrated by a man? How did it negotiate the literary and political status of a text at odds with the masculine aesthetics of Russian realism at that time?

The lowest bar for considering a literary text metafictional is the presence in the text of narrative self-reflection, i.e. an articulated awareness of the ontological difference between the events narrated in the text and the reality in which the reader empirically finds herself. This awareness is often expressed through directly initiated communication with 'the reader' as the narrator's rhetorical addressee and a 'receiver' of the text's overall message as described in Jakobson's model of literary communication.[47]

In its most obvious instance, the meta-nature of the literary text becomes apparent in the act of narrative metalepsis, when one or more rhetorical entities of the text cross ontological levels within it. In narratology, metalepsis is 'any intrusion by an extradiegetic narrator or narratee into the diegetic universe (or by diegetic characters into a metadiegetic universe, etc.)'.[48] Alongside these extreme cases of ontological transgression, there exist a number of less obvious self-conscious narrative strategies (or, to use Gerald Pierce's term, 'metanarrative signs') that, if employed consistently, reinforce the reader's engagement with a literary text and shape its reception in singular, specific ways. A failure to acknowledge the particular effect the use of these techniques has on the text's reception, functioning, afterlife and reputation distorts our understanding of its history and promotes misinterpretations. Aiming to compensate for this omission in the previous scholarship, my narratological analysis of the three novels focuses on their explicitly metafictional passages. I single out instances of major and minor narrative metalepses, including not only overt but also implicit ontological frame-breaks like the conventional asides addressed to the implied reader.

In terms of categorising the rhetorical entities of the text such as 'author', 'reader' and 'narrator', I am relying on the modern updated version of Wayne Booth's and Wolfgang Iser's typologies of the 'implied reader' and the 'implied author' as revised by Gerald Prince, Wolf Schmid and Shlomith Rimmon-Kenan.[49] Most importantly,

I follow contemporary scholars in distinguishing between the 'implied' reader, the 'ideal reader' and 'narratee'.

The 'implied reader', or 'intended reader', who

> is not fixed in the text but exists merely in the imagination of the author and who can be reconstructed only with the latter's statements or extra-textual information, does not form a part of the work. Such a reader belongs exclusively to the sphere of the real author, in whose imagination he or she exists.[50]

The 'ideal' or 'model reader' is an implied reader who is ideally suited to receiving the author's message and interpreting it correctly. Both implied and model readers exist on the same ontological level as the implied author.

Narratee, on the other hand, 'is the agent addressed by the narrator', and 'is, by definition, situated the same narrative level as the narrator'.[51] This distinction allows me to conceptualise and analyse the constitutive difference between, for example, Chernyshevskii's intended readers (the censors), model readers (the subscribers to the journal in which the novel was published) and narratees ('the perspicacious reader', 'the good public', 'the female reader') or Panaeva's implied readers (again, the journal's audience), ideal readers (the proponents of women's rights, aware of her identity as a woman) and narratees ('the poor women, 'the young men', etc.).

Similarly, in all the three close readings, I distinguish between 'biographical authors' of the texts (the actual historical figures Nikolai Chernyshevskii, Aleksei Pisemskii and Avdot'ia Panaeva), the 'implied authors', and the narrators of the three novels. The narrators share their creators' biographies to varying degrees: Chernyshevskii's narrator is an unnamed amalgam of his past (published), current (incarcerated) and future (liberated) selves, whereas the narrator in *Vzbalamuchennoe more* is explicitly referred to as 'Pisemskii the realist writer'.[52] Avdot'ia Panaeva's relation to her explicitly male narrator is the most complex of the three, and implies a challenge of the prescriptive contemporary discourses of femininity. In order to analyse this challenge from the point of view of narratology, I rely on the concept of 'narrative transvestism' developed by Madeleine Kahn.[53]

Despite being closely related to their real-life counterparts, the 'implied authors' of the three texts are nonetheless ontologically distinct. As a stable, consistent entity, the implied author of the text is a construct inferred and assembled by the reader.[54] The gap between the reality of the author's situation and the reader's perception of it is particularly obvious in the example of Chernyshevskii and Panaeva. Whereas it has been suggested that the real-life author of *Chto delat'?* had no meaningful connections to established underground revolutionary movements,[55] the implied author of the novel is presented as someone whose help is vital for the young revolutionaries like his character Rakhmetov.[56] In the case of Avdot'ia Panaeva, the implied author of her novel is 'Nikolai Stanitskii', her carefully constructed male-writer persona that she had maintained since her first publications in the early 1850s.

Finally, I use the idea of narrative levels to describe the changing positions of the narrator in each of the three texts, as well as to define their role in the functioning of narrative metalepses. For the purposes of my analysis, I adopt Gérard Genette's definition of 'narrative metalepsis' (noted above) as 'the transition from one narrative level to another'.[57] The 'extradiegetic' narrator occupies the highest (diegetic) level of narrative and does not take part in any of the narrated events. An 'intradiegetic' narrator occupies the next level in the hierarchy (hypodiegetic level) and naturally features in the overall story. The narrator who oscillates between different levels of the narrative is defined as 'metadiegetic'. The extent to which extra-, intra- and metadiegetic 'narrators are absent or present in the story they narrate'[58] also varies. The 'heterodiegetic' narrator does not participate in the story, whereas the 'homodiegetic' narrator can turn into a character of his own story.[59] These characteristics of Chernyshevskii's, Pisemskii's and Panaeva's narrators are discussed in detail, as is the degree of their narrators' perceptibility and reliability.

On the one hand, as David Shepherd noted, 'little, if anything, is to be gained by supplementing the bibliographies of Waugh, Hutcheon, and others with Russian and Soviet titles simply to prove that in this, as in other areas, Russian and Soviet literature, despite its many historical handicaps, has not fallen too far behind global trends'.[60] On the other hand, the inherent self-consciousness of the Russian novelistic tradition remains largely unexamined. The texts that comprise it are, therefore, excluded from the general accounts — an essential consideration and, ultimately, a reason for the use of the analytic apparatus, developed by the theory of metafiction, in this book.

Notes to the Introduction

1. A. S. Pushkin, *Polnoe sobranie sochinenii*, 10 vols (Moscow and Leningrad: Izdatel'stvo Akademii nauk SSSR, 1949), v: *Evgenii Onegin. Dramaticheskie proizvedeniia*, p. 93.
2. A. S. Pushkin, *Eugene Onéguine: A Romance of Russian Life in Verse*, trans. by Henry Spalding (London: Macmillan, 1881), p. 118. Although considered 'crude' by Pushkin scholars, Lt. Col. Henry Spalding's 1881 version of this stanza does the best job of transposing Pushkin's playful rhyme into English, which is why I have chosen it here. For an authoritative overview of translations of various texts by Pushkin and specifically on Spalding, see Lauren C. Leighton, 'Pushkin and Problems of Translation', in *The Pushkin Handbook*, ed. by David M. Bethea (Madison: University of Wisconsin Press, 2005), pp. 334–51.
3. Iu. N. Tynianov, 'O kompozitsii "Evgeniia Onegina"', in *Poetika, istoriia literatury, kino* (Moscow: Nauka, 1977), pp. 52–78 (p. 68). Without acknowledging the source, Tynianov here refers to a contemporary anonymous review of *Evgenii Onegin* that mentioned its 'Sternian warts': 'наросты к рассказу, по примеру блаженной памяти Стерна'. Anonymous, 'Evgenii Onegin. Roman v stikhakh. Soch. Aleksandra Pushkina', *Atenei*, 2 (1828), 76–89 (p. 80).
4. Vladimir Nabokov, 'Commentary to *Eugene Onegin*', in *Eugene Onegin: A Novel in Verse*, trans. and comm. by Vladimir Nabokov, 4 vols (New York: Bollingen Foundation, 1964), II: *Commentary on Preliminaries and Chapters One to Five*, pp. 470–71.
5. 'некоторый метатекст, трактующий вопросы поэтической техники.' Iu. M. Lotman, *Roman A. S. Pushkina "Evgenii Onegin": Kommentarii. Posobie dlia uchitelia* (Leningrad: Prosveshenie, 1983), pp. 250–51. Both Lotman and Nabokov consider these lines a direct polemic with and possibly even a quote from earlier lyrics by Zhukovskii and Sumarokov. Lotman examines this phenomenon in the context of renewed interest in the problems of Russian versification, resurrected in the 1810s because of discussions of Russian hexameter. Ibid.
6. 'Почтить память можно не только кажденнем "благовонной травы", но веселым делом разрушения.' V. B. Shklovskii, '"Evgenii Onegin" (Pushkin i Stern)', in *Pushkin: Pro et contra*, ed. by V. M. Markovich and G. E. Potapova, 2 vols (St Petersburg: Izdatel'stvo russkogo khristianskogo gumanitarnogo instituta, 2000), I, 490–504 (p. 504).

7. For a fundamental study, bringing in a variety of primary sources, see B. F. Egorov, *Izbrannoe, Esteticheskie idei v Rossii XIX veka* (St Petersburg: Letnii sad, 2009), as well as Charles A. Moser, *Esthetics as Nightmare: Russian Literary Theory, 1855–1870* (Princeton: Princeton University Press, 1989).
8. The narrative practice in question is interchangeably referred to either as 'metafiction' or 'self-conscious fiction' in the core studies on the subject, among which the most significant are: Patricia Waugh, *Metafiction: The Theory And Practice of Self-Conscious Fiction* (London: Routledge, 1984); Linda Hutcheon, *Narcissistic Narrative: The Metafictional Paradox* (Waterloo, Ont.: Wilfrid Laurier University Press, 1980); Robert Alter, *Partial Magic: The Novel as a Self-Conscious Genre* (Berkeley: University of California Press, 1975); Rudiger Imhof, *Contemporary Metafiction: a Poetological Study of Metafiction in English since 1939* (Heidelberg: Winter, 1986); Robert Scholes, *Fabulation and Metafiction* (Urbana: University of Illinois Press, 1979); Inger Christensen, *The Meaning of Metafiction: A Critical Study of Sterne, Nabokov, Barth and Beckett* (Bergen: Universitetsforlagen, 1981); Margaret A. Rose, *Parody//Meta-Fiction: An Analysis of Parody as a Critical Mirror to the Writing and Reception of Fiction* (London: Croom Helm, 1979). Often, 'metafiction' assumes postmodernist connotations, whereas 'self-conscious fiction' remains a broad category, including almost any example of self-aware writing practice.
9. Waugh, *Metafiction*, p. 2.
10. Mark Currie, 'Introduction', in *Metafiction*, ed. and introduced by Mark Currie (London: Longman, 1995), pp. 1–21 (p. 1).
11. In his 1995 study 'Metapoesis', Michael Finke refers to a metapoetic literary tradition the development of which he charts from Pushkin to Chekhov (Michael Finke, *Metapoesis: The Russian Tradition from Pushkin to Chekhov* (Durham, NC and London: Duke University Press, 1995).
12. For a comprehensive analysis of metafiction as a literary phenomenon and academic discipline see Currie, 'Introduction', pp. 6–15; or, for a more partial review, Robert Spires, 'Introduction: The Metafictional Mode', in *Beyond the Metafictional Mode: Directions in the Modern Spanish Novel* (Lexington: University Press of Kentucky, 1984), pp. 1–18.
13. William H. Gass, *Fiction and the Figures of Life* (New York: Knopf, 1970), p. 25.
14. See, for instance, John Barth, 'The Literature of Exhaustion', *The Atlantic Monthly*, 220.2 (1967), 29–34.
15. Currie, 'Introduction', pp. 7–11. Hutcheon also singles out 'Jakobson and his model of communication' as the point after which literature and literary criticism have become increasingly self-conscious (Hutcheon, *Narcissistic Narrative*, p. xv).
16. Waugh, *Metafiction*, p. 2.
17. See Imhof, *Contemporary Metafiction*, pp. 10, 32–33; Waugh, *Metafiction*, pp. 3, 7–13.
18. Y. H. Zhao, 'The Rise of Metafiction in China', *Bulletin of the School of Oriental and African Studies, University of London*, 55.1 (1992), 90–99 (p. 95).
19. Owen Hodkinson, *Metafiction in Classical Literature: The Invention of Self-Conscious Fiction* (London and New York: Routledge, 2016).
20. See Waugh, *Metafiction*; Imhof, *Contemporary Metafiction*; Hutcheon, *Narcissistic Narrative* (1980).
21. See Waugh, *Metafiction*, p. 5 on metafiction making Bakhtin's idea of the dialogic potential of the novel explicit; or Hutcheon's chapter on parody that borrows heavily from Tynianov's theories: Linda Hutcheon, 'Thematising Narrative Artifice: Parody, Allegory, and the Mise En Abyme', in *Narcissistic Narrative*, pp. 48–58.
22. See Alter, *Partial Magic*; Christensen, *The Meaning of Metafiction*.
23. A brief chronology of the studies of Russian metafiction can be traced from David Shepherd's *Beyond Metafiction: Self-Consciousness in Soviet Literature* (Oxford: Clarendon, 1992), via Mark Lipovetskii's *Russkii postmodernizm: ocherki istoricheskoi poetiki* (Ekaterinburg: Ural'skii gosudarstvennyi pedagogicheskii universitet, 1997), to Nina Kolesnikoff's *Russian Postmodernist Metafiction* (New York: Peter Lang, 2001). Gary Saul Morson's 1978 article ('Reading between the Genres: Dostoevsky's *Diary of a Writer* as Metafiction', *Yale Review*, 68 (1978), 224–34), was published well ahead of the 1990s but draws on methodology that precedes works by Scholes, Hutcheon and Waugh. Morson looks at *Diary of a Writer* as 'fiction about the nature of fiction making'; and sees it as consisting of 'metastatements', or 'semifictions'. Morson's analysis is

based on the findings of Gregory Bateson's 'meta-science' theory (*Steps to an Ecology of Mind* (Chicago: University of Chicago Press, 1972) and Erving Goffman's ideas of 'frame analysis' (*Frame Analysis: An Essay on the Organization of Experience* (Harmondsworth: Penguin, 1975)). Contemporary Russian studies of metafiction sometimes still take no account of the theories of self-consciousness or metanarrative developed outside of the Russian-speaking academia. A good is example of one such recent 'isolationist' study is M. A. Khatiamova's *Formy literaturnoi samorefleksii v russkoi proze pervoi treti XX veka* (Moscow: Iazyki slavianskoi kul'tury, 2008), that traces the history of Russian studies of metafiction back to the Moscow-Tartu school, and the works of Z. Mints, I. Smirnov, R. Timenchik, V. Toporov, Iu. Lotman and others.

24. D. M. Segal, 'Literatura kak vtorichnaia modeliruiushchaia sistema', in *Literatura kak okhrannaia gramota* (Moscow: Vodolei, 2006), pp. 11–50; 'Literatura kak okhrannaia gramota', ibid., pp. 50–156.
25. Ibid., p. 68. Segal's defined his 'metapoetics' as a general feature of the 'specifically Russian tradition of literary modelling'. Ibid., pp. 52–53.
26. Segal's insights and frequent use of the prefix 'meta-' in Russian structuralism (as in Iurii Lotman's commentary to Pushkin cited above) paved way for Mark Lipovetskii's argument for the applicability of the theory of metafiction to modernist and postmodernist Russian prose in his *Russkii postmodernizm: ocherki istoricheskoi poetiki*. Lipovetskii's study first came out in Russian under this title in 1997 and then two years later became available in English as *Russian Postmodernist Fiction: Dialogue with Chaos* (New York: M. E. Sharpe, 1999). Lipovetskii revised Segal's approach to Russian modernist metanarratives in the light of contemporary theories of metafiction, as developed by Patricia Waugh, Linda Hutcheon, Rudiger Imhof and Inger Christensen. He then applied the newly developed methodology to texts by Vladimir Nabokov, Andrei Bitov, Viktor Erofeev, Venedikt Erofeev, Sasha Sokolov, Tat'iana Tolstaia, Viacheslav Pietsukh and Dmitrii Prigov. In Russian scholarship, Lipovetskii's study remains a rare example of a work on the subject that is aware of its Western counterparts.
27. Finke, *Metapoesis*, p. 20.
28. Molly Brunson, *Russian Realisms: Literature and Painting, 1840–1890* (DeKalb: Northern Illinois University Press, 2016); *Russian Writers and the Fin de Siècle: The Twilight of Realism*, ed. by Katherine Bowers and Ani Kokobobo (Cambridge University Press, 2015); *Sovremennik protiv Moskvitianina: literaturno-kriticheskaia polemika 1850-kh gg.*, ed. by A. V. Vdovin, K. Yu. Zubkov, A. S. Fedotov (St Petersburg: Nestor-Istoriia, 2015). Other examples of recent scholarship on the subject include Ani Kokobobo's *Russian Grotesque Realism* (Athens, OH: Ohio State University Press, 2018) and Sarah Ruth Lorenz's 'Visionary Mimesis' (unpublished doctoral thesis, University of California, Berkeley, 2012).
29. Waugh, *Metafiction*, p. 5. Waugh's position interestingly echoes Segal's opinion on the limitations of pre-modernist metafictions. Ibid., pp. 31–33.
30. Ibid., p. 11.
31. Alter, *Partial Magic*, p. 116.
32. Metafiction's long lineage was acknowledged by its other leading theorist, Linda Hutcheon, who added Denis Diderot to the list of indisputably metafictional writers alongside Cervantes and Stern. Hutcheon insisted that 'metafiction is not new', going as far as to argue for a separate metafictional tradition chronologically parallel with that of classical realism: Sterne alongside Richardson and Defoe, Diderot preceding Balzac. Hutcheon saw the modern novels that she was most interested in ('a kind of fiction which began to run rampant in the 1960s') as heirs to earlier, eighteenth- and nineteenth-century works of fiction, with their 'critical awareness and diegetic self-consciousness' (Hutcheon, *Narcissistic Narrative*, pp. 1, 8–9, 44). For critics such as Imhof, Christensen and Hutcheon, the application of the methodological apparatus of metafiction to texts from before the 1960s is not only possible, but absolutely essential for their understanding of modern texts. There is among them a shared understanding that tracing the lineage of metanarratives is necessary for placing them in the history of literature and isolating their influence on later literary works.
33. Ann Jefferson, *Reading Realism in Stendhal* (Cambridge: Cambridge University Press, 1988), p. xiii.

34. Ibid., p. 4.
35. Victor Terras, 'Realism', in *Handbook of Russian Literature* (New Haven: Yale University Press, 1985), pp. 363–67 (p. 365).
36. See, for example, René Wellek's insightful 'outsider's' view of the Soviet debate on realism in 'The Concept of Realism in Literary Scholarship', in *Concepts of Criticism*, ed. by Stephen G. Nichols, Jr. (New Haven: Yale University Press, 1973), pp. 222–56 (p. 222–23).
37. Henry James, 'From the Preface to *The Tragic Muse*', in *The Portable Henry James*, ed. by John Auchard (London: Penguin, 2004), pp. 476–77 (p. 477).
38. Lidiia Ginzburg, *O psikhologicheskoi proze* (Moscow: Intrada, 1999), p. 244.
39. For a recent discussion of the mimetic (both visual and verbal) qualities of Tolstoi's texts, see Brunson, *Russian Realisms*, pp. 100–27.
40. For a timeline of the development of Russian realism, see Terras, 'Realism', pp. 363–67.
41. Wellek, 'Concept of Realism, p. 229.
42. 'Поэт жизни действительной', 'совершенной истины жизни' in V. G. Belinskii, 'O russkoi povesti i povestiakhh g. Gogolia ("Arabeski" i "Mirgorod")', in *N. V. Gogol' v vospominaniiakh sovremennikov*, ed. by S. I. Mashinskii (Moscow: GIKHL, 1952), pp. 340–48.
43. In *Metapoesis*, Finke presents an insightful analysis of Gogol''s *Teatral'nyi raz'ezd posle predstavleniia novoi komedii* (1836; 1842), championing its metapoetic nature. Finke argues that this 'playlet' presented Gogol''s metapoetic musings on the nature of communication between the dramatist and his public in contemporary theatre. Written as a reaction to the staging of *Revizor* (1836), the play was ostensibly about the author's attempts to find out how the public reacted to his latest play. However, Finke suggests that the play was 'overtly about poetics, from start to finish' (p. 24) and should be read in the framework of the poetics of vaudeville — the most popular dramatic genre in Russia at the time when Gogol''s plays were staged. The play's 'self-reflexivity and flaunting of generic rules' worked to the effect of producing 'in the wider public the shock of recognition and greater understanding of its own responses'. Finke, *Metapoesis*, p. 30.
44. Donald Fanger, *Dostoevsky and Romantic Realism* (Chicago: University of Chicago Press, 1974), p. vii.
45. For more on the transformation of aesthetic ideals into social and self-representation in Pushkin, Lermontov and Gogol', see William Mills Todd III, *Fiction and Society in the Age of Pushkin: Ideology, Institutions, and Narrative* (Cambridge, MA: Harvard University Press, 1986).
46. Wellek, 'Concept of Realism', p. 228. On contemporary tensions between 'realism' and 'naturalism' across Europe and Russia, see ibid., pp. 233–38.
47. According to Jakobson's model, the biographical author in this model is a 'sender', and the literary text (novel) is a 'channel'. Whether metanarrative could be considered a 'code' or a 'function' in this model is a question of some contention between theorists of metafiction. For more on the application of Jakobson's model of communication and Bakhtin's idea of 'metalinguistics' as mentioned in the *Problemy poetiki Dostoevskogo* (1963), see Finke, *Metapoesis*, pp. 5–18; Hutcheon, *Narcissistic Narrative*, p. 44; Todd, *Fiction and Society in the Age of Pushkin*, pp. 47–49; Gerald Prince, 'Metanarrative Signs', in *Metafiction*, ed. by Currie, pp. 55–71, pp. 55–58; Waugh, *Metafiction*, p. 37.
48. Gérard Genette, *Narrative Discourse: An Essay in Method*, trans. by Jane E. Lewin (Ithaca, NY: Cornell University Press, 1980), pp. 234–35. The rhetoric of this process has been examined by two generations of narratologists from Gérard Genette to Mieke Bal (ibid., pp. 231–37; Mieke Bal, *Narratology: Introduction to the Theory of Narrative* (Toronto: University of Toronto Press, 2009), pp. 58–60); its complex epistemological nature had been most aptly addressed in Michael Riffaterre's *Fictional Truth* (Baltimore: Johns Hopkins University Press, 1989), whereas its political dimension had been explored in Terry Lovell's *Pictures of Reality: Aesthetics, Politics and Pleasure* (London: BFI Publishing, 1980).
49. Shlomith Rimmon-Kenan, *Narrative Fiction: Contemporary Poetics* (London: Methuen, 1983); Wayne C. Booth, *The Rhetoric of Fiction* (Harmondsworth: Penguin, 1987); Wolfgang Iser, *The Implied Reader: Patterns of Communication in Prose Fiction from Bunyan to Beckett* (Baltimore: Johns Hopkins University Press, 1974); Wolf Schmid, 'Implied Author', in *The Living Handbook of Narratology*, <hup.sub.uni-hamburg.de/lhn/index.php ?title=Implied Author &oldid=2068>

[accessed 9 August 2019]; Gerald Prince, *Narratology: The Form and Functioning of Narrative* (Berlin: Mouton, 1982).
50. Schmid, 'Implied Author'.
51. Rimmon-Kenan, *Narrative Fiction*, p. 104.
52. A. F. Pisemskii, *Polnoe sobranoe sochinenii*, 8 vols (St Petersburg: Izdatel'stvo tovarishchestva A. F. Marks, 1910–11), IV: *Starcheskii grekh. Bat'ka. Vzbalamuchennoe more. Russkie lguny. Ocherki* (1910) [henceforth *Vzbalamuchennoe more*], p. 434.
53. Madeleine Kahn, *Narrative Transvestism: Rhetoric and Gender in the Eighteenth-Century English Novel* (Ithaca, NY: Cornell University Press, 1991).
54. Rimmon-Kenan, *Narrative Fiction*, p. 87.
55. A. A. Demchenko and E. I. Pokusaev, *N. G. Chernyshevskii: nauchnaia biografiia* (Saratov: Izdatel'stvo Saratovskogo universiteta, 1992), pp. 223–50.
56. Chernyshevskii, *Chto delat'?*, ed. by T. I. Ornatskaia and S. A. Reiser (Leningrad: Nauka, 1975), p. 208.
57. Genette, *Narrative Discourse*, p. 234.
58. Rimmon-Kenan, *Narrative Fiction*, p. 95.
59. My summary of the typology of narrators is based on the classification used by both Genette (*Narrative Discourse*, pp. 212–37) and Rimmon-Kenan (*Narrative Fiction*, pp. 87–106)
60. Shepherd, *Beyond Metafiction*, pp. 9–10.

CHAPTER 1

❖

The Political Self-Conscious: The Russian Novel in the 1860s

At first glance, metafiction — introspective, playful and self-centred — should be concerned least of all with ideology and politics. And yet, despite its narcissism,[1] self-conscious fiction is no less concerned with the world outside its boundaries than with itself. One of its primary and universally acknowledged aims is to examine the epistemological and ontological relation of narrative to reality (with reality often personalised in the figure of an implied reader) external to the fictional world. Its secondary but no less important function is highlighting the philosophical and ideological implications of the nature of these relations.

Throughout the late twentieth and the twenty-first centuries, postmodern literary and historiographical metafictions challenged dominant political narratives through inspecting the principles of their linguistic construction. Defamiliarisation, a technique often adopted in self-conscious fiction, made the linguistic structures of power visible by transferring self-awareness from the text to the reader, thus problematising the effects produced by the dominant narrative. As Linda Hutcheon noted, it aimed 'to demystify power [...] to reveal it in all its arbitrariness' and to 'call attention to authority structures in such a way as to subvert the Romantic ideology of the myth of originality that once subtended them'.[2]

In the past forty years, the rise of metafiction as a critical discipline has demonstrated the crucial role played by ideological self-awareness for this narrative mode. It is no surprise that metafiction developed particular ideological subtypes, dealing with the collective consciousness of a marginalised social group that questioned the conventions defining its way of life. This type of fiction examined how such groups were represented in dominant narratives and then, through appropriation and reclaiming, forged a new discursive and political identity for them.[3] The political subplot in postmodern metafiction was already apparent in the texts of its early practitioners, such as the *Tel Quel* group in France and *Gruppo 63* in Italy, partly because of the heightened ideological self-consciousness of the 1960s, but also because ideological self-awareness remains the most fundamental feature of metafiction of any period. By its nature of being self-conscious, metafiction questions — linguistically, philosophically and politically — manifestations of the ideological status quo in contemporary culture. In the concluding chapter of the first edition of *Metafiction* (1984), Waugh noted that the question of whether aesthetically 'radical' texts are also politically radical is an issue of 'crucial importance', 'which may only be resolved once post-modernism has itself become a post-phenomenon'.[4] In this chapter, I suggest that this question could be no less fruitfully explored by looking back into metafiction's realist past rather than only into its post-postmodernist future.

Novelists as Citizens

Patricia Waugh's argument against the application of the theory of metafiction to pre-postmodern texts, mentioned in the introduction to this study, rests on the assumption of a lack of ideological self-consciousness in nineteenth-century authors. Frame-breaking narratives, the critic maintains, did not challenge the ultimate mimetic illusion but, on the contrary, reinforced it, precisely because the authors saw no danger in accepting a linguistically constructed picture of reality as one that is actually true.[5] But was this type of world-view really such an obstacle to enquiries into the ontological status of fiction and its ideological implications?

As Ann Jefferson noted in her study of Stendhal, it would have never occurred to the French writer, 'living in the age of positivism [...] to doubt the reality of reality'.[6] And yet he was preoccupied by the fact that 'representations have their own stylistic momentum as well as mimetic veracity and [...] that copying of nature cannot easily be safeguarded'.[7] Despite being philosophically of a positivist persuasion, Stendhal was concerned with the fact that realistic narratives do not actually reflect reality; what they end up reproducing are the accepted codes of realistic depiction, familiar and easy to interpret for both writer and reader. Precisely because they are so easy to absorb and interpret, the clichés ('vulgar', 'common' and 'prosaic')[8] replace the reader's own personal perception, making her moral and intellectual agenda redundant. This, though obviously not an example of the poststructuralist awareness of reality as a linguistic construct, betrays a sophisticated concern on the part of a nineteenth-century realist writer with the ontological and epistemological nature of fiction and, moreover, its ideological implications. If the reader accepts the ready-made view of reality, there is no need for her to work out her own.

Stendhal's concern was not unique among realist novelists, and would have been shared by many in Russia. In mid-nineteenth-century Russian fiction, the characters created by many authors, including Ivan Goncharov, Ivan Turgenev, Fedor Dostoevskii, Nikolai Chernyshevskii, Avdoti'a Panaeva, Nadezhda Khvoshchinskaia, Evgeniia Tur, Aleksei Pisemskii, Nikolai Leskov and Lev Tolstoi, were forging moral consciousnesses of their own (with varying degrees of success) amid the plurality of ideologies of the age. In criticism, the question of verisimilitude and its utilitarian purposes dominated aesthetic debates between journalists, philosophers and writers for over twenty years.[9]

The aesthetic debates that raged among the Russian intellectuals of the 1860s are a well-studied episode in both the history of literature and history of ideas. Because of the period's significance for the Soviet cultural and literary canon,[10] the Soviet scholarship on the 1860s is both vast and extremely ideologised. The most influential Soviet study of the period, Boris Egorov's *Bor'ba esteticheskikh idei v Rossii 1860-kh godov* [Struggle of Aesthetic Ideas in 1860s Russia], was revised by its author in 1991 and largely rid of its Marxist-Leninist methodological apparatus.[11] Together with Charles Moser's 1989 *Esthetics as Nightmare: Russian Literary Theory, 1855–1870*, a contribution on the same subject from the other side of the Iron Curtain, these works serve as a solid foundation for modern interdisciplinary scholarship on the period. New, insightful studies, such as Victoria Frede's 2011 analysis of the history of 'radical' emotions in the 1860s, or Laurie Manchester's recent work,[12] prove that Egorov's and Moser's initial thematic and chronological focus withstood the test of time: philosophy, literature and politics in the 1860s *did* converge in a very specific way that is worth further investigation. My analysis in this book narrows down their focus even further and uses the three novels, Chernyshevskii's *Chto delat'?*, Pisemskii's *Vzbalamuchennoe more* and Panaeva's *Zhenskaia dolia*, as a sort of triangular magnifying lens that exposes the specifics of the theory and practice of a particular genre, the increasingly metafictional realist novel, at the time.

Deep involvement in politics is one of the constant features of Russian literature, whose history is commonly held to begin with *Slovo o polku Igoreve* [The Tale of Igor's Campaign], a piece of literary fiction of strategic ideological importance. In the 1860s, this inherent characteristic became even more prominent, when highly politicised literary texts, actively promoted by publishers and enthusiastically received by readers, proliferated to the point of becoming mainstream. By that time, a large number of published novels had an — often overt — ideological agenda.

This development does not look particularly surprising in the broader context of Russian literary history. The Horatian ideal of the Poet Citizen, inherited from the classical tradition, was adopted by literary elites in the eighteenth century and remains in use to this day.[13] By the mid-nineteenth century, historical circumstances were actively encouraging this approach. Despite gradual relaxation of censorship regulations from the end of the reign of Nicholas I onwards, literary fiction still remained one of the very few open forums for the discussion of radical political and philosophic ideas. Consequently, it was considered necessary to keep this forum free from the static noise of a 'pure art' preoccupied with artistic concerns rather than problems of social governance. This efficient literary policy, which was practised by the editorial boards of popular literary journals such as *Sovremennik*, ensured the dominance of the doctrine of utilitarian writing, the most influential of the several approaches to art and aesthetics preached by the key radically minded players on the literary scene of the period: Nikolai Chernyshevskii, Nikolai Dobroliubov, Dmitrii Pisarev and, later on, Maksim Antonovich.

The publication of Turgenev's *Ottsy i deti* [Fathers and Children] in 1862 heralded the inclusion of fictional forms into ideological debates and consolidated groups of intellectuals at the opposing ends of the radical/conservative divide. The utilitarian impulse was so powerful that even writers at the other end of the ideological spectrum, such as Aleksei Pisemksii or the author of the theory of 'immoral aesthetics' Konstantin Leont'ev, saw fiction principally as a vehicle of ideas, and only secondarily as a form of art. As Turgenev pointed out in a letter to the publisher Mikhail Katkov in 1862, his 'main desire was to set in motion two or three ideas — and it seems that I have succeeded'.[14]

Although broadly concerned with aesthetics in general, a lot of the 1860s discussions focussed specifically on literature and its social obligations. As noted by Moser, 'Literature was indeed [...] the nervous system of society, it provided the channels of society's consciousness or self-consciousness.'[15] In a kind of a metaleptic ouroboros, literary works of the period were created with a heightened awareness of current aesthetic debates, themselves heavily influenced by the critics' political and ideological allegiances. Fictional narratives, especially novels, became a form of argument in a political debate, with their authors fully intending them to be interpreted as such.

Moreover, writers published critical articles and critics tried their hands at fiction, examining what they were doing and why. The realist novel, the most well-known genre of nineteenth-century Russian literature, occupied a specific place in this system of aesthetic coordinates. As a genre of imaginative literature widely practised at the time, it was an object of philosophical deliberations on the role of literature in society. At some point, however, it also became a form in which these deliberations were presented to the public, thus balancing the genre precisely at the crossing of what the French critic Gérard Genette called a sacred ontological frontier, the boundary between the world in which the story is told and the world of which it is telling.

Self-Consciousness and the Russian Novel

The first secular and original prose experiments in Russia (if still close to folklore and the oral tradition) were the Petrine tales, which, by the mid-eighteenth century, were superseded by the first Russian novels: Fedor Emin's *Nepostoiannaia fortuna, ili prikliucheniia Miramonda* [Fickle Fortune, or Adventures of Miramond] (1763), Mikhail Chulkov's *Prigozhaia povarikha* [Comely Cook] (1770) and Matvei Komarov's *Milord Dzhordzh* [Milord George] (1782). In his study *The Rise of the Russian Novel: Carnival, Stylization, and Mockery of the West*, David Gasperetti argued against the common view that, in the eighteenth century, 'Russian writers, especially novelists, are supposed to have indiscriminately imitated a vast array of foreign models'.[16] Gasperetti believed that the authors' response to Western culture was 'more circumspect': Emin, Chulkov and Komarov were imitators of Western literary styles, yet, in many ways, they 'attacked these conventions as being incapable of representing Russian cultural reality'.[17] Using a particular type of metaliterary parody — stylisation — early Russian novelists questioned 'not just the conventions but the very worldview that prevailed in the foreign-inspired literature of their day'.[18]

Building on Gasperetti's findings, I would suggest that the very first appropriation of the novelistic form in Russia was thus acutely self-conscious, questioning the ability of an essentially foreign form to accommodate a native reality and, typically for metafiction, challenging the 'uncritical acceptance of the authority of the written word'.[19] Because of the authors' nationalist and aesthetic concerns, the novel, already inherently self-conscious as a form, became even more so in eighteenth-century Russia. The 'strong metaliterary impulse'[20] can thus be charted from early Russian novels into the nineteenth century, a period in which the novel remained a popular but still unstable form.

Perhaps the otherwise inexplicable growth[21] and success of the novel in Russia in the nineteenth century can be explained partly by the genre's intense self-awareness. For almost a century until the 1870s, when Turgenev's popularity won Russian novels an international prominence and made them into a marketable export, Russia's most brilliant literary minds were experimenting with the genre. The tendency to replace the mimesis of product (reality) with the mimesis of process (portraying reality)[22] — a sure sign of the dominance of self-consciousness in literary narratives — was prioritised in the three most prominent pre-realist Russian novels of the nineteenth century: Pushkin's *Evgenii Onegin*, Lermontov's *Geroi nashego vremeni* (1841) and Gogol''s *Mertvye dushi* (1842). As William Mills Todd III astutely observed, the twentieth-century canonisation of these texts as classics 'smoothed away much of their abrasiveness, that is, their self-consciousness and critical intentionality',[23] and yet these very features remained a constant in the Russian novelistic tradition of subsequent years.

The bestselling book of the early 1830s, Faddei Bulgarin's picaresque novel *Ivan Vyzhigin, ili Russkii Zhil' Blaz* [Ivan Vyzhigin, or The Russian Gil Blas] (1829), though popular, struck the well-read public as outdated and kitsch, as Pushkin was quick to notice.[24] Pushkin himself was interested in a different kind of novelistic genre: an experimental, introspective, still uncertain form whose inherent metafictional potential could be teased out through the contemporary fashion for Romantic irony. Pushkin's intention was to write an experimental novel in verse, exploring the boundaries of the genre, observing how it functions and sharing these observations with his readers. Meanwhile, Lermontov's psychological insights into his protagonist Pechorin's incessant introspection advanced, as Donna Tussing Orwin noted in 2007, 'self-consciousness as a national trait of the Russian literary tradition'.[25] In 1842, the publication of *Mertvye dushi* further established self-consciousness as a significant trend in the development of the novel in Russia. Gogol''s parodic work, wavering between romantic irony and realist representation, was a masterpiece precisely because it never settled for one or the other.

Alongside the magisterial novelistic tradition, which would later be critically re-conceptualised as pre-realist,[26] there ran also a secondary line of narratives aimed at less sophisticated readers: Aleksandr Vel'tman's *Strannik* [Wanderer] (1831), Vladimir Odoevskii's *Russkie nochi* [Russian Nights] (1843), as well as Aleksandr Bestuzhev-Marlinskii's novellas. Metafictional narrative strategies, evident in these texts, were, as David Shephard noted, 'part and parcel of the ferment of the institutionalization and the professionalization of Russian letters'.[27] Unlike its European counterpart, this line did not run independently of the realist canon; it merged with it, picking out metafictional strategies from the commonly shared pool of literary devices and professional anxieties.

With the advent of Realism in the 1840s, Russian self-conscious narratives did not go into 'eclipse', as, according to Robert Alter, happened in Europe.[28] Instead, they proliferated within an intellectual climate of heightened literary introspection and ideological self-awareness.

From 'Poetry of Reality' to 'Feats of Denunciation'

In Russia, prose gained an equal standing with poetry by the end of the first half of the nineteenth century, surpassing it in seriousness and eventually becoming the medium of choice for literary expression and open debate. In this unique atmosphere, it became increasingly important for those involved in literary production to establish patterns of interaction between literature and reality. Both critics and writers were constantly engaged in the process of working out not only the degree of 'truthfulness' of any given narrative, but, more importantly, also its ideological value.

The 1850s saw a gradual transition from concerns with degrees of verisimilitude to a new understanding of the role that literature was to play in society. In the twenty years of aesthetic debates that raged after Belinskii died in 1848, the idea of Russian realism underwent a remarkable transformation from the 'poetry of reality' [poeziia real'nosti] to a 'feat of denunciation' [oblichitel'nyi podvig].[29] By the middle of the 1860s, the introspection of psychological prose turned towards the urgent questions of utility, morality and truth and their representation in literary texts.

The high-profile intellectual debates of the 1860s made Russian writers reflect on their vocation and its utilitarian purposes. For many, to be a writer meant to engage with social reality in a productive way and to engineer change through the truthful representation of social ills or the convincing description of an attractive alternative. The traditional view of nineteenth-century Russian literary politics holds it to be very polarised: Slavophiles vs Westernisers, Moscow traditionalists vs St Petersburg innovators, utilitarians vs proponents of pure art, and so on. What lends this picture more sophistication is an understanding that the conflicting sides were united in their dissatisfaction with the current political situation, and that the tension between the opposing sides resulted in creative outputs of varying literary quality and political impact. The polemics that began as articles and literary reviews then progressed towards larger literary forms, with the most popular pieces playing a role not only in literary but also in social life, functioning as mass communication media.[30]

The practice became so widespread that, in addition to the major literary figures of the era (such as Nikolai Chernyshevskii, on one side of the debate, or Sergei Aksakov, on the other), comparatively minor writers began to contribute to the discussion, capitalising on the trend. Moser's contention that the radicals dominated the sphere of literary criticism and the conservatives the sphere of literary works[31] holds true only if we continue to employ the traditional binary approach. For every committed revolutionary of the left and unyielding conservative of the right, there were a number of opportunists in between. Their wavering positions might have been due to genuine changes of views or to the need to make a living by publishing a number of articles in different journals.

Some writers enjoyed a level of popularity and recognition that would have been difficult to achieve at a time of a different literary fashion (Fedor Reshetnikov, whose novella *Podlipovtsy* [People from Podlipov] (1864) was published by Nekrasov because of the contemporary trend for gritty ethno-realism, is a good example). Others relied on a fine understanding of the literary craft in order to carry them through: 'I, although only a poor writer, understand nevertheless the requirements of true art',[32] claimed Chernyshevskii in *Chto delat'?* (1863). Chernyshevskii's irony aside, the literary scene in the 1860s was teeming with people of little or no literary training, trying their hand as writers and journalists, sometimes out of conviction and often as a response to a growing demand. Some of them would go on to make a substantial contribution to contemporary literature and theatre.

Radical, Conservative, and Feminist Metafictions

The synchronised momentum of thrusting out novelistic 'arguments' from all sides of the ideological debate was exemplified in the almost simultaneous publication of three novels in 1862–63: Nikolai Chernyshevskii's *Chto delat'?*, Aleksei Pisemskii's *Vzbalamuchennoe more* and Avdot'ia Panaeva's *Zhenskaia dolia*.

Nikolai Chernyshevskii, a proponent of radical criticism and an influential co-editor of *Sovremennik*, wrote his novel in four months, while imprisoned in the Peter and Paul fortress. Because of the conditions of Chernyshevskii's imprisonment, *Chto delat'?* did not go through the usual drafting process and was published without revision in *Sovremennik* in 1863, issues 3–5.

In 1863, Aleksei Pisemskii's views on aesthetics were diametrically opposed to Chernyshevskii's. Despite Pisemskii's generally conservative leanings, the writer's allegiances alternated throughout his life. At the time when *Vzbalamuchennoe more* was published, Pisemskii's disgust for the radical aesthetics matched Chernyshevskii's fondness for it and both writers were prepared to go to great literary lengths to make their respective positions clear and easy to digest for their readers. *Vzbalamuchennoe more* was written after Pisemskii's return from a short visit to Europe (which he found alien and overrated[33] — impressions that further exacerbated his usual vitriolic style) and published in Mikhail Katkov's *Russkii vestnik* [Russian Herald] also in 1863, issues 3–8.

Avdot'ia Panaeva's *Zhenskaia dolia* was published a year before *Chto delat'?* and *Vzbalamuchennoe more*, in 1862. A hostess of *Sovremennik*'s literary salon and Nikolai Nekrasov's lover and co-author, Panaeva was a successful writer in her own right who had by 1862 already published more than ten popular short novels. Like the rest of Panaeva's fiction, *Zhenskaia dolia* offered a contribution to the debate on 'the woman question', that is, 'a public discussion of social and economic changes in women's lives'.[34] Serialised in three parts, it appeared in *Sovremennik* in March, April and May 1862, issues 3–5.

Despite the fact that academic studies of Chernyshevskii's oeuvre vastly outnumber those on Pisemskii and Panaeva, it is remarkable that the critical literature on all the three writers mention metaliterariness as one of the most important problems raised by studying their work.[35] Utilising a mix of gothic, melodramatic and sensationalist narrative modes, *Chto delat'?* combined Chernyshevskii's latest insights into aesthetic theory with the by then already old-fashioned reader-oriented poetics typical of the eighteenth-century novels. The text aspired to present a 'dictionary of contemporary life',[36] looking back to the self-conscious Enlightenment narratives of Diderot and the Encyclopaedists. In *Chto delat'?*, an authoritative and often patronising narrator discussed the structure of the novel and voiced his doubts about his readers' predilection for happy endings and 'unnecessary melodrama'. Through the story of Vera Pavlovna's ideological awakening, related by a highly self-conscious narrator, Chernyshevskii aimed to encourage his readers to question their ideological assumptions and contemplate the ontology of fiction and the relationship of art and reality.

Despite the fact that Pisemskii's works are frequently considered, unproblematically, as second-rate examples of realist fiction typical of the later stages of the naturalist school, the metafictional elements in his 1863 novel are clearly noticeable. Alongside the main character Aleksandr Baklanov *Vzbalamuchennoe more* features an omniscient narrator, who, halfway through the novel, suddenly turns out to be a real-life writer, Aleksei Pisemskii. The Pisemskii narrator/character then proceeds to expound his views on contemporary literature and to read the novella *Starcheskii grekh* [The Old Man's Sin] (actually published by Pisemskii in 1860) to Baklanov and his lover. The first-person narrator thus engages with the characters of the novel despite having claimed elsewhere that they are 'completely fictional characters',[37] creating an ontologically confusing metafictional web of relations, not unlike the much later example of the narrator entering his own narrative in postmodern metafiction.

Avdot'ia Panaeva's novels were aimed at a general audience, and, as the critic Dmitrii Pisarev commented, were even perceived to compromise the lofty ideals of the radical movement by oversimplifying them.[38] *Zhenskaia dolia* presented a typical enough narrative of escape from oppressive family circumstances through marriage,[39] and yet it contained overt metanarrative elements. Although different from philosophical queries of the kind found in *Chto delat'?* or the metaleptic narrator/character confusion of *Vzbalamuchennoe more*, Panaeva's constant asides to 'the reader' and reflections on the nature of literary fiction demonstrated the popularity and spread of self-conscious literary techniques among the contemporary writers, varying from experimental to cliché.

The intellectual climate of the 1860s, a decade in which literature and criticism fused with politics, produced metafiction almost by necessity. The oversaturation of the public sphere with ideology led to a surge of metafictional practices in contemporary literature, and metafictional narratives and instances of self-conscious narration became common in the works of writers belonging to different ideological camps, from radical to conservative. Aside from the three novels examined here, instances of metafictional narration can be found in the works of other less well-known novelists of the period who have since fallen off the critical radar almost completely. Writers such as Konstantin Leont'ev, Viktor Askochenskii, Vasilii Avenarius and others offered their views on topical issues, publishing 'statements in their own defense in which they were almost obliged to deal with fundamental esthetic questions'.[40] While discussing the problematic aesthetic aspects of imaginative literature, they also reflected on the ontology of fiction and the epistemology of political thought.

The chapters that follow showcase various uses of the same narrative strategy — metanarrative — in the three representative literary texts of the period. Moreover, since the case studies offered in the three chapters include novels by writers from across the ideological spectrum, the study as a whole establishes the persistence of metafictional narrative strategies throughout the expanse of the mid-1860s literary scene.

The questions of the relationship between the ideal and the real in literary verisimilitude occupied the most brilliant — and some not quite so brilliant — minds of the era. In the context of an examination of narrative self-consciousness, these can be seen as larger philosophical enquiries into the ontology of fiction. The uneasy task of negotiating the degree of truthfulness of a realistic representation so that its ideological message is not compromised remained the subject of a decade-long debate, still reverberating in Pisemskii's outcry of 1872:

> Meanwhile, the novel, it seems, becomes more and more just a literary chronicle of the times and a faithful helpmeet of history, whereas our demented critics keep shouting at the novelists: 'do not dare to tell the truth, lie and lie, so that you do no harm to our trends, imposed from above'.[41]

The obsession of contemporary fiction with ideological self-awareness facilitated further enquiries into the epistemology of ideological beliefs. Narrators in novels with an ideological agenda kept drawing attention to the artificiality and the constructed, manipulative nature of their texts, thereby prompting their readers to question the larger political narratives that they were expected to perceive as natural and take for granted. If the suspension of disbelief and complete subjugation of the reading public could not be sustained in fiction, neither should it be expected to prevail in political life. This intention would permeate both the form and the content of published works, and produce the peculiar fusion of ideological *Bildungsroman* and political *Künstlerroman* (with Chernyshevskii's *Chto delat'?* and *Prolog* [Foreword], Pisemskii's *Vzbalamuchennoe more*, and Panaeva's novel being obvious examples) as a logical consequence of the specific intellectual atmosphere of the period.

Notes to Chapter 1

1. I use this term as adopted by Linda Hutcheon in her 1980 study, in which she suggests working towards an appropriation of also 'other potentially pejorative terms, such as introspective, introverted, and self-conscious, [that] are likewise meant to be critically neutral' (Hutcheon, *Narcissistic Narrative*, p. 1).
2. Ibid., p. xvi.

3. See, for example, Madelyn Jablon, *Black Metafiction: Self-Consciousness in African American Literature* (Iowa City: University of Iowa Press, 1997).
4. Waugh, *Metafiction*, p. 149.
5. Ibid., pp. 31–33.
6. Jefferson, *Reading Realism in Stendhal*, p. xiii.
7. Ibid., p. 25.
8. Ibid.
9. For a comprehensive overview, see Charles A. Moser, 'The Disputants and Their Journals', in *Esthetics as Nightmare: Russian Literary Theory, 1855–1870* (Princeton: Princeton University Press, 1989), pp. 3–87.
10. For a discussion of the Soviet ideological appropriation of the myths and tropes of 1860s, see Katerina Clark, *The Soviet Novel: History as Ritual* (Bloomington: Indiana University Press, 2000), pp. 8–9.
11. B. F. Egorov, *Izbrannoe, Esteticheskie idei v Rossii XIX veka* (St Petersburg: Letnii sad, 2009).
12. Laurie Manchester, *Holy Fathers, Secular Sons: Clergy, Intelligentsia, and the Modern Self in Revolutionary Russia* (DeKalb: Northern Illinois University Press, 2008).
13. See, for example, contemporary poetry: D. L. Bykov and M. O. Efremov, *Grazhdanin Poet. 31 nomer khudozhestvennoi samodeiatel'nosti. Grazhdane besy* (Moscow: KoLibri, 2012).
14. Translated and quoted in Susan Fusso, *Editing Turgenev, Dostoevsky and Tolstoy: Mikhail Katkov and the Great Russian Novel* (DeKalb: Northern Illinois University Press, 2017), p. 95.
15. Moser, *Esthetics as Nightmare*, p. 260.
16. David Gasperetti, *The Rise of the Russian Novel: Carnival, Stylization, and Mockery of the West* (DeKalb: Northern Illinois University Press, 1998), p. 4.
17. Ibid.
18. Ibid., p. 5.
19. Ibid., p. 66.
20. Ibid.
21. For a discussion of the 'swiftness' of the novel's rise in Russia, see Richard Freeborn, *The Rise of the Russian Novel: Studies in the Russian Novel from 'Eugene Onegin' to 'War and Peace'* (Cambridge: Cambridge University Press, 1973), p. 1. For a recent narratological perspective, see Victoria Somoff, *The Imperative of Reliability: Russian Prose on the Eve of the Novel 1820–1850* (Evanston: Northwestern University Press, 2015).
22. Hutcheon, *Narcissistic Narrative*, p. 4.
23. Todd, *Fiction and Society in the Age of Pushkin*, p. 8.
24. On Pushkin's uneasy relationship with Bulgarin, see Vassilii Gippius, 'Pushkin v bor'be s Bulgarinym v 1830–1831 gg.', *Pushkin: Vremennik Pushkinskoi komissii*, 6 (1941), 235–55. For more on Bulgarin's rise to fame and fortune see A. I. Reitblat, *Faddei Venediktovich Bulgarin: ideolog, zhurnalist, konsul'tant sekretnoi politsii: Stat'i i materialy* (Moscow: Novoe literaturnoe obozrenie, 2016).
25. Donna Tussing Orwin, *Consequences of Consciousness: Turgenev, Dostoevsky, and Tolstoy* (Stanford: Stanford University Press, 2007), p. 10. Orwin makes a point that echoes Gasperetti's, assessing metaliterary techniques as a way of coping with foreign cultural influences: 'Russian psychological prose emphasises self-consciousness and its effects. This characteristic developed partly because Russians acquired their knowledge of modern individualism through foreign models. Raised in a society that privileged the communal over the individual, they could not completely internalise behaviour that they admired and imitated, so they began to observe themselves from a distance, and ironically. First imitation of foreign models, and then the psychological effect of this behaviour in turn became a well-known theme in Russian fiction.' (ibid.)
26. Terras discusses the process and consequences of Soviet reconceptualisation of the nineteenth-century Russian canon in Terras, 'Realism', p. 365.
27. Shepherd, *Beyond Metafiction*, p. 5.
28. See, for example, Alter, 'The Self-Conscious Novel in Eclipse', in *Partial Magic*, pp. 84–138.
29. D. I. Pisarev, 'Realisty', in *Literaturnaya kritika*, 3 vols (Leningrad: Khudozhestvennaia literatura, 1981), II, 6–54 (p. 10).

30. Umberto Eco, for example, calls the 'popular novel' 'one of the most spectacular examples [...] of the mass communication media'. See Umberto Eco, *The Role of the Reader: Explorations in The Semiotics of Text* (Bloomington: Indiana University Press, 1984), p. 141. According to Moser, the shift of the polemic from the pages of journals 'into the pages of creative literature' occurred around 1860–61 (Moser, *Esthetics as Nightmare*, p. 32).
31. Moser, *Esthetics as Nightmare,*, p. xv.
32. N. G. Chernyshevsky, *What Is to Be Done?*, trans. by Michael Katz (Ithaca: Cornell University Press, 1989), p. 308.
33. Charles A. Moser, *Pisemsky: A Provincial Realist* (Cambridge, MA: Harvard University Press, 1969), p. 120.
34. Jane Costlow, 'Love, Work, and the Woman Question in Mid-Nineteenth-Century Women's Writing', in *Women Writers in Russian Literature*, ed. by Toby W. Clyman and Diana Greene (Westport: Greenwood Press, 1994), pp. 66–76 (p. 61). For comprehensive bibliography on the subject of the woman question see also ibid., pp. 72–73.
35. On Chernyshevskii, see: Irina Paperno, *Semiotika povedeniia: N. G. Chernyshevskii: Chelovek epokhi realizma* (Moscow: Novoe literaturnoe obozrenie, 1996), pp. 23, 25; see also U. A. Gural'nik's survey of the definitions of genre in critical literature on Chernyshevskii in *Nasledie N. G. Chernyshevskogo-pisatelia i sovetskoe literaturovedenie* (Moscow: Nauka, 1980), pp. 143–44. On Pisemskii: Moser, *Esthetics as Nightmare*, p. 143. On Panaeva and metafiction in Russian women's writing, see: Jane Costlow, 'Love, Work, and the Woman Question in Mid-Nineteenth Century Women's Writing', pp. 66–76; Joe Andrew, 'Telling Tales: Zhukova as Metaliterary Author', in *Vieldeutiges Nicht-zu-Ende-Sprechen: Thesen und Momentaufnahmen aus der Geschichte russischer Dichterinnen*, ed. by Arja Rosenholm and Frank Göpfert (Fichtenwalde: Göpfert, 2002), pp. 113–29.
36. In a letter to his wife of 1862, Chernyshevskii wrote that he was planning to write a multi-volume *Critical Dictionary of Ideas and Facts* [Критический словарь идей и фактов]. N. G. Chernyshevskii, 'Letter to O. S. Chernyshevskaia from 5 October 1862', in *Polnoe sobranie sochinenii* [henceforth *PSS*], 15 vols (Moscow: GIKHL, 1939–53), XIV: *Pis'ma 1838–1876 godov* (1949), p. 456.
37. A. F. Pisemskii, *Polnoe sobranoe sochinenii*, 8 vols (St Petersburg: Izdatel'stvo tovarishchestva A. F. Marks, 1910–11), IV: *Starcheskii grekh. Bat'ka. Vzbalamuchennoe more. Russkie lguny. Ocherki* (1910) [henceforth *Vzbalamuchennoe more*], pp. 304–05.
38. 'This writer (N. Stanitskii) is permanently employed by *Sovremennik*, and permanently desecrates with his pretentious sentences the bright and wide-reaching ideas which have been developed in this journal before, by actually intellectual and active people'. D. I. Pisarev, 'Kukol'naia tragediia s buketom grazhdanskoi skorbi', in *Polnoe sobranie sochinenii*, 6 vols (St Petersburg: Izdatel'stvo F. Pavlenkova, 1894–1907), IV (1894), pp. 147–96 (p. 148), first published in *Russkoe slovo*, 8 (1864), 1–58.
39. For more on narratives of escape, see Catriona Kelly, *A History of Russian Women's Writing, 1820–1992* (Oxford: Clarendon Press, 1994), pp. 59–79.
40. Moser, *Esthetics as Nightmare*, p. 32.
41. A. F. Pisemskii, 'Letter to N. S. Leskov from 12 April 1872', in *Pis'ma*, ed. by M. K. Kleman and A. P. Mogilianskii (Moscow: Izdatel'stvo Akademii nauk SSSR, 1936), p. 245 (translated by Moser, *Esthetics as Nightmare*, p. 185).

CHAPTER 2

A Matter for Debate

When Nikolai Chernyshevskii was arrested on 7 July 1862, it seemed that his participation in public life had come to an end. He was imprisoned on charges of sedition, treated as a dangerous political criminal and isolated from the outside world. Chernyshevskii was not even permitted to write until October 1862, when, having repeatedly petitioned the authorities to allow him to work on commercial translations to support his family, he was finally given enough ink and paper.[1] And yet on 9 February 1863, no less than six months after its editor's arrest, the cover of *Sovremennik* announced:

> Для 'Современника', между прочим, имеются: 'Что делать?', роман Н. Г. Чернышевского (начнется печатанием со следующей книжки).
>
> [*Sovremennik* has acquired, among other things, *What Is to Be Done?*, a novel by N. G. Chernyshevskii (its publication will begin from the next issue onwards).][2]

This lavishly advertised novel, Chernyshevskii's first and most successful, was written during his imprisonment in the Peter and Paul Fortress, where he was waiting for the Investigative Committee to examine his case and schedule a trial. Despite his relative inexperience as a writer of fiction,[3] Chernyshevskii chose to express his novel's didactic message through a series of complex metafictional narrative strategies. As Gary Saul Morson has noted, *Chto delat'?* 'consists of [a] constant alternation of narrative and metanarrative' so prominent that it 'often resembles a sort of socialist Sterne, a didactic Don Quixote'.[4] The use of these techniques, deeply rooted in the literary culture of the period, allowed Chernyshevskii to present a sophisticated argument on politics and aesthetics that would remain his most significant literary achievement.

An archpriest's son from Saratov, a wealthy merchant city in the south of Russia, Chernyshevskii (1828–89) established a successful career in St Petersburg in the 1860s. He took his university degree in philosophy in 1851 and three years later settled in the capital. When his initial plan for an academic career fell through (Chernyshevskii's master's thesis *Esteticheskie otnosheniia iskusstva k deistvitel'nosti* [The Aesthetic Relations of Art to Reality] (1853) was so controversial that it took the university authorities three years to process it),[5] he found other employment. He worked first as a teacher, then as a journalist, and finally as an editor and literary critic at *Sovremennik*, one of the leading 'thick'[6] journals of mid-nineteenth-century Russia. Founded by Aleksandr Pushkin in 1836, through the years this journal had been edited by a succession of literati, from P. A. Viazemskii, A. A. Kraevskii and V. F. Odoevskii to P. A. Pletnev. Finally, Pletnev sold *Sovremennik* to Ivan Panaev and Nikolai Nekrasov in 1846. By that time, the journal was struggling with just 223 subscribers and a print run of 300–400 copies (by comparison, its closest rival *Otechestvennye zapiski* [Notes of the Fatherland] circulated 5,000 copies in the same year). Recruited as part of Nekrasov's strategy for the journal's revival, Chernyshevskii joined *Sovremennik* in 1853 and oversaw its literary policy for more than a decade.

Relieved from his duties as an editor after his arrest, from 14 December 1862 to 4 April 1863 Chernyshevskii worked on *Chto delat'?* in his cell. He composed a single draft of the text that would be only marginally revised before publication — limited availability of paper and ink, as well as the looming threat of a complete ban on writing, made editing very difficult. In addition, all of Chernyshevskii's correspondence, including draft pages of the novel, had to pass through the Investigating Committee in charge of pursuing his court case. On 15 January 1863, having finished the first two chapters of *Chto delat'?*, Chernyshevskii passed them on to the Committee along with a letter to his wife. The manuscript was, miraculously, deemed harmless by the censors, and by 4 February it was already with Nekrasov at *Sovremennik*. But this turned out to be just the first of many hurdles on the novel's way to its readers.

As Avdot'ia Panaeva recalled in her memoirs, Nekrasov was so excited to have received it that he accidentally lost the first part of the manuscript. While Nekrasov was on his way to the publisher Wolf, whose printing presses were located near the editors' office on Liteinyi Avenue, it must have accidentally fallen off his carriage. Thanks to a kindly passer-by who brought it to *Sovremennik*'s office to claim the promised reward, the manuscript was recovered the next day. Such was Nekrasov's relief that he had given the man much more money that initially advertised.[7] Encouraged by the near miraculous recovery of the precious manuscript and the ease with which the chapters passed the first round of censors, Nekrasov then advertised the novel on the cover of *Sovremennik's* January–February issue.

Nekrasov's excitement was understandable. By 1863, much of the journal's success rested on the texts produced or commissioned personally by Chernyshevskii and after his arrest the journal's remaining editors struggled to appoint an editorial board that would keep *Sovremennik* going in the same fashion. The timing was also auspicious: since June 1862 *Sovremennik*, often in trouble with the censors, had been out of circulation for eight months by the order of the Censors' Committee. In general, *Sovremennik*'s relationship with the Russian government was a web of familial and professional connections: Ivan Panaev's uncle V. I. Panaev held one of the highest posts at court as a director of chancery for the ministry of the court [direktor kantseliarii ministerstva dvora]. The influential censor A. V. Nikitenko, a member of the Committee for Book Publishing [Komitet po delam knigipechataniia] since 1859, worked as *Sovremennik*'s first editor in 1847.[8] In a similar fashion, much of the Committee's good will rested on the editors' personal relationship with the censors that ensured timely payments of appropriate bribes. Ivan Panaev's death in 1862 and

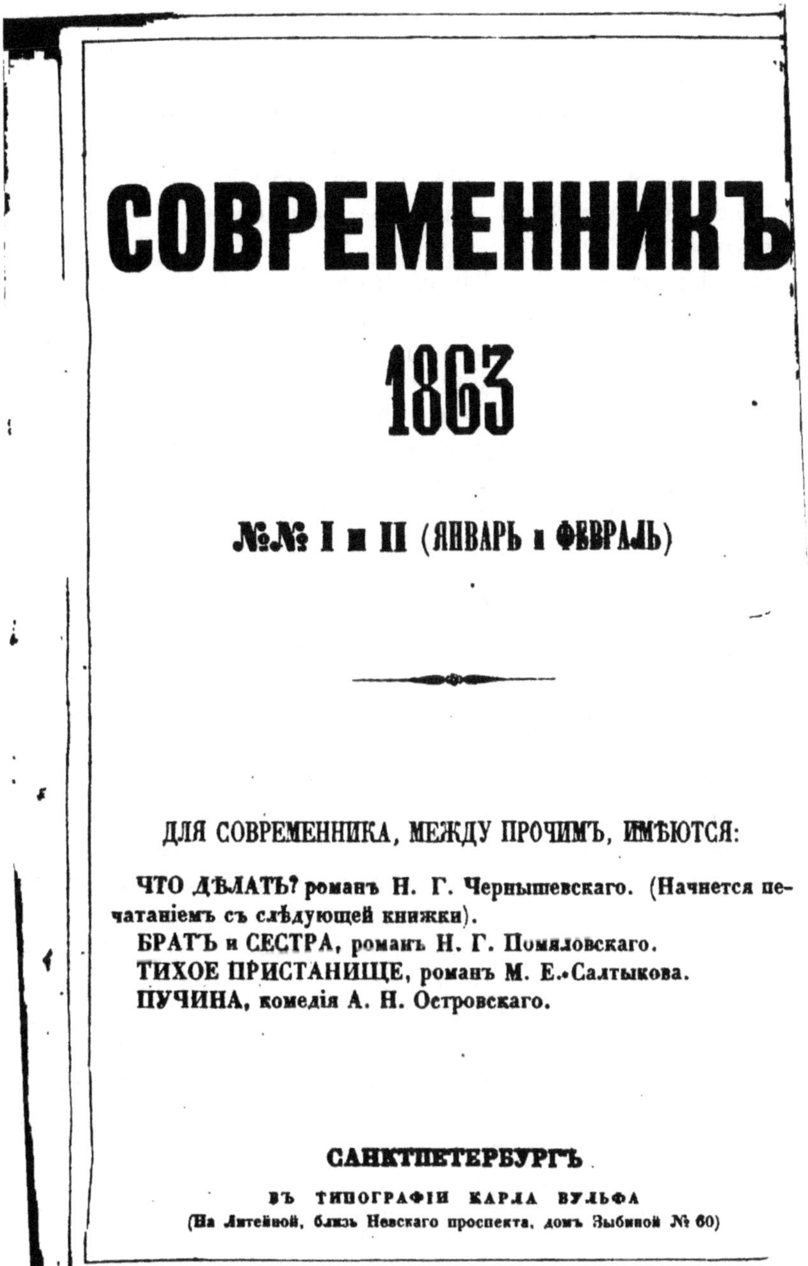

СОВРЕМЕННИКЪ

1863

№№ I и II (ЯНВАРЬ и ФЕВРАЛЬ)

ДЛЯ СОВРЕМЕННИКА, МЕЖДУ ПРОЧИМЪ, ИМѢЮТСЯ:

ЧТО ДѢЛАТЬ? романъ Н. Г. Чернышевскаго. (Начнется печатаніемъ съ слѣдующей книжки).
БРАТЪ и СЕСТРА, романъ Н. Г. Помяловскаго.
ТИХОЕ ПРИСТАНИЩЕ, романъ М. Е. Салтыкова.
ПУЧИНА, комедія А. Н. Островскаго.

САНКТПЕТЕРБУРГЪ

ВЪ ТИПОГРАФІИ КАРЛА ВУЛЬФА
(На Литейной, близъ Невскаго проспекта, домъ Зыбиной № 60)

FIG. 2.1. *Sovremennik*, 1–2 (1862), cover.

Chernyshevskii's arrest soon after left Nekrasov to negotiate with the committee on his own, and ensuring the readers' support for his publication was a priority. And so the first issue of the journal published after an eight-month break had to reassure the readers that, despite his arrest, Chernyshevskii was still contributing to *Sovremennik*, even if in a different capacity. Announcing the journal's latest prestigious acquisition, Nekrasov publicly reinstated Chernyshevskii's connection to *Sovremennik* and proved that it had not been diminished by his new status as a political inmate.

Chernyshevskii's arrest followed an incriminating campaign orchestrated by the government. The writer was accused of composing an inflammatory proclamation and apprehended on the evidence of a report submitted to the police by one of his close acquaintances, Vsevolod Kostomarov.[9] In the atmosphere of general political unrest caused by the St Petersburg fires of May 1862,[10] Chernyshevskii was held in the Peter and Paul Fortress for over a year awaiting trial. Finally, as a part of the government's campaign against political activists, Chernyshevskii was convicted and, after a mock execution in May 1864, exiled to Siberia for twenty years. In 1887 he was allowed to move to Astrakhan and then to Saratov, where he settled for only four months before his death in 1889.

While in exile, Chernyshevskii composed two unfinished novels (*Prolog* [Foreword] (1867–70) and *Povesti v povesti* [Novellas within a Novella] (1863)), a number of short prose pieces, and a twelve-volume translation of Georg Weber's *Allgemeine Weltgeschichte* [General World History] (1884–88). Despite Chernyshevskii's continued importance for nineteenth-century Russian radicals,[11] none of these texts became as popular and influential as *Chto delat'?*. Although *Chto delat'?* was banned immediately after publication, it had nonetheless become a key text for the widespread underground radical movement. Popular among young idealist readers, at some point it was picked up by a fourteen-year-old Vladimir Ul'ianov. The novel did not impress him at first, but eventually became much appreciated by its probably most influential reader. In Lenin's own words, *Chto delat'?* '[had] ploughed him up'[12] and he remained a devoted reader of Chernyshevskii ever after.

Before the novel's explosive nature, so noticeable in hindsight, became obvious to the censors, *Sovremennik* managed to publish the entire text of *Chto delat'?* in its March, April and May issues.[13] Very soon issues of the journal containing the novel were confiscated from the booksellers and the only editions available to readers were either smuggled in from abroad or produced illegally.[14] The demand, however, was so high that, according to contemporary accounts, bound pages of the March–May issues of *Sovremennik* containing the novel were sold for up to 25 roubles. By the end of the century, the price for a copy of the original *Sovremennik* 1863 issues went as high as 60 roubles.[15] Testimonials about the novel's popularity abound in numerous private documents, from recollections of retired revolutionaries to the literary memoirs of the members of the establishment, such as the publishing tycoon Aleksei Suvorin or the painter Il'ia Repin. In 1906 the ban was lifted, and by 1917 *Chto delat'?* had been reissued four times. By 1975, the novel had gone through sixty-five editions in the Soviet Union in Russian[16] with the print run coming up to more than 6 million copies.

Chto delat'? tells the story of Vera Pavlovna Rozal'skaia and her forward-minded lovers, the medical students Lopukhov and Kirsanov. Soon after publication, Chernyshevskii's novel became known as the gospel of Russian political radicalism: dealing with contemporary issues, it offered a whole generation an example of how to channel their revolutionary aspirations into productive activity. And yet, despite its utilitarian purpose, the novel featured extensive use of metanarrative, a strategy designed to emphasise the text's artificiality and ontological ambiguity.

In this chapter, I will look into this strategy in detail, analysing Chernyshevskii's understanding of the ontology of literary fiction in the context of contemporary public debates on politics and aesthetics. Through a close reading of the novel's metafictional passages in its final version and earlier drafts, focusing particularly on instances of metalepsis, I will examine the fluid boundaries of material reality as represented in the novel. Multiple crossings of the metaphysical border between literary fiction and 'the matter' of objective reality throughout the novel create, I argue, an intentionally unresolved ontological ambiguity that was essential for expressing Chernyshevskii's political and aesthetic argument in a literary form.

A very popular object of both Soviet and early post-Soviet literary studies in Russia (albeit for different reasons), this novel has not been traditionally approached as an intentionally metafictional text. However, considering how prominent metanarrative strategies are in the novel, it seems appropriate at this stage to examine briefly how scholars of Chernyshevskii engaged with this narrative phenomenon. Aside from positioning my own study in relation to this vast and important body of critical work, this short overview also contributes to a wider discussion initiated in the introduction to this book: if metafiction was such an important part of the Russian literary tradition as recent scholarship suggests, how did Slavic studies conceptualise it before the general theory of metafiction was developed in the 1970s?

The majority of academic studies on Chernyshevskii were published in Russia and the Soviet Union in the period from the 1910s to the 1980s,[17] before the theory of metafiction was integrated into the field of Russian studies. And yet, metanarrative featured so prominently in *Chto delat'?* that Soviet scholars found various ways of analysing it with the help of available methodologies. The novel's metalepses were conceptualised as aberrations of the narrative voice, or its equivalents in terms of Soviet literary criticism, the 'image of the author' [obraz avtora] and the 'author-narrator' [avtor-povestvovatel'].[18] The existence of the multiple narrative voices was explained by employing definitions such as 'authorial thought' [avtorskaia mysl'].[19] This 'authorial thought' was defined as a combination of disembodied narrative voices that provided reflections on general philosophical, historical, ethical and aesthetic topics, and emphasised the difference between the voice of the author and the voices of his characters. Instances of metanarration in the novel were described as extra-diegetic 'out-of-plot elements'[20] that merged the novel's 'inner' and 'outer' plots. The essence of metalepsis — a transgression of narrative levels within the text — was interpreted as a crossing of those multiple plot lines.[21] Neither G. E. Tamarchenko nor Iu. K. Rudenko, the two Soviet scholars of Chernyshevskii's work specifically interested in structural properties and theorising of Chernyshevskii's narrative, nor other major Chernyshevskii scholars, such as N.

A. Verderevskaia, M. T. Pinaev or P. A. Nikolaev, distinguished between frame-breaking and non-frame-breaking metalepses in the novel. As a result, the Soviet critics have analysed the narrator's interaction with his character Rakhmetov and the 'perspicacious reader' as events happening on the same ontological level. Other instances of the narrator's turning into a character were also addressed mainly in the context of plot dynamics. Instead, the critics focused on the 'supplementary' (Tamarchenko) or 'framing' (Rudenko) plot of the author–reader relationship. The genealogy of this plot was traced to Pushkin's 'lyrical asides' and Gogol''s polemics with the antagonistic reader in *Mertvye dushi*.[22]

In the same vein, the traditional Soviet interpretation of the text's intentional ambivalence was based on the assumption that Chernyshevskii wrote *Chto delat'?* in 'Aesopian language'.[23] The use of this writing technique, obscuring the political argument with a fable-like plot, presumably helped Chernyshevskii to fool the censors and smuggle his ideas out to *Sovremennik*'s subscribers, who would be able to decode his veiled messages.[24] Most importantly, Rudenko has identified the novel's dual preoccupation with the 'aesthetics of the novel, persistently discussed in the novel's text itself', as well as its focus on didacticism.[25] The narrator [obraz rasskazchika] fulfilled not just the traditional function of authenticating the verisimilitude of the 'new people' but also acted as the reader's mentor, whose didactic intent affected all the narrator/reader communication. Later, in 1981, Gary Saul Morson would refer to this effect as 'didactic frame-breaking', '"baring" by exaggeration the devices it employs'.[26]

Outside Russia, Andrew Drozd, in his 2001 study *Chernyshevskii's What Is to Be Done?: A Reevaluation*, briefly focused on metanarrative in *Chto delat'?* in his close reading of the novel's preface. Drozd noted the novel's structural similarity to Laurence Sterne's fiction and acknowledged 'the constant alteration of the illusion of reality followed by the smashing of that illusion' as one of the 'organizing principles'[27] of the novel. Gary Saul Morson's analysis of the novel in *The Boundaries of Genre: Dostoevsky's Diary of a Writer and the Traditions of Literary Utopia* (1981) also emphasised the metaliterary nature of the text. Self-referentiality in *Chto delat'?*, according to Morson, was aimed at debating the form of the novel while practising it, 'constantly discussing, incorporating, and parodying the novel's traditional forms and plots'.[28] In *Esthetics as Nightmare*, Charles Moser noted that metalepsis in the novel showcased the narrator's 'didactic role: he is a mentor who tells his readers precisely what to think, comments sarcastically on their more blatant stupidities, and generally leads his ideologically uninitiated readers by the hand'.[29] Moser traced the use of this device to Pushkin and pointed out the contemporaneous use of it in Aleksei Pisemskii's *Vzbalamuchennoe more*. Finally, in his reading of the metapoetics of Russian literature, Michael Finke discussed the meta-textuality of the novel's preface in the introduction to his study of metanarrative in Gogol', Pushkin, Dostoevskii, Tolstoi and Chekhov.

Thus, it is safe to say that the prominence of metanarrative in *Chto delat'?* was so remarkable that it was noticed by Chernyshevskii scholars both in Russia and abroad, even despite the obvious methodological constraints of Soviet literary studies. However, the critics' preoccupation with Chernyshevskii's political views often led to a simplified interpretation of the narrative strategies used in his texts. In the case of metanarrative, this complex phenomenon had been conceptualised in the reductive terms of the 'author/reader' opposition. Such oversimplification failed to consider the essential problems of narrative perception and focalisation levels, the use of metalepsis and the parallax effect,[30] mimetic referentiality and narrative negotiation.

The present study does not aim to substitute one term for another by turning the already existing discussion of the 'image of the author' into a discussion of a 'narrative voice'. By drawing attention to the ontological irregularities of narration in *Chto delat'?* and conceptualising them as metafiction, I hope to contribute to the recently initiated process of the novel's re-evaluation and to point out its relevance for new, revised theories of Russian literary realisms.[31]

Negotiating Boundaries of Reality in *Chto delat'?*

Chernyshevskii's first serious attempt at literary fiction, *Chto delat'?* was thematically connected to the articles he published earlier, in 1860–61, particularly the 'Anthropological principle in philosophy' [Antropologicheskii printsip v filosofii] (1860) and 'Is this a beginning of change?' [Ne nachalo li peremeny?] (1861). These articles addressed some general social, political and aesthetic issues that were current in public debates at the time,[32] but focused particularly on a problem that was of great importance to Chernyshevskii personally: the relationship between art, specifically literary fiction, and reality. The elimination of the ontological divide between art and reality was Chernyshevskii's chief philosophical concern, indicative of his deep engagement with the development of literary aesthetics in Russia both as a theoretical discipline and as an applied methodology of criticism.

If the general trajectory of Chernyshevskii's intellectual development took him from the critique of Hegelian idealism to championing the anthropological materialism of Ludwig Feuerbach,[33] his views on the ontology of fiction were formed under the more immediate influence of Vissarion Belinskii. The leading Russian literary critic of the 1840s (also wooed by Nekrasov to join the revived *Sovremennik* in 1846), Belinskii struggled to incorporate Hegel's understanding of the dualism of form and content, as well as intent and ideal, into his readings of contemporary Russian fiction. Chernyshevskii inherited this preoccupation, which resulted in a theoretical argument with the German idealist aesthetics that he constructed in his master's thesis and a practical argument with contemporary fiction that he took up in his literary criticism. Ever since the publication of *Esteticheskie otnosheniia iskusstva k deistvitel'nosti* in 1853, Chernyshevskii had been campaigning for a new type of literature to become mainstream. His dissertation, dedicated to proving the superiority of reality over its representation in art, advocated a 'utilitarian' approach to art and prioritised its didactic potential. As a critic, Chernyshevskii praised a 'responsible' type of writing that addressed social and political problems and offered ways of solving them, thus changing reality through art.[34] The idea of a utilitarian approach to literature was inspired both by the desire to eliminate conceptually the difference between art and reality and the desire to affect reality directly through the medium of art.

As Irina Paperno has pointed out, Chernyshevskii's idea of realism was based on the rejection of 'philosophical idealism for positivism, theology for Feurbachian anthropology, traditional Christian ethics for English utilitarianism, constitutional liberalism for socialism and radicalism, and romantic aesthetics for the aesthetics of realism'.[35] Paperno analysed the effect this *Weltanschauung* had on Chernyshevskii's ideas of literary aesthetics. The issue of the ontology of literary fiction or, as Paperno refers to it, 'the issue of the relations between literature and reality and, in the long run, the function of literature in real life' was a key concept in the contemporary aesthetics of realism that was fascinating both Chernyshevskii and his disciples, the young 'radical critics' such as Nikolai Dobroliubov and Dmitrii Pisarev.[36]

It was precisely through an attempt to transgress the ontological border between artistic representations of reality and objective reality itself in literary fiction that Chernyshevskii and his followers tried to reconcile the principles of realist aesthetics with the didactic impulse of utilitarian art. According to Paperno, on the one hand the intention of realism (as proclaimed by radical critics) was the direct and precise representation of social reality, as close to the empirical object, or as true to life, as possible. ('Truth' [istinnost'], or authenticity of representation, became the central aesthetic category, more important than 'Beauty'). On the other hand, realism clearly had a didactic intent and wished to have a direct impact on reality. Thus, literary characters and literary situations were claimed to have been derived from 'life itself' and thereafter, 'returned to reality' and offered to society as examples worthy of imitation in real life.[37] As Lidiia Ginzburg noted in her discussion of Chernyshevskii's writings, 'literature and reality were working together. Literature fixated the events of reality and brought it back in a considered, structured form, for future reproduction'.[38]

Particular importance in this situation was bestowed on the literary critic, who had to become a mediator between literature and reality.[39] In Chernyshevskii's understanding, literature itself 'served as an intermediary between man and reality', evaluating and explaining 'the phenomena of real life, thereby making them accessible to human understanding and catalyzing action'.[40] As a result of this approach, radical criticism's arguments often produced an ontological confusion between 'the realms of literature and real life', in which 'the literary world was easily and eagerly equated with the real world'.[41] The boundary between the physical matter of objective reality and the imaginary substance of literary texts became a subject of constant debate.

In line with the argumentation put forward in Chernyshevskii's articles, in *Chto delat'?* manifestations of this ontological ambivalence are found throughout the novel. On the level of literary discourse, the novel makes liberal and frequent use of metanarrative, questioning the act of composing literary fiction in the process of doing it. On the level of plot and system of characters, the novel offers two final scenes, one of which involves a metaleptic appearance of a character who could be identified as the author of the same narrative. Finally, on the level of symbolic imagery, a persistent metaphor of narrative as 'performance' or 'spectacle' conveys the idea that nothing is what it seems to be: characters assume new identities, act under false pretences and much of the 'evidence' they encounter along the way, such as official documents certifying death, ownership or marriage, prove to be unreliable.

Chernyshevskii's reliance on the style he had developed as a literary critic naturally led him to adopt a particular way of communicating with the reader throughout the text of the novel. Addressing the reader directly, sometimes as an ally and sometimes as an adversary, was intended to recreate the rhetorical construct of the intellectual community that the thick journals projected. In *Chto delat'?*, Chernyshevskii the author merged with Chernyshevskii the critic in the figure of a self-conscious narrator, an embedded mediator between the text and the reader, providing meta-reflection on the process of composing a work of fiction relevant to contemporary political struggle. In a way, *Chto delat'?* presented the readers with an ultimate conflation of a thick journal's content: a work of literary fiction with a suggested interpretation already integrated into the text. Traditionally interpreted as a legacy of Romanticism in Chernyshevskii's prose,[42] this literary strategy, I would argue, was much more typical of its time than has been previously acknowledged.

This conflation of literary and publicistic discourse was not unique to Chernyshevskii. Rather, it was typical for writers who shared the radical critics' ideological and aesthetic views. These writers aimed to, as one of the Soviet critics put it with a Shklovskii-inspired structuralist insight, 'express themselves as directly as possible', in order to 'not just show, but explain, interpret for the reader the meaning of their story [...] to state their own opinion of it', with 'their literary devices often bared'.[43] Their overall method could be characterised as, in the same study of these 'democratically minded' writers, 'an alternation of mimesis and diegesis, bordering on journalism', 'featuring an exploring, experimenting author'.[44] In this way, the intellectual, political and, one can say, discursive climate of the 1860s, stylistically and philosophically influenced by the radical 'realist' [real'nye] critics, makes Chernyshevskii's liberal use of metanarrative much less of an old-fashioned oddity on the contemporary literary scene than it might have appeared to be.

Contemporary reviews of *Chto delat'?* were sharply polarised. After the novel's publication in *Sovremennik*, Chernyshevskii became one of the most high-profile writers and political prisoners in the country. His notoriety exacerbated the virulence of the critics' attacks and reaffirmed the loyalty of his supporters. Immediate negative reactions, such as F. M. Tolstoi's ('Rostislav') article 'Lzhemudrost' geroev g. Chernyshevskogo' [False Wisdom of Mr Chernyshevskii's Characters] in *Severnaia pchela* [Northern Bee], were swiftly answered by arguments in support of the novel, such as V. S. Kurochkin's ('Znamenskii') feuilleton 'Pronitsatel'nye chitateli (Iz rasskazov o starykh liudiakh)]' [Perspicacious Readers (From Stories of Old People)] in *Iskra* [Spark], *Sovremennik*'s weekly supplement.[45] Later on, N. N. Strakhov's cautious support, voiced in his article 'Schastlivye liudi' [Happy People], contrasted with D. I. Pisarev's enthusiastic approval in 'Novyi tip' [New Type]. Among conservatives, N. S. Leskov offered a compassionate reading of the novel in *Severnaia pchela*, whereas A. A. Fet, together with V. P. Botkin, delivered a scathing attack on Chernyshevskii's personality and political views in an article submitted to *Russkii vestnik*.[46]

The reviewers were mostly concerned with endorsing or rejecting the novel's political message and rarely commented on the text's literary merits (most agreed it had no literary merit at all). The reviews testify that the original quality of the novel's self-referentiality and metalepses was obscured by its topicality and direct approach to the most sensitive current questions such as radical social reform or sexual liberation. However, a few astute remarks from the critics can help us reconstruct the effect the novel's metafictional narrative must have had on its first readers.

Leskov's article 'Nikolai Gavrilovich Chernyshevskii v ego romane "Chto delat'?"] [Nikolai Gavrilovich Chernyshevskii in his novel *What Is to Be Done?*] made it obvious that contemporary readers agreed with Chernyshevskii's claim that a 'true' story is valuable even if it is aesthetically imperfect. Leskov acknowledged the circumstances that led Chernyshevskii to write a work of fiction ('he was forced to manufacture a novel because of circumstances beyond his control: a necessity for action and an inability to accomplish it in any different form') and maintained that discussing the novel's artistry [khudozhestvo] was beside the point: 'and so, anyone who will try, at length, to prove the novel's failure as a work of belles-lettres, will be wasting their time and effort'.[47] However, Chernyshevskii's use of narrative strategies common to journal polemics (addressing the reader, using the narrator as a mediator between the story and its audience, authenticating the narrative through claims of personal experience) did not pass unremarked. Maintaining that 'Mr Chernyshevskii is a journalist, and a journalist of a certain well-known school',[48] Leskov pointed out one of the most significant features of the novel's poetics: its merging of the literary and publicistic discourse that upset the usual division of narrative levels typical for literary fiction.

Nikolai Solov'ev, sharply denouncing both Chernyshevskii's views and *Sovremennik*'s general literary policy in an article 'Teoriia bezobraziia' [Theory of Ugliness], noted that 'the author speaks the most in this novel'. He drew attention to the novel's highly theoretical abstractions in which 'thoughts play the role of feelings' and 'life has been sacrificed to the freedom of thought, has become a victim of theory'.[49] The narrator's various strategies of authentication seem to have been successful, according to Nikolai Strakhov's article, in which he noted that the 'direct statements the novel makes about the existence of the new people cannot be in any doubt [...] These new people exist'.[50] The staunchly conservative review by Fet and Botkin interpreted the novel's playfulness as 'grimaces in the worst taste', '[full of] lisping contradictions, voluntary and involuntary stammers of our novelist'.[51]

The absence of further notes on the novel's self-reflexivity in the multiple critical articles is partly explained by the 1860s trend for turning literary reviews into polemic pieces. Owing to the novel's topicality, reviews of *Chto delat'?* were often used as a chance to polemicise with the author's supporters and enemies. An exchange between Saltykov-Shchedrin and Zaitsev is a good example of this practice. In their pieces in *Sovremennik*'s chronicle 'Nasha obshchestvennaia zhizn'' [Our social life][52] and *Russkoe slovo* [Russian word],[53] the two critics used Chernyshevskii's novel as an excuse to address each other's political views. Even though verisimilitude, or lack thereof, in Chernyshevskii's text was announced as the topic of their discussion, in fact the critics were busy debating whether Russian society has any need of the real 'new people'.[54] A conservative but sympathetic critic, A. M. Bukharev, stated directly: 'If you will, I will use Mr. Chernyshevskii's novel to explain what we really need to do, considering the intellectual and the spiritual state of our society and our fatherland'.[55] Another reason for the scarcity of such remarks specifically on the novel's narrative structure, as Igor' Kondakov has suggested, would have been the novel's withdrawal from the public sphere almost immediately after its publication.[56]

Because of Chernyshevskii's established career as a literary critic, the narrative voice of the novel must have seemed an extension of Chernyshevskii-the-critic's voice into literary fiction itself. It was probably too obvious to pay it any attention, to the point that some reviewers, like V. Kurochkin in his playful article, adopted the tone of the conversation with the perspicacious reader to deal with the novel's detractors.[57] The self-referential style of polemical articles of the thick journals would have been expected from a writer of Chernyshevskii's political and aesthetic persuasion. It came as a logical consequence of his declared interest in bridging the ontological gap between literature and reality, equating the description of radical change and its implementation with its enactment.

The novel's multiple metalepses repeatedly merged the semi-fictional world of the narrator with the world of his addressee, the perspicacious reader. Opening with two chapters that exposed the power of narrative manipulation, *Chto delat'?* featured a narrator and characters that straddled the ontological boundary between the world in which the story was told and the world of which it told. Liberal use of authenticating strategies such as introducing the narrator as an eye-witness of the events, incorporating financial and statistical documents as well as references to real-time events into the literary text, brought the characters' world as close to the readers as possible. Metafiction was precisely the type of narrative best suited for such a goal — as a method of ontological enquiry in fiction, it fitted Chernyshevskii's general approach to literature as a theorist and a practitioner. In the following close reading of the novel's metafictional passages, I analyse the introductory chapters as metadiegetic prolepses and explore the relationship between the novel's unreliable metadiegetic narrator and his multiple addressees. Finally, I focus on the novel's most significant metalepses and the way they are used to maintain an intentional ontological ambiguity throughout the entire text.

Drawing the Reader In: Metadiegetic Prolepses

Similar to the majority of novels published at the time, *Chto delat'?* came out serially: its first chapters appeared in print while the rest of the text was still a work in progress. Chernyshevskii passed the manuscript to Nekrasov part by part, as soon as he finished writing it. Consequently, Chernyshevskii would not have seen the text as a whole: neither in proofs, nor in its published version, since he was not allowed to receive daily newspapers or journals. While writing, Chernyshevskii had less and less time for editing as the time went on — he was often questioned by the Investigating Committee, providing oral and written statements for his trial all through spring and summer that year.[58] At the same time, he was busy working on two commercial translations in order to earn money.[59] To add to these demands on his time, his supply of writing paper was also gradually diminishing and he resorted to reusing the margins of previously discarded pages.

As a result, there is a discernible difference between the pre-drafted chapters of the novel that benefited from Chernyshevskii's brisk but careful editing and those composed without any preliminary drafts. The first four edited chapters are noticeably more coherent than chapters 5 and 6, written directly as a fair copy. The small alterations of the first draft, made when Chernyshevskii was writing out fair copies of chapters 1–4, have been carefully preserved and published as a part of the 1975 academic edition of *Chto delat'?*.[60] When finished, the novel was, according to A. N. Pypin, Chernyshevskii's cousin and an editor at *Sovremennik*, 'published without any omissions'.[61] The close reading of the novel's passages that I offer below compares the first draft to the version of the text published in *Sovremennik* in 1863, examining the changes that were made in the novel's metafictional passages. These changes, never previously examined in detail, show exactly how the novel's ontological ambiguity — its stylistic trademark, and, I argue, one of the reasons for its lasting cultural influence — was created.

The idea of writing a fictional piece that would allow him to reach readers from the Peter and Paul Fortress took shape quite soon after Chernyshevskii was imprisoned. Despite his long career as a journalist, Chernyshevskii was not an experienced fiction writer and his choice to start working on a 'a fictional story' [belletristicheskii rasskaz][62] would not have been obvious. In many ways, his decision to turn to a novelistic form was purely practical. As a sole provider for his family, Chernyshevskii was concerned about the loss of income that naturally followed his incarceration. According to *Sovremennik*'s business correspondence, to alleviate his position Nekrasov promised to pay 4,000 roubles for a novel.[63]

Initially, Chernyshevskii planned a multi-volume *Istoriia material'noi i umstvennoi deiatel'nosti chelovechestva* [History of Material and Intellectual Activity of Humankind] that would have been followed by *Kriticheskii slovar' idei i faktov* [Critical Dictionary of Ideas and Facts] based on it.[64] However, it soon became clear that, since he was writing for the sake of the general good of society, in order to 'explain to people what truth is and how they should think and live',[65] he had to look for a form that, above all, would be accessible to readers. Very confident of his abilities,[66] Chernyshevskii intended to rework the material intended for *Istoriia* 'in the lightest, most popular spirit, almost in the manner of a novel, with anecdotes, scenes and witticisms, such that even people who read nothing but novels would read it'.[67]

Aware of the contemporary public's reading tastes and habits, Chernyshevskii was conscious of the fact that the readers' interest had to be captured and retained from the beginning.[68] With this in mind, he started the novel by, in his own words, putting some 'bait' on the narrative 'hook' in two introductory chapters titled 'The Fool' and 'The First Consequence of this Foolish Affair'. With the exception of these two introductory chapters, the rest of the novel followed a linear plot.

Chapter 1, 'Vera Pavlovna's Life with Her Family', introduced the novel's protagonist, Vera Pavlovna, and told the story of her life up to the point when her unwanted suitor Storeshnikov proposed marriage. Chapter 2, 'First Love and Legal Marriage', described first Vera's courtship and then her marriage to her brother's tutor, the young medical student Lopukhov. Lopukhov, a progressive young man, married Vera in order to free her from the tyranny of her parents' household and to help her start an independent life. The rest of the melodramatic plot unfolded in the following three chapters: 'Marriage and Second Love', 'Second Marriage' and 'New Characters and a Conclusion'. Vera set up her own household and then, after a series of inspiring dreams, a sewing cooperative. The readers found out that after Vera fell in love with her husband's best friend Kirsanov, her husband Lopukhov faked his suicide to free her to marry her new true love. Lopukhov then departed for America, only to come back shortly after under the new name of Charles Beaumont.[69] Upon his return, he also fell in love again and married a young heiress. Reconciled, the two couples continued to socialise and work together to hasten the arrival of the fair future. The novel wound up with an enigmatic short chapter titled 'Change of Scene', set in the near future of 1865. It featured 'a lady in mourning' and 'a man of about thirty years old', who are usually considered to be the representations of Chernyshevskii's wife Olga and himself in the future, after he is freed from imprisonment by a change of political regime.[70]

The two introductory sub-chapters of the novel are often overlooked in close readings of *Chto delat'?* in favour of the famous preface. And yet, they are crucial to any attempts to interpret the rest of the novel. These scenes not only 'hook' the readers' attention but also foreshadow the kind of interpretative effort that will be required from them throughout the novel. The very first instalment of the novel's text, its metadiegetic prolepsis, is a meditation on the power of interpretation and the dangers of constructed narratives. A prolepsis, in Rimmon-Kenan's apt definition, is 'telling the future before its time', 'replac[ing] the kind of suspense deriving from the question "What will happen next?" by another kind of suspense, revolving around the question "How is it going to happen?"'.[71] In the opening sub-chapters of Chernyshevskii's novel, the narrative figure of prolepsis is used as a cunning metadiegetic preview of the novel's entire epistemological relationship with its readers.

The novel's first chapter opens with an account of a suicide that has been reported in one of the big St Petersburg hotels. A man had checked in but then disappeared from his room during the night. A police officer, arriving at the scene, finds a suicide note and explains to the bemused hotel staff that the man who shot himself on the nearby bridge last night must have been their guest. However, the mystery of the hotel guest remains unresolved as no body is found.

The arriving police official is interpreting the events for the hotel staff who are waiting to see what his visit could illuminate ('they sent for the police; now everyone was waiting to see what would happen'). Having discovered the note, he announces: 'Так вот оно, штука-то теперь и понятна, а то никак не могли сообразить!' [So that's it! Now it's all clear. No one could make head or tail out of it.] He then tells the story that will be repeated and discussed by the servants: 'Рассказ полицейского чиновника долго служил предметом одушевленных пересказов и рассуждений в гостинице. История была вот какого рода.' [For a long time afterward the policeman's story [rasskaz] served as the subject of animated retelling and discussion in the hotel. The story [istoriia] goes as follows.][72] These two lines make use of two words routinely used in Russian to describe a narrative, 'rasskaz' and 'istoriia'. Here, however, they are used as two nouns emphasising the distinction of the event [istoriia][73] and the narrative [rasskaz] that was constructed around it. The narrative here is an interpretation of factual events, produced by the agent of the state power to be disseminated and internalised ('served as the subject of animated retelling and discussion') by the public (here, symbolically, 'the servants' [prisluga]).

The novel proceeds to describe the confrontation between the police officers and passers-by at the scene of the crime. While attempting to make sense of what has happened, a mass of passers-by spontaneously breaks up into two groups: a 'conservative majority' [konservativnoe bol'shinstvo] that believes the man had shot himself and a 'progressive' minority [progressisty] who believe that a more complex series of determinations are likely to be at play. The two groups differ in the interpretation of the event but agree on their judgement of the perpetrator, whom they declare to be a 'fool' [durak]. In the end, after a hat with a bullet hole is found in the river, the conservative interpretation finally wins over 'the spirit of denial and progress'.[74]

The opening scene of the novel offers its readers a symbolic model of the origin, transmission and interpretation of narratives, pointing out the ideological motivations behind different interpretations. In the overall structure of the novel, it acts as metadiegetic prolepsis, building up a particular kind of 'interpretational' suspense. The story catches up with the 'bait' cast at the very beginning of the novel at the end of chapter 3, when Rakhmetov presents Vera with a note from Lopukhov, explaining the reasons behind his mysterious disappearance and fake suicide. The readers, now armed with hindsight, are reminded about this model of the interpretative apparatus offered to them earlier as a warning.

This account of a sensational event is followed directly by a scene of domestic happiness, disrupted by the news of the same mysterious death. In the sub-chapter 'The First Consequence of this Foolish Affair', the readers are thus plunged into the action *in medias res*. The second introductory chapter functions as an additional 'hook' for the readers' attention: no explanation is given as to who the characters in this scene are or how they are connected to the rest of the story that unfolds in the next six chapters.

Following these two introductory chapters[75] comes the novel's preface, quite possibly the most analysed three pages of Chernyshevskii's entire oeuvre and one of the overtly metafictional parts of the novel. If the first two instalments are written in the intentionally brisk style of contemporary realist narratives (the works Chernyshevskii was hoping to emulate included texts by N. G. Pomialovskii or N. V. Uspenskii),[76] the preface opens with a direct appeal to the reader and proceeds with an extreme narrative self-consciousness. Almost immediately, it set up the novel's main rhetorical opposition of the narrator and his multiple addressees, and established its governing discursive principle of ontological uncertainty.

In keeping with the previous two sub-chapters, the preface functioned as a secondary explanatory prolepsis that was even more explicitly metadiegetic. Openly addressing the issue of literary conventions and the role of the reader in the functioning of a literary work, the preface also referred to the 'future before its time',[77] but this time in terms of the readers' future interaction with the text itself. Partly evoking the typical rhetoric of the thick journals' editor's letters and partly emulating the didactic asides from the novels of Laurence Sterne and Henry Fielding,[78] the preface defined the manner of the novel's narrative voice that would be sustained throughout the entire text. Moreover, through the constant use of the word 'audience' [publika], referring to the reading public but also evoking spectators at the theatre, the preface establishes the metaphor of narrative as a performance that is carried on throughout the novel and culminates in the title of the final chapter, 'Change of Scene' [Peremena dekoratsii]. Referring back to the first of the introductory sub-chapters, this metaphor presents the text of the novel as a performance open to multiple interpretations.

The main agent of performing the narrative is, of course, the novel's maverick narrator. Constantly engaging his addressees and interlocutors in direct dialogue, he directs the readers' attention to the aspects of the text that he wants to emphasise (for example, his thoughts on the 'new people' and their progressive way of life) and distracts them from the issues that might obstruct the novel's dissemination (the implied author's connection to underground political movements, or the fact that the novel was written by a convicted political criminal).

Thus, the performativity of the novel's metadiegetic prolepses served both practical and conceptual purposes. Simultaneously warning the readers of the dangers of authoritative interpretations and delivering a didactic message, the metalepses draw them into the world of the novel in an efficient and playful way.

The Perspicacious Narrator...

Following the two introductory sub-chapters, the oft discussed preface of the novel introduced a self-conscious narrator, whose patronising treatment of his (perspicacious or otherwise) readers has become one of the most recognisable literary features of *Chto delat'?*. The narrator also remained the main agent of metanarrative throughout the novel.

In his various roles, the narrator features in transgressive conversations with the perspicacious reader, in both the metaleptic scenes involving the character

Rakhmetov and the novel's ambivalent final chapter. Unlike the narrator in Pisemskii's *Vzbalamuchennoe more*, who introduces himself as 'Monsieur Pisemskii',[79] the narrator in *Chto delat'?* is an amalgam of its creator's current and future selves. The presently incarcerated literary critic, novelist and social commentator addresses his loyal readers throughout the novel, while his future self, freed from prison, appears only in the last chapter. This layered narratorial presence can be unpacked with the help of a few clues.

The narrator made several references that make it possible to identify him with the biographical author, Nikolai Chernyshevskii. In the chapter describing the narrator's meeting with the character Rakhmetov, the narrator notes that he is a 'treasured' person for a young radical to know.[80] Later on, discussing Vera's desire to become a medic, he reminisces about a fire that he helped to put out as a child.[81] Both of these remarks referred to Chernyshevskii's own position in society and incidents from his own childhood, even if the narrator was never identified by name in the final version of the novel. Initially, however, Chernyshevskii gave the narrator his own name, 'Nikolai'. He then changed the name to 'Vladimir', and finally settled on no name at all. The draft of the first chapter lists among other *dramatis personae*: 'a person, narrating [Nikolai] Vladimir Petrovich Turchinov'.[82] In the scene of the narrator's meeting with Rakhmetov, he is referred to mysteriously as 'Mr. N.'. This progression of changes suggests that Chernyshevskii saw the character partly as his alter ego but did not want to make the connection between himself and the narrator of his text too explicit.

Ontologically, the narrator here occupies the transgressive position of a character who is anchored in reality outside of the fictional text, who features in the text, but who also exists in the realm of fictional projections into the future. Even though at first he appears in the guise of a conventional omniscient narrator, this figure's ontological ambivalence, put forward in the preface in such a bold way, is retained throughout the text of the novel through the device of narratorial asides. His inability to settle on either one side or the other of the ontological divide forms one of the building blocks of the novel's general ontological ambiguity. The narrative itself emphasises the narrator's volatile status by drawing attention to the different ways in which he relays Vera's story.

Following immediately after the preface, the first chapter, 'Vera Pavlovna's Life with her Family', sets a date for the beginning of the novel (1852, sometime before the unspecified date when the narration itself commences). Describing Vera's neighbours, the narrator briefly notes 'I don't know who now resides in the fourth-floor apartment…', only to disappear again for the next few chapters. Later on, he reappears, professing his allegiance to one of character's style of speech: 'Just like Julie, I too like to call vulgar things by their real names'.[83]

The first of the authorial intrusions quoted above would not stand out to Chernyshevskii's contemporaries. Indeed, similar asides, indicating the presence of an omniscient narrator, proliferate in the works of mid-nineteenth-century writers of various ideological persuasions, from Goncharov and Turgenev to Pisemskii and Gertsen. The second aside, however, is indicative of a specific role the narrator would play at a later stage in Chernyshevskii's novel.[84]

Soon after the narrator admits his propensity for rude expressions, he recalls the promises made in the preface, once again warning the reader about the kind of narrative he is offered:

> Если бы я хотел сочинять трескучие столкновения, я б и дал этому положению трескучую развязку; но ее не было на деле; если бы я хотел заманивать неизвестностью, я бы не стал говорить теперь же, что ничего подобного не произошло; но я пишу без уловок и потому вперед говорю: трескучего столкновения не будет, положение развяжется без бурь, без громов и молний.[85]

> [If I wanted to create powerful confrontations, I would provide a thunderous resolution for this predicament. In fact it was not like that at all. If I wanted to entice you with uncertainty, I wouldn't be telling you now that nothing of the sort took place. But since I am writing without setting any traps, I'll say in advance that there will be no thunderous confrontation; this predicament will be resolved without storm, thunder or lightning.][86]

Here, the narrator purports to follow a particular style of storytelling to which he pledged himself when launching his narrative. Its main purpose is to be true to life, because the truthfulness of the story compensates for its artistic imperfections. The disgraceful tricks have only been used at the beginning to lure the reader in, but now, the story will be told exactly as it happened and no manipulation of the reader's attentions and sympathies will occur. Moreover, the narrator promises that in the future the story will unfold with minimum dramatic effect. It seems that the narrator is setting out a binding contract with his readers — in fact, if his readers have any understanding of how literary fiction works, they should be able to notice that the restrictions he places on himself run counter to any dynamic narrative developments.

The narrator disguises the obvious falsity of his promises by fashioning the image of the reader as both a demanding contractual partner and an accomplice. By explaining his actions in advance, the narrator aims to transform the reader from a passive recipient of the text into its active interpreter. It is not a coincidence that he next addresses the reader in a companionable, almost conspiratorial way:

> Читатель, ты, конечно, знаешь вперед, что на этом вечере будет объяснение, что Верочка и Лопухов полюбят друг друга? — Разумеется, так.[87]

> [Dear reader, you know, of course, well in advance that there will be a conversation between Verochka and Lopukhov which will clear up the misunderstanding between them and that they will fall in love. That goes without saying.][88]

The narrator is styling himself as thoughtful and caring ('I am forewarning the reader about everything...')[89] and saying there cannot possibly be any hidden meaning in his words:

> Я не из тех художников, у которых в каждом слове скрывается какая-нибудь пружина, я пересказываю то, что думали и делали люди, и только; если какой-нибудь поступок, разговор, монолог в мыслях нужен

для характеристики лица или положения, я рассказываю его, хотя бы он и не отозвался никакими последствиями в дальнейшем ходе моего романа.⁹⁰

> [I am not the sort of author whose every word hides some kind of surprise. I describe what people thought and what they did, and that's all. If some action, conversation, or internal monologue is needed to characterise a person or situation, then I'll relate it, even if it should prove to have no influence on the future course of my novel.]⁹¹

In fact, the events in the novel resolve themselves in a most melodramatic fashion when Vera and Lopukhov elope and marry in secret, and so the reader's expectations are ultimately betrayed. Chernyshevskii thus creates an original type of an unreliable narrator, whose unreliability manifests itself not in the usual untruthful representation of the events. Rather, it lies in his readiness to test the boundaries and ultimately betray the unspoken rules of the narrator/audience relationship that have been established at the outset of the narrative. He is not unreliable in what he tells, but unreliable in how he promises to deliver this information. The narrator breaks almost all the promises he has made, purposefully jolting the readers out of interpretative complacency and drawing their attention to the mechanics of narrative manipulation. As a result, in *Chto delat'?*, as H. Porter Abbott notes in his definition of narratorial unreliability, 'the narration itself — its difficulties, its liability to be subverted by one's own interests and prejudices and blindness — becomes part of the subject'.⁹²

The narrator consistently emphasises the difference between facts and their interpretation. Chapter 1 starts with a description of the contested ownership of the apartment block where Vera's parents live. According to the sign on the building, it belongs to one Storeshnikov, but in fact it is his widow who actually owns the entire building.⁹³ In his meeting with the narrator, Rakhmetov asks for Mr. N's help with some unnamed underground activity, but Mr. N refuses because that is 'simply not what he does'. Rakhmetov then calls Mr. N a liar and the narrator admits in hindsight that indeed he was 'forced to say not what he believes' [govoril emy ne to, chto dumal].⁹⁴ These constant discrepancies between what things are and what they look like urge the readers to remain vigilant towards multiple possible interpretations of the events.

Throughout the novel, metanarrative is used to discuss the type of text the narrator is presenting to his audience. A type of an interpretative commentary on the unfolding narrative runs through the novel, uniting the narrator and the readers in a companionable 'we': 'we shall now see how she acquired this proof'.⁹⁵ This commentary keeps up the interpretative rhetoric of Chernyshevskii's journal articles but it also maintains the channel of communication between the narrator and the reader.

Aside from the narrator, the preface also introduced his addressees and interlocutors — an implied audience. This implied audience consisted of three different types of readers: a perspicacious male reader [pronitsatel'nyi chitatel'] (the narrator's antagonist), ordinary male and female readers [chitatel', chitatel'nitsa] (open to the narrator's arguments), and, finally, 'the audience' [publika] for whose benefit the narrative is put together and with whose opinion the narrator is most concerned. The division into these groups was, with rare deviations, sustained throughout the entire novel, but the preface itself focused specifically on this further sub-categorisation of readers: dividing them into female and male readers.

Ever since Nikolai Karamzin asserted that sophisticated literary discourse should emulate the speech of society ladies and aim to have them as readers,[96] the image of the female reader had gained particular significance in Russian literary polemics. This issue became even more prominent in the 1860s when the debates around the woman question, carried out on the pages of the influential Russian thick journals, diverted attention to the literary aspects of the female emancipation movement.[97] The gendered nature of the discussion of types of readership in the preface was further exacerbated by the fact that 'audience' [publika] in Russian is a feminine noun. The dialogue therefore turns, naturally, into that of a male writer and his female addressee.

The intuitive but sometimes naïve and easily distracted female reader was juxtaposed with the male reader, who is arrogant and prone to erroneous judgements. Most importantly, this split in the novel's 'audience' evoked the division of the public into conservatives and progressists, outlined in the opening sequence 'The Fool'. The reasons for which the male reader was mocked in the preface are also reminiscent of the earlier passage: just as the servants of the hotel cannot make any sense of the story without the official version of the narrative provided by the police officer, the reader 'knows only what is said to [him]' [znaesh' tol'ko to, chto tebe skazhut].[98] The reading public has a typically female literary taste for engaging narratives, but most importantly, it lacks proper aesthetic judgement. The narrator's main problem with his reading public's incompetence lies in its inability to distinguish between aesthetically pleasing texts that reflect reality and artless texts that aim only for verisimilitude. Thus, the discussion of the issue of 'artistic talent' in the preface introduced the contested aspect of Chernyshevskii's aesthetic theory of realist fiction — the paradox of mimetic verisimilitude.

Chernyshevskii's arrogant narrator easily antagonises modern readers and critics. However, read in the historical and political context of the novel's publication, the rhetoric of the preface comes across as not just derisive, but also cautionary. The narrator, echoing the point of the novel's introductory chapter, scolds the readers for being too naïve in presuming the benevolent agenda of the source from which a narrative originates:

> сам ты ничего не знаешь, не знаешь даже того, что тем как я начал повесть, <u>оскорбил, унизил тебя</u>. Ведь ты не знал этого, — правда? — ну, так знай же![99]

> [Why, you know nothing at all by yourself! You don't even know that in the way I started this work I <u>insulted you and humiliated</u> you. You did not know that, did you? Well, now you do!][100]

This unsophisticated rhetorical trick guaranteed that every reader would count herself a part of the privileged minority rather than the despised majority. In addition, these insistent warnings to the reader drew attention to the public's susceptibility to ideological manipulation through narratives, including those of literary fiction. Thus, the abuse of the unsuspecting reader functions, in fact, as a symbolic representation of the dangers that a lack of awareness of any narrator's agenda could bring.

Couched in the terms of an ironic dialogue with the readers, as in the example above, the preface plays out Chernyshevskii's inner conflict of compromising literary aesthetics in order to put forward his own agenda. The narrator communicates the author's anxiety about going against his own better aesthetic judgement to reach a wider public that usually does not engage with sophisticated literary texts. Having 'low opinion' and being 'angry' at the readers' base tastes, Chernyshevskii did not have any illusions about the amount of dry moralising the public can absorb. In his articles, he repeatedly stated (following Belinskii) that the reading public is the real arbiter of literary success and the real guide to its development: 'The power of the reading public in literary affairs is limitless. Literature becomes what the public wants it to be.'[101]

Concluding the preface, the narrator states:

> Есть в тебе публика, некоторая доля людей, — теперь уже довольно значительная доля, — которых я уважаю. [...] Но с ними мне не нужно было объясняться. Их мнениями я дорожу, но я вперед знаю, что оно за меня. Добрые и сильные, честные и умеющие... [Вы] недавно начали возникать между нами, но вас уже не мало, и быстро становится все больше. Если бы вы были публика, мне уже не нужно было бы писать; если бы вас еще не было, мне еще не было бы можно писать. Но вы еще не публика, а уже вы есть между публикою, — поэтому мне еще нужно и уже можно писать.[102]

> [Yet there is among you, dear readers, a particular group of people — by now a fairly sizeable group — which I respect. [...] There is no need to offer them any explanation. I value their opinion, but I know in advance that they're on my side. Good, strong, honest, capable people — you have only just begun to appear among us; already there's a fair number of you and it's growing all the time. If you were my entire audience, there'd be no need for me to write. If you did not yet exist, it would be impossible for me to write. But you're not yet my entire audience, although some of you are numbered among my readers. Therefore it's still necessary and already possible for me to write.][103]

Indeed, explaining his views to like-minded supporters did not present a challenge to someone as well trained in political discussion as Chernyshevskii was by 1863, at the pinnacle of his journalistic career. A traditional interpretation of this passage in the criticism on Chernyshevskii explains it by asserting the author's awareness of the censor and the need to 'smuggle out' the true content of his novels to the readers.[104] I would argue that, perhaps more importantly, the preface demonstrated Chernyshevskii's awareness of the rules he had to obey to retain the reader's favour. As a utilitarian and a materialist, committed to the ideals of Enlightenment,[105] Chernyshevskii saw nothing wrong in using a work of literature as a means to a didactic end. At the same time, as a publicly recognised authority on contemporary literature, he was uneasy about the compromises required to cater to the tastes of a general reading public. In his opinion, he had to 'humiliate himself' by submitting his writing skills to the requirements of an accessible narrative:

> Ты, публика, добра, очень добра, и потому ты неразборчива и недогадлива. [...] Не осуждай меня за это, — ты сама виновата; твоя простодушная наивность принудила меня унизиться до этой пошлости.[106]
>
> [You, the public, are kind, very kind indeed, and therefore undiscriminating and slow-witted. [...] Don't condemn me for it: you deserve all the blame. It's your own simple-minded naivete that compelled me to stoop to such vulgarity.][107]

Despite being repulsed by the literary vulgarities, Chernyshevskii has a clear idea of how to use them:

> Я употребил обыкновенную хитрость романистов: начал повесть эффектными сценами, вырванными из средины или конца ее, прикрыл ее туманом. [...] я должен был забросить тебе удочку с приманкою эффектности.[108]
>
> [I employed the conventional ruse of a novelist: I began my tale with striking scenes taken from the middle or the end, and I shrouded them with mystery. [...] I was obliged to bait my hook with striking scenes.][109]

Now that the readers' interest had been captured, the story could go on for its original purpose — to dispel confusion and teach a lesson:

> Не будет ни эффектности, никаких прикрас. Автору не до прикрас, добрая публика, потому что он все думает о том, какой сумбур у тебя в голове, сколько лишних, лишних страданий делает каждому человеку дикая путаница твоих понятий.[110]
>
> [There will be neither striking scenes nor embellishments. The author is in no mood for such scenes, dear public, because he keeps thinking about the confusion in your head, and about the useless, unnecessary suffering of each and every one of us that results from the absurd muddle in your thoughts.][111]

Later on in the novel, its self-reflexive hero Rakhmetov, describing the turn the story had taken, would lament the fact that 'instead of simple conversations of the most serene sort, such a heart-rendering melodrama arose'.[112] Despite the fact that, as Peter Brooks pointed out in his study of European melodrama, 'the novel during the nineteenth century [...] still maintained an unembarrassed relation to popular entertainment',[113] Chernyshevskii was palpably resentful about the fact that he had to present his educating story in a ruse of a 'stupid melodrama', full of 'torment over trifles and crises over nonsense'.[114] Most of the narrator's dialogues with his multiple narratees centred on precisely the same problem of aesthetic compromise. It was, however, his transgressive interaction with his usual addressee, the perspicacious reader, that truly upset the novel's ontological unity.

... and his Omniscient Reader

The figure of the perspicacious reader, an annoying, all-pervasive presence who had ruined the experience of reading this novel for many an actual reader, is integral to the text's overall structure, as well as to the functioning of metanarrative in *Chto delat'?*. The novel's ontological ambiguity rests on multiple transgressions of ontological levels, or metalepses, and a significant number of those involve the narrator's interaction with his preferred narratee. In a reversal of the typical narrator/narratee relationship, the author playfully imposes his own omniscience onto the reader. When, as it would, the reader's knowledge invariably falls short of the desired level, this produces a noticeable comic effect that enlivens the (otherwise admittedly sometimes dry) pages of Chernysheskii's novel.

The 'perspicacious sort of reader' [pronitsatel'nyi sort chitatelei] first appears early in the novel, in one of the first descriptions of the representatives of 'the strange young people' [strannaia molodezh'], Lopukhov and Kirsanov. In this scene, the young doctors discuss how best to help their new female friend, Vera, without once discussing whether she is attractive. The narrator implies that, prone to misinterpreting what he reads, this reader thinks the new people strange and uninterested in aesthetics, misunderstanding their preoccupation with Vera's well-being rather than her beauty. In order to draw attention to his characters' support for ideas of female emancipation, Chernyshevskii emphasises their attitude to Vera as a fellow human being rather than an attractive woman. As integral as the introductory chapters of the novel for plot development, this scene is equally symbolic: it touches on the main argument of contemporary debates of literary aesthetics, the confrontation between the 'real'/realist' and 'aesthetic' critics. Representing the 'majority of professional litterateurs' [bol'shinstvo zapisnykh literatyrnykh liudei] and 'aesthetic litterateurs' [esteticheskiie literaty],[115] the perspicacious reader is immediately styled as the narrator's ideological adversary.

Throughout the novel, the perspicacious reader continues to represent all the 'authors and literary hacks' [literaty i literaturshchiki],[116] a class of people who know their own mind and are unlikely to change it. 'Well, God be with you, whatever you say, for there is no way to talk you out of it',[117] notes the resigned narrator. As an adversary of both the narrator and the 'new people', the perspicacious reader also has a remarkable double among the novel's characters: Vera's mother, Maria Alekseevna. Maria Alekseevna's role in the novel is significant: she is a catalyst of most of the events in the first part of the novel. In addition, she is a concrete embodiment, a personification, of the 'Old People' from whom Vera, Lopukhov, Kirsanov, Rakhmetov and their friends aim to distinguish themselves. Maria Alekseevna is often mentioned in self-conscious authorial asides. For example, discussing her powers of reasoning, the narrator sarcastically notes: '[she] studied the same rule of logic that I too learned by heart'.[118] The scenes featuring Maria Alekseevna are usually accompanied by a commentary on the style in which they are narrated: the fact that they resemble a farce ('pokhodiat na fars') is out of the narrator's control ('reshitel'no protiv moei voli'), despite the danger they pose of turning the narrative into 'vaudeville'. The reason for the inclusion of these scenes, the narrator maintains, is to convey the events exactly as they happened no matter how much that might compromise the overall artistic value of the work:

> Но я рассказываю дело не так, как нужно для доставления мне художнической репутации, а как оно было. Я как романист очень огорчен тем, что написал несколько страниц унижающихся до водевильности.[119]
>
> [But I'm recounting this affair the way it happened, rather than the way needed to establish my artistic reputation. As a novelist I very much regret that I wrote several pages in which I stooped to the level of vaudeville.][120]

By this point, an attentive reader will have noticed that the narrator's claims are not to be trusted. The narrator's running commentary in these scenes is emphasised by the direct interpretative rhetoric. The descriptions of events are accompanied by a number of statements such as: 'I start explaining' [prinimaius' ob'iasniat'];[121] 'I say this to justify' [govoriu v opravdanie];[122] 'I say this not in jest' [ne shutia govoriu];[123] 'I express my respect, sing praises' [vyrazhaiu svoie uvazhenie, proslavliaiu],[124] etc.

At one point, the narrator initiates a brief but direct dialogue with Maria Alexeevna:

> — Довольны ли вы, Марья Алексеевна?
> — Что, батюшка мой, мне быть довольной-то? Обстоятельства-то мои плоховаты?
> — Это и прекрасно, Марья Алексеевна.[125]
>
> ['Are you content, Marya Aleksevna?' 'What should I be satisfied with, my good sir? My circumstances are rather poor, aren't they?' 'That's as it should be, Marya Aleksevna.'][126]

Ontologically transgressive (the author is talking to his own character), this dialogue is reminiscent of the conversations the narrator often holds with his adversary, the perspicacious reader. In fact, it appears that Maria Alekseevna and the perspicacious reader share a common feature: both are representatives of the old, un-enlightened and non-progressive people. The style of the dialogues with the perspicacious reader often veers towards conversational, with refrains and a specific colloquial rhythm.[127] This type of language is used to present Maria Alekseevna's speech, too. Of all the characters, Maria Alekseevna comes closest to being the embodiment of the implied perspicacious reader. Her relationship with Vera and Lopukhov becomes, in effect, a micromodel of Chernyshevskii's relationship with an ideal censor, firmly conservative and easy to fool. In a neat case of life emulating art, the history of the novel's own miraculous progress through the hands of the various censors, described in the beginning of this chapter, shows that such a relationship was indeed possible in reality.

The characters of the novel and its implied readers are able to decode the novel's actual message with varying degrees of success. Throughout the text, Chernyshevskii constructs a sophisticated hierarchical system of the characters' and readers' ability to interpret the events that happen on both sides of the ontological divide. In one of the novel's most humorous passages, Maria Alekseevna and Storeshnikov completely misinterpret the titles of the books that Lopukhov has brought for Vera.[128] Whereas Maria Alekseevna's ignorance remains static, Vera gains more insight the closer she is drawn to the New People. At first, she also interprets Lopukhov's words about his fiancé in a conventional way, but having read the books he supplied her with, she is able to see though his metaphors. In Chernyshevskii's understanding, the spiritual and political development of an individual is seen partly as a process of honing skills of effective interpretation.

Similarly, the perspicacious reader, styled as the narrator's adversary, is unable to interpret the events of the novel. He is stubbornly, hopelessly ignorant, even though he thinks himself to be a connoisseur of the arts. Even when the 'general public', amenable to the narrator's arguments, can be trusted to understand the text on its own, the perspicacious reader needs further clarification. He is, however, cunning and suspects that he is not told everything there is to know: for example, after Rakhmetov is introduced, the perspicacious reader suspects that the narrator has ties with other political radicals.[129]

Another typical representative of the older generation, Maria Alekseevna, misinterprets most of what happens to Vera in the first chapter of the novel, even though she is suspicious that she is being fooled. Her daughter Vera, as the readers are constantly reminded, is not particularly special, and neither is the general reading public.[130] Thus, the contrast between Vera and her mother on the level of the system of characters is echoed in the contrast between the general public and the perspicacious reader on the level of the novel's implied readers. The continuous use of the same device, metalepsis, draws attention to this structural parallel.

The perspicacious reader is the narrator's persistent addressee:

> Однако же, как мы с проницательным читателем привязаны друг к другу. Он раз обругал меня, я два раза выгнал его в шею, а все-таки мы с ним не можем не обмениваться нашими задушевными словами; тайное влечение сердец, что вы прикажете делать!'[131]
>
> [My, how attached we've become, the perspicacious reader and I. He insulted me, I threw him out on his ear twice, and still we go on exchanging our innermost thoughts. A secret attraction of hearts! What can we do about it?][132]

Echoing the dialogue quoted above, perspicacious reader gains his own voice in the chapter following Rakhmetov's introduction. In this instance, just like Maria Alekseevna, the perspicacious reader engages in a direct dialogue with the narrator. An illusion of the perspicacious reader's autonomy is created and sustained: his judgements appear to be not just separate but contrary to the narrator's. This conflict plays out in a revealing conversation about the details of Lopukhov's fake suicide:

> Теперь проницательный читатель уже не промахнется в отгадке того, кто ж это застрелился. 'Я уже давно видел, что Лопухов', говорит проницательный читатель в восторге от своей догадливости. Так куда ж он девался и как фуражка его оказалась простреленною по околышу? 'Нужды нет, это все шутки его, а он сам себя ловил бреднем, шельма', ломит себе проницательный читатель. Ну, бог с тобою, как знаешь, ведь тебя ничем не урезонишь'.[133]
>
> [Surely now the perceptive reader can no longer fail to guess who it was who

shot himself. 'I've known for some time that it was Lopukhov,' he says, thrilled by his own perspicacity. Well then, what's become of him? How was it that his cap was shot right through the band? 'There's no need for that! It was merely one of his tricks. And he himself was helping to drag the river for his own corpse, that rascal!', proclaims the perceptive reader. Well, God be with you, whatever you say, for there is no way to talk you out of it'.][134]

The perspicacious reader's bad literary and artistic taste or, sometimes, a complete absence thereof, is ridiculed throughout the novel. In *Chto delat'?*, the inability to make 'correct' aesthetic judgements is equal to the lack of an enlightened political judgement: 'You're very poor, my dear sir, on those aesthetic deliberations you so love...'[135]; 'You're very poor, my dear sir, in your understanding of the way decent people think...'.[136]

The ideological conflict between the narrator and the perspicacious reader reaches its climax in a scene of direct discursive confrontation. Finally, the narrator can no longer tolerate the reader's ignorance and tries to dispatch him altogether. In the novel's most ontologically transgressive scene, the perspicacious reader once again interrupts the flow of the narrative with his unwanted comments:

> А я знаю... Что это? знакомый голос... Оглядываюсь... так и есть! он, он, проницательный читатель, так недавно изгнанный с позором за незнание ни аза в глаза по части художественности; он уж опять тут, и опять со своею прежнею проницательностью, он уж опять что-то знает! — А! я знаю, кто писал... Но я торопливо хватаю первое, удобное для моей цели, что попалось под руку, — попалась салфетка, потому что я, переписав письмо отставного студента, сел завтракать — итак, я схватываю салфетку и затыкаю ему рот: 'Ну, знаешь, так и знай; что ж орать на весь город?'[137]

> ['Oh, I know...' What's that? A familiar voice... I turn around to look... Sure enough! It's him, the perspicacious reader, recently banished in disgrace for his total ignorance of the ABC's of art. Here he is again, once more with his old perspicacity, claiming that he knows something! 'Oh, I know who wrote that...' I hastily seize the first convenient object that comes to hand which will suit my purpose — it's a napkin, because having transcribed the letter written by the former medical student, I have just sat down to lunch. So I seize a napkin and stuff it in his mouth. 'Well, what if you do! Is that any reason to shout it from the rooftops?'][138]

The comic effect here is achieved, as often before in the conversations with the perspicacious reader, through a mix of colloquial and literary language. This passage presents a complete ontological break, a metalepsis. The narrator, interrupted during the physical act of writing, interacts with an imagined reader of his text. The napkin, stuffed in the reader's mouth, is left over from narrator's breakfast, which he had straight after copying Lopukhov's letter. The letter itself is quoted in full just before this passage, which creates an illusion of immediacy in this transgression of ontological levels.

This metaleptic exchange continues a few pages later, when the perspicacious reader frees himself from the constraints of the napkin. He continues to protest, arguing with the narrator about the characters' behaviour and morality, and finally directly challenges the narrator's moral unreliability, exclaiming 'And the author is an immoral man!'. 'Splendid, you have guessed it!', admits the narrator, steering the discussion towards his favourite topic, the paradox of mimetic verisimilitude: 'It's all too contrived, too exalted. Life is much simpler'.[139]

The irony in this passage, as before, is centred on the unreliability of the novel's narrator. Despite all the mocking that the perspicacious reader receives for his backward aesthetic preferences, the events of the novel unfold precisely in a way that this type of reader would expect. The demands of the accessible and entertaining narrative prevail over the narrator's own preference for dense realist description. The narrator's ambivalent opinion of his own role in relating this story is expressed in the last line, which leaves the question of the narrator's reliability open.

The perspicacious reader is constantly proven wrong, sometimes via a simple two-step rhetorical strategy. First, the narrator creates the illusion of agreement with the perspicacious reader but then proves him wrong. An example of such a strategy is a discussion about blue stockings, in which the narrator creates the impression that he is discussing Vera. In the middle of the discussion, the narrator turns the insult around by attacking the perspicacious reader to prove that one can be a bore and a nitwit irrespective of gender.[140]

The device of the free indirect speech that is used for the perspicacious reader throughout the novel (with the exception of the direct dialogical confrontations) interestingly mirrors the use of this device elsewhere in the text. Chernyshevskii used free indirect speech liberally if not excessively, both as a means of characterisation and psychological insight as well as for comic effect. Widespread use of this narrative technique also provides a fluid focalisation pattern that allows for a seamless change of the point of view. Thus, the use of free indirect speech allows the reader to encounter and understand now the point of view of the narrator, now the characters, and sometimes even the perspicacious reader's points of view without perceiving a break of the diegetic unity of the text.

Acting as the narrator's interlocutor and functioning as an object of ridicule, the figure of the perspicacious reader is not as one dimensional as it seems. The analysis of the metalepses in which this figure features demonstrates that he bears the weight of the majority of the ontological breaks in the texts, as well providing Chernyshevskii with an extra focaliser alongside the narrator and the characters.

In the final scene of the novel, 'Change of Scene', the figure of the perspicacious reader is used one last time to bring the ontological ambiguity of the text to the fore. Relating the story of a seemingly innocent summer outing in 1865, the chapter features 'a lady in mourning' and 'a man of about thirty years old'. Introduced at the very end of the novel, these figures enjoy an intentionally ambivalent ontological status. Over the years, the scholars have built various elaborate hypotheses according to which this lady in morning represents Chernyshevskii's wife, Ol'ga Chernyshevskaia, to whom the novel is dedicated.[141] If this interpretation is followed through, the man who joins the lady in mourning on her trip to the shopping gallery would be none other but Nikolai Chernyshevskii himself. The action of this last chapter takes place two years into the future in 1865, two years after the summer party described in the previous chapter, a time when Chernyshevskii's trial would have come to an end.

As has been noted above, throughout the novel the persona of the narrator does not steer too far from the biographical persona of the implied author, Nikolai Chernyshevskii. The narrator presents himself also as a writer, a successful, respected professional. He is older than the New People but he socialises in the same circles as Lopukhov and Kirsanov, and knows them well. He is familiar with their way of life and customs, enjoys their trust, and attempts to relate their story accurately and without bias.

Major ontological transgressions in the novel happen in the scenes of the narrator's engagement with the figure of the perspicacious reader, who personifies the conservatives among the novel's implied readers. In these scenes, free indirect speech assigned to the figure of the reader becomes direct dialogue, and a discursive confrontation takes place. In the final scene of the novel, a similar confrontation takes place, when the narrator engages in another direct dialogue with an unhappy reader, unconvinced by this bold description of the events that have not yet happened.

This brief, final conversation with the readers (both perspicacious adversaries and trusting supporters) at the very end of the novel's text is significant structurally, discursively and metaphorically. In this scene, political, social and narrative upheavals all reach their climax. A political change that made the release of the prisoner possible is celebrated in a society of young people, the like of which has never been seen before: they flout social conventions, exchange partners and involve women in productive, if small-scale, industrial activity. In a manner similar to medieval utopias, the narrative achieves an apocalyptic carnivalesque climax where all the rules are broken; the narrator tells of the events that have not yet happened, the characters meet their creator the author; the past meets the future.

Throughout the novel, the transgression of ontological levels in *Chto delat'?* is intentionally noticeable for the reader, jolting him out of the experience of a realist narrative into an acknowledgement of the ease with which any story and its reception can be manipulated. The introduction in the last scene of two characters, who, like the narrator, exist on both ontological planes (both in the novel and in the reality it portrays), maintains this ontological confusion until the last lines of the text.

The role of the perspicacious reader in the ontology of this novel thus reveals itself to be at least twofold. On the one hand, as the narrator's preferred narratee, this figure serves as a rhetorical tool for breaking through and transgressing the ontological levels of the text. The frame-breaking metalepses, such as the one in which the narrator assaults the reader with a napkin, form the core of the most overtly metafictional moments of the novel.

On the other hand, in many cases, the perspicacious reader stands in for the novel's most demanding implied reader — the government censor. Ironically, the historical circumstances of the novel's famously miraculous passing (almost uncensored) through a number of government agencies indicate the success of Chernyshevskii's chosen technique. An unsophisticated rhetorical trick — a continuously staged confrontation between the narrator and the perspicacious reader — encouraged the readers to distance themselves from the perspicacious reader's opinions. This, in turn, ensured that the interpretational model offered by the narrator overrode other, more subversive, readings of the text.

The Rakhmetov Metalepsis

Even though the ontological discrepancies are evident in Chernyshevskii's treatment of all of his characters, nowhere are they more prominent than in the parts of the text that feature Rakhmetov. Rakhmetov is first mentioned in the novel as a minor character, one of Lopukhov's friends who visit his and Vera's house during their marriage. He is described as 'horrible' [uzhasnyi][142] and unfriendly. After Lopukhov's staged suicide, Rakhmetov reappears to comfort Vera and offer inspiring advice.

Chapter 9, 'An Extraordinary Man' [Osobennyi chelovek], relates the story of Rakhmetov's life and includes one of the novel's most interesting metalepses — the story of narrator's meeting with Rakhmetov. Chernyshevskii clearly anticipated that a re-introduction of a minor character into a story that had previously centred on Vera Pavlovna's life might seem arbitrary to his readers. Hence, the re-introduction of Rakhmetov in this chapter is followed by no fewer than two additional chapters in which the 'introduction of the character' as a literary device[143] is debated and discussed in detail.

Rakhmetov belongs to a select group of people of a 'particular breed' [liudi osoboi porody][144] whom the narrator knows personally, a 'living proof' that the new kind of people can come from a traditional background. Chernyshevskii here uses a particular strategy of authentication typical for a realist narrative where the existence and, even more importantly, verisimilitude of a particular character is proved and enhanced by an eye-witness testimony provided by the most authoritative source in a fictional universe — the narrator. Considering that by now the readers have been deceived by the narrator multiple times, the use of this strategy emphasises not just the unreliability of this particular account, but also the questionable nature of the overall claims of authenticity that are typical for realist narratives in general. In order to grant the character the necessary ontological autonomy, in this chapter the narrator emphasises Rakhmetov's special status by discursively downplaying the subject–object opposition typical for the narrator–character relationship.

First, the narrator effaces his own singularity. Throughout the character's introduction the narrator keeps referring to himself as a part of the larger group, 'our circle', as he calls it. The rhetorical entity of the first person singular ([ia]) gently mocks the outstanding people he met and then seamlessly transforms into the 'we' ([my]) of Rakhmetov's admirers:

> 'Над теми из них, с которыми я был близок, я смеялся. [...] Я люблю смеяться над такими людьми. [...] И знали мы, что наш знакомый

Рахметов проживает в год рублей 400. [...] Наш Рахметов из какой-нибудь захиревшей и обеспоместившейся ветви Рахметовых [...] Никто из нас не знал, что у него не 400, а 3 000 рублей дохода.'[145]

[I used to laugh at those particular individuals, my intimate friends, when I was alone with them. [...] I love to laugh at such people. [...] We knew that our friend Rakhmetov lived on an income of about 400 roubles a year. [...] Our Rakhmetov was a member of some declining branch of the family [...] Therefore none of us knew that instead of 400 roubles, he had an income of some 3,000 roubles.][146]

The narrator first encounters Rakhmetov as another member of Lopukhov's and Kirsanov's friendship circle and offers an account of this earlier meeting. Remarkably, this first confrontation can be read as a reverse metaphor of an author's relationship to his character:

Через минуту Рахметов сел прямо против меня, всего только через небольшой стол у дивана, и с этого-то расстояния каких-нибудь полутора аршин начал смотреть мне в лицо изо всей силы. Я был раздосадован: он рассматривал меня без церемонии, будто перед ним не человек, а портрет, — я нахмурился. Ему не было никакого дела. Посмотревши минуты две-три, он сказал мне: 'г. N., мне нужно с вами познакомиться. Я вас знаю, вы меня — нет...'.[147]

[A minute later Rakhmetov sat down directly across from me, with only the small table near the sofa between us; from a distance of some one and a half arshins he began to stare at my face with all his might. I was annoyed. He examined me without ceremony, as if I were a portrait and not a person. I frowned, but it made no difference to him. After staring at me for two or three minutes he said, "Mr. N., I must make your acquaintance. I know you, but you don't know me'.][148]

The usual balance of narrative power here is subversively undermined: the character approaches the narrator as a 'portrait' rather than a 'person', as well as having the advantage of already knowing about his existence but remaining himself unknown. This mimics the position in which characters stand in relation to their narrators, of whom they are presumably unaware despite the fact that the narrators are privy to their most intimate thoughts.

The chapters following the account of the narrator's meetings with Rakhmetov explain the reasons for the character's introduction into the narrative in which he had not featured before and will not feature further. This explanation is effected through a device of initiating a dialogue with the 'perspicacious reader', familiar to the readers from the preface. Rakhmetov, the narrator explains, is described in great detail because otherwise the reader would not know that such people could exist — the reader's imperfect vision would not let him recognise such outstanding specimens if he met them outside the pages of this book. Moreover, Rakhmetov's sudden appearance as a 'main' [glavnyi] character is misleading, as he will not play an important role in the novel's plot. A subtle discursive metalepsis is exercised here through a zeugma of 'leaving the room' and 'leaving the story'.[149]

[...] когда Рахметов, поговорив с Верою Павловною, уйдет, то уже и совсем он уйдет из этого рассказа, и что не будет он ни главным, ни неглавным, вовсе никаким действующим лицом в моем романе.¹⁵⁰

[Well in advance I'll tell you that after he's finished his little chat with Vera Pavlovna, Rakhmetov will take his leave; with that, he'll also take his leave from my narrative. He'll play neither a principal role nor a secondary one, nor any role at all in the rest of my novel.]¹⁵¹

In this passage, the terms of the narrator/reader relationship are dramatically emphasised. The narrator 'tells' and 'describes' ([skazhu, rasskazhu, opishu, rasskaz, opisaniie]): in a 600-word passage these verbs and their derivatives occur no less than eighteen times, whereas the readers 'see' ([videt', vidat', uvidet'], used six times). This emphasis on the visual character of the reader's perception is fully in tune with the novel's continuous metaphor of performativity and spectacle, reflected in the chapter headings and authorial asides. Here, it is realised on the level of metanarrative, giving the readers instructions not only about how to interpret the offered narrative but specifying the means through which this interpretation has to be carried out.

The visual aspect of the reader's interaction with the text is further explored through the use of typography in a manner reminiscent of Laurence Sterne. The reader is invited to make his own guess about the artistic reasons behind the introduction of Rakhmetov as a character:

Зачем же он введен в роман и так подробно описан? Вот попробуй, проницательный читатель, угадаешь ли ты это? А это будет сказано тебе на следующих страницах [...] так это я скажу тебе в конце главы, угадай-ко теперь, что там будет сказано: **угадать нетрудно**, если ты имеешь хоть малейшее понятие о **художественности**, о которой ты так любишь толковать, — да куда тебе! Ну, я подскажу больше чем половину разгадки: Рахметов выведен для исполнения главнейшего, самого коренного требования **художественности**, исключительно только для удовлетворения ему; ну, ну, **угадай хоть теперь**, хоть теперь-то **угадай**, какое это требование, и что нужно было сделать для его удовлетворения, и каким образом оно удовлетворено через то, что показана тебе фигура Рахметова, остающаяся без всякого влияния и участия в ходе рассказа; **ну-ко, угадай**. Читательница и простой читатель, не толкующие о художественности, они знают это, а попробуй-ко угадать ты, мудрец. Для того и дается тебе время, и ставится, собственно, для этого длинная и толстая черта между строк: видишь, как я пекусь о тебе. Остановись-ко на ней, да и подумай, не отгадаешь ли.¹⁵²

[But why then was he introduced and described in such detail? Well, my perspicacious reader, wouldn't you like to guess the reason? You'll be told why a few pages hence [...] I'll explain it all to you at the end of this chapter. You may want to **guess** now what you'll be told then. It's not hard to **guess** if you've even the least notion of **art**, about which you so love to blather. But how could you **guess**? Well, I'll prompt you with more than half the answer: Rakhmetov has been introduced to fulfill the principal, most fundamental, requirement of **art**, and exclusively to satisfy it. Well, well, can you **guess** now? At least you can **guess** what this requirement is, what was needed to satisfy it, and how it was satisfied by the introduction of Rakhmetov, even though he has no influence

сказа;—ну-ко, угадай. Читательница и простой читатель, не толкующіе о художественности, они знаютъ это, а попробуй-ко угадать ты, мудрецъ. Для того и дается тебѣ время, и ставится собственно для этого длинная и толстая черта между строкъ: видишь, какъ я некусь о тебѣ. Остановись-ко на ней, да и подумай, не отгадаешь ли.

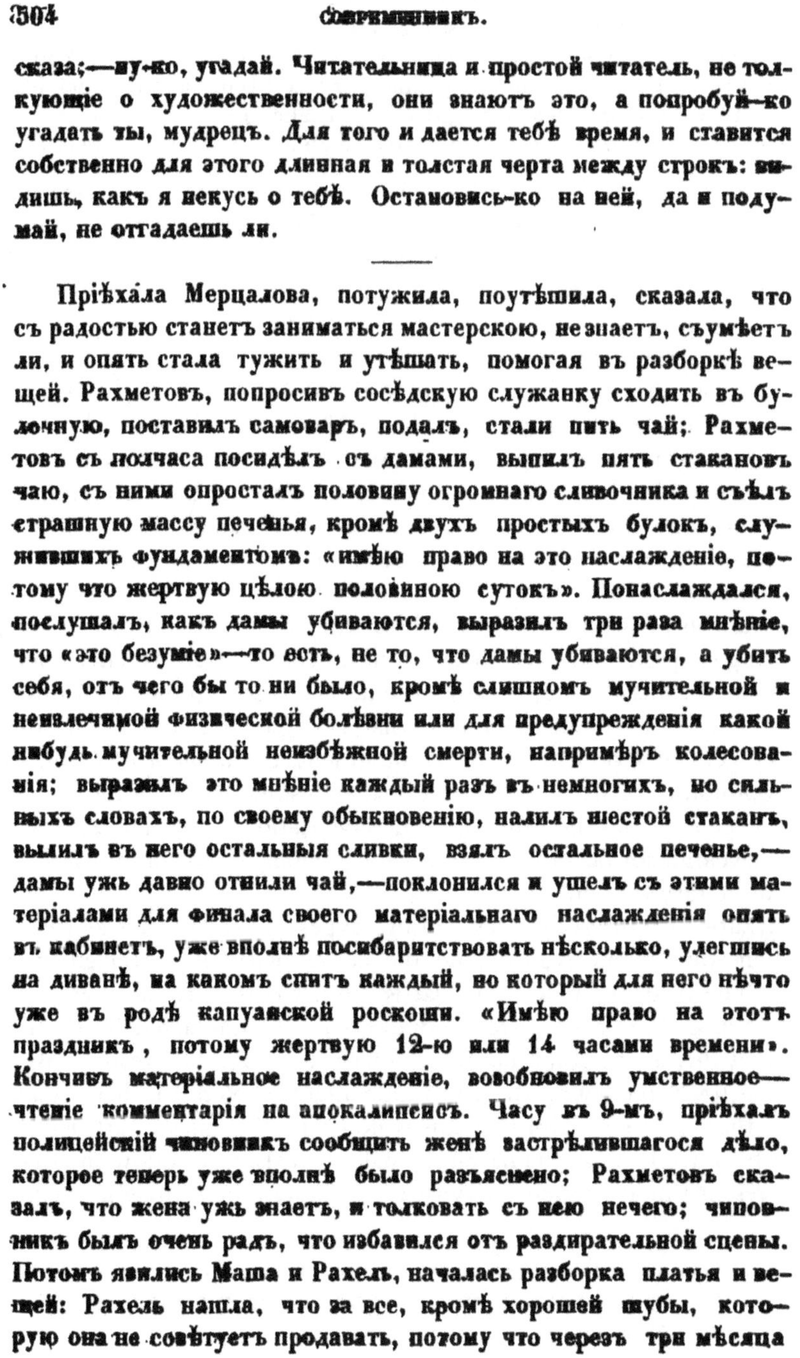

Пріѣхала Мерцалова, потужила, поутѣшила, сказала, что съ радостью станетъ заниматься мастерскою, не знаетъ, съумѣетъ ли, и опять стала тужить и утѣшать, помогая въ разборкѣ вещей. Рахметовъ, попросивъ сосѣдскую служанку сходить въ булочную, поставилъ самоваръ, подалъ, стали пить чай; Рахметовъ съ полчаса посидѣлъ съ дамами, выпилъ пять стакановъ чаю, съ ними опросталъ половину огромнаго сливочника и съѣлъ страшную массу печенья, кромѣ двухъ простыхъ булокъ, служившихъ фундаментомъ: «имѣю право на это наслажденіе, потому что жертвую цѣлою половиною сутокъ». Понаслаждался, послушалъ, какъ дамы убиваются, выразилъ три раза мнѣніе, что «это безуміе»—то есть, не то, что дамы убиваются, а убить себя, отъ чего бы то ни было, кромѣ слишкомъ мучительной и неизлечимой физической болѣзни или для предупрежденія какой нибудь мучительной неизбѣжной смерти, напримѣръ колесованія; выразилъ это мнѣніе каждый разъ въ немногихъ, но сильныхъ словахъ, по своему обыкновенію, налилъ шестой стаканъ, вылилъ въ него остальныя сливки, взялъ остальное печенье,—дамы ужь давно отпили чай,—поклонился и ушелъ съ этими матеріалами для финала своего матеріальнаго наслажденія опять въ кабинетъ, уже вполнѣ посибаритствовать нѣсколько, улегшись на диванѣ, на какомъ спитъ каждый, но который для него нѣчто уже въ родѣ капуанской роскоши. «Имѣю право на этотъ праздникъ, потому жертвую 12-ю или 14 часами времени». Кончивъ матеріальное наслажденіе, возобновилъ умственное—чтеніе комментарія на апокалипсисъ. Часу въ 9-мъ, пріѣхалъ полицейскій чиновникъ сообщить женѣ застрѣлившагося дѣло, которое теперь уже вполнѣ было разъяснено; Рахметовъ сказалъ, что жена ужь знаетъ, и толковать съ нею нечего; чиновникъ былъ очень радъ, что избавился отъ раздирательной сцены. Потомъ явились Маша и Рахель, началась разборка платья и вещей: Рахель нашла, что за все, кромѣ хорошей шубы, которую она не совѣтуетъ продавать, потому что черезъ три мѣсяца

FIG. 2.2. 'Natasha Mertsalova arrived...' N. G. Chernyshesvkii, *Chto delat'?*, *Sovremennik*, 1863 (95), p. 504.

or importance in the rest of the story. **Come now, guess**! My female reader and the common reader who doesn't go on at length about **art** already know the answer. But you, my wise male reader, you too must try to **guess**! You can have as much time as you need; for that purpose I'll put a long, thick black line between sections. See what good care I take of you? Pause over it and reflect as to whether you will or won't be able to guess the answer.]¹⁵³

The passage indeed concludes with a short thick line, a common text paragraph divider sign in publications at that time. In the next paragraph, conventional storytelling is resumed: 'Natasha Mertsalova arrived...' (see Figure 2.2).¹⁵⁴ The hypertrophied orality of the narrator's chant engages the reader verbally, whereas his visual engagement is maintained through the use of unsophisticated but cunningly used graphic means.

A comparison with the draft version of the novel reveals that Chernyshevskii significantly expanded this passage in the final version of his text.¹⁵⁵ The earlier version has no examples of repetition, neither of the verbs nor of the commands to the readers, which makes it an aesthetically smoother but rhetorically weaker version of the same text. The draft also contains no graphic interaction with the reader. It seems that the changes were aimed at intensifying the reader's involvement with the text.

The discussion of Rakhmetov's worth for the current narrative is continued in the following chapter, 'A Conversation with the Perspicacious Reader Followed by his Expulsion'. In this chapter, debating the necessity of introducing Rakhmetov as a character morphs into a discussion of what any character is in a work of literary fiction: an agent of action, the voice of judgment, or an agent of truth. Offering contrary opinions, the narrator and the reader resume the ongoing discussion of aesthetics in general and the function of literary fiction. Thus, an issue of plot and character development becomes a pretext for a wider discussion of the nature and purposes of literary fiction.

The narrator and his addressees, various types of readers, act as two sides in an argument on literary realism and the authenticity of portrayed events and characters. The reader's supposition that Rakhmetov is introduced as an agent of action (he brings Vera a note from Lopukhov) is counteracted by the narrator's assertion that this is not Rakhmetov's primary function. The reader's assumption that Rakhmetov is introduced to pass a judgement on Vera and her friends is also refuted by the narrator's claim that this is not what the rules of art demand. The reason for his introduction, the narrator finally reveals, is to follow the first rule of art: to represent things in such a way that the readers could imagine them exactly as they are:

> Первое требование художественности состоит вот в чем: надобно изображать предметы так, чтобы читатель представлял себе их в истинном их виде.¹⁵⁶

> [The first requirement of art is as follows: one must always depict objects so that the reader can perceive their true form.]¹⁵⁷

So it follows that the character of Rakhmetov is introduced to provide the reading public with another example of a 'New Man'. At this point of the chapter, the narrator's playful tone becomes serious, and, most importantly, his addressee changes from the reader to the public:

> Ну, слушай же. Или нет, не слушай, ты не поймешь, отстань, довольно я потешался над тобою. Я теперь говорю уж не с тобою, я говорю с публикою, и говорю серьезно.[158]
>
> [Well then, listen here. Even better, don't listen, since you won't understand. Leave me alone. I've made fun of you long enough. Now I'll speak with the public instead of with you, and I'll be very serious.][159]

This change exposed the true purpose of this argument: to draw the readers' attention to the degree of verisimilitude in the portrayal of the novel's various characters. The novel's didactic message demanded a certain degree of authenticity in terms of the events that it related. At the same time, the manner of the narrator's argument with his addressees ensured his monopoly on the correct 'reading' of these characters and events, which needed to be communicated to the general reading public, whose interpretative apparatus was deemed, for now, to be inadequate. It was for the benefit of the public that the epic 'larger than life' character of Rakhmetov illuminated the characters of Vera, Lopukhov and Kirsanov, and made them look ordinary rather than 'lofty and beautiful'.[160]

Introducing Rakhmetov in these chapters, Chernyshevskii triggered a metaliterary discussion of the text's aesthetics and structure. Apart from discussing the principles of character description, Chernyshevskii here resurrected debates on aesthetics, including on aspects of imagery, plot and narrative dynamics, all of which were initiated in the novel's preface.

'They are real, and so are you'

Beginning in the preface, the novel's ontological ambiguity is purposefully maintained throughout the text, particularly through the uncertain ontological status of the novel's characters, including the narrator. The draft version of the novel contains, towards the end, a passage in which the narrator unequivocally claims that he is recounting the stories of 'factual new people'.[161] No such note remains in the final version of the text, where the ontological status of the characters is left deliberately ambiguous, leading the readers to believe that the new people of the novel could equally be either real or fictional figures. The elimination of this note is purposeful. The carefully maintained ambiguity of the novel's ontological status does not only accord with Chernyshevskii's general philosophical agenda, but it is also a typical rhetorical modus operandi that he used throughout his earlier writings. Had the passage remained in the final version of the novel, it would have functioned as a final rhetorical bookend for the narrator's dialogue with his readers in the preface.

The passage in question follows the announcement of Lopukhov's (now called 'Beaumont') wedding to Katerina Polozova and the admission that the two families have become very close and would now be friends for a long time. Judging by its position in the draft text, this lengthy passage, discussing real 'facts' behind the novel's plot, has been substituted in the final published version by this note:

> Живут ладно и дружно [...] Но из этого еще не следует, чтобы мой рассказ о них был окончен, нет. [...] Я еще имею рассказать о них много, и ручаюсь, что продолжение моего рассказа о них будет гораздо любопытнее того, что я рассказывал о них до сих пор.[162]

> [They live cheerfully and amicably. [...] But it doesn't follow that my story is at an end. [...] I've much more to tell about them and I guarantee that the continuation of my story will be even more engrossing than what I've told you thus far.][163]

The original passage raises several issues that are of crucial importance for understanding Chernyshevskii's own view of the ontology of his narrative.

Firstly, the narrator of this passage states that the text he offers to the reader is not a novel ('I do no aspire to have written a novel) but rather 'just a story about one of my good friends and people close to her'.[164] Since real life does not abide by the laws of literature, he claims, the story needs to be brought to an end, even if, by novelistic standards, it has reached its climax and does not require further elaboration. Secondly, the narrator feels the need to clarify exactly what has been artistically invented and what has been copied from reality in his story:

> ...мне нужно объясниться с публикою о том, до какой [степени] участвовали в моем рассказе вымысел и многое [ли] в нем изменено против того, как было на самом деле.[165]

> [... I need to explain to the public to which degree an invention took part in my story and how many changes have been made to the account of what had actually happened.]

He then proceeds to explain that even though the names of his characters are fictional, they are in fact real people, and the events they live through have also actually happened at some point in the past ('facts that my good friends have lived'). These 'facts', however, had to be embellished:

> Я для тебя должен был завить и закудрявить простой ход дела, потому что тебе он показался бы уже слишком прост, то есть, по-твоему, груб, прозаичен, безнравственен.[166]

> [For you I can curl and brush up the simple course of events? Because you would have thought it too simple, that is, as you say, rude, prosaic, immoral.]

Having explained himself, the narrator concludes the passage with a promise to finish the story.

The omission of this passage in the final version of the novel is partly a result of Chernyshevskii aiming for more stylistic and rhetorical finesse. Sequential comparison of the draft to the finished text shows that the majority of the changes that Chernyshevskii made were clarifications and intentional blunting of the most direct arguments. It is also a further indication of Chernyshevskii's continuing preoccupation with the dilemma of didacticism and realist representation: the constant negotiation between the degree of truthfulness and aesthetics in a didactic text. The argument, started in the preface, continues with a question: is the main purpose of art to represent reality as truthfully as possible or is it allowed to augment reality so that the didactic effect is heightened? In this passage, Chernyshevskii states clearly that the story is presented in the form of a novel to educate its readers, and so both the events and the characters are embellished for effect. They need, however, also to be realistic to be believable as role-models. The truncated version of the above passage that has survived into the novel's final version omits this explanation. Instead, it promotes an intentional ontological ambiguity that affords ample opportunity for metanarrative and ontological frame-breaking and particularly metalepsis.

The novel's subtitle *From Tales about New People* clearly indicates that the story is told mainly in order to introduce its characters. The problem of establishing their historical authenticity has spawned an entire sub-industry in Chernyshevskii studies.[167] One of the reasons why the issue has attracted so much attention over the years is this intentional ambiguity, a metaleptic confusion, that the text itself promotes. The passage from the novel's draft, quoted above, is a literary mystification, as it has now been established that Chernyshevskii did not have any actual prototypes for his characters. According to Reiser, he might have been inspired by the biographies of people he knew but even in this case they would have resembled his characters much less than the passage suggests.[168] So are Vera Pavlovna, her friends and the *osobennyi chelovek* Rakhmetov portrayed as real people whose story is told by the narrator, who personally knows them, or are they framed as purely fictional characters invented in order to tell an edifying story? The narrator's position on that varies throughout the novel.

On the one hand, he claims to be telling the story of an actual woman, Vera Pavlovna Rozal'skaia, with her explicit 'permission' [rasskazyvaiu (s eie soglasiia)]'.[169] On the other hand, throughout the novel the narrator converses with his characters (Vera,[170] or her mother, Maria Alexeevna[171]), negotiating with them their role in the narrative's progression. Similarly, the stories of the New People are often claimed to be accounts of true events.[172] Throughout the text the narrator makes sure the reader does not forget that he personally met the people he is describing: when Vera is reading Lopukhov's letters, the narrator tells us he is by now used to the antics of 'these people', having spent a lot of time in their company.[173] However, at the same time, the New People are described as 'types' [tipy] with 'typical features'.[174] Even the 'extraordinary man' Rakhmetov, perhaps because of the contemporary literary preoccupation with 'typologies', is described as a representative of a wider community of unusual people.[175] Alongside the narratorial asides and multiple metalepses, these constant oscillations in the characters' ontological status maintain the intentional ontological ambiguity that becomes one of the defining features of the novel.

★ ★ ★ ★

The close reading of the novel's metafictional passages offered in this chapter demonstrates the remarkable prominence of metanarrative in *Chto delat'?*. The novel's metadiegetic prolepses, unreliable narrator, the delicate balance of multiple narratees, as well as the continuously maintained ambiguity of its characters' ontological status, aid the creation of a sophisticated metafictional text that questions its own functions in the process of performing them.

Introducing multiple narratees, as well as exploiting typography to emphasise the ontological ambiguity of his texts, Chernyshevskii used narrative techniques that would have been familiar to him from the works of Laurence Sterne and Henry Fielding. In an innovative way, he adapted these techniques for the purpose of reflecting on current debates on politics and the aesthetics of realist fiction. Indeed, Chernyshevskii turned to metafiction as the most suitable means of communicating his publicly stated philosophical concern with the ontology of literary fiction to a wider audience than the readers of his critical articles.

Taking into account recent advances in the field of Chernyshevskii studies, my aim was to focus on how Chernyshevskii's use of metanarrative, particularly metalepsis, in *Chto delat'?* affected the novel's structure, system of characters and plot dynamic. I suggest that the novel's neglected introductory passages, along with the much-studied preface, function as explanatory metadiegetic prolepses, offering readers a model of the interpretative effort that would be required from them throughout the text. From the introductory chapters onwards, Chernyshevskii's readers are constantly reminded of the dangers of discursive manipulation; both explicitly, in the narrator's asides, and implicitly, by being confronted with the narrator's unreliability. Since the narrator in *Chto delat'?* consistently breaks the promises he makes in his metaliterary observations, I argue that Chernyshevskii's text features an unusual type of unreliable metadiegetic narrator.[176]

Starting with the novel's preface, the narrator's self-reflexive commentary establishes a 'direct causality between the events of the metadiegesis and those of the diegesis, conferring on the second narrative an explanatory function'.[177] The metaphor of theatrical performance, running from the opening scene through the entire novel, performs a similar function, subtly reminding the readers about the difference between reality and its artistic representation. The ability to distinguish between the two is repeatedly shown to be necessary for making a sound political and aesthetic judgement. The perspicacious reader, for instance, who is unable to tell bad art from good, is equally hopeless in the matters of recognizing the progressive ways of the New People. This ongoing narrative self-reflection is performed alongside more overt instances of metanarrative in the novel, such as the frame-breaking metalepses of the dialogues with the perspicacious reader.

The ontological ambiguity merges the planes of the implied author and the narrator, creating an illusion of Chernyshevskii's presence in his own story. By employing the narrator as an eye-witness, Chernyshevskii lends the story further credibility, as do the narrator's multiple references to events that were similar to what had happened in Chernyshevskii's life. The state of ontological confusion is purposefully maintained throughout the text, as demonstrated by my analysis of the ontological status not just of the narrator and his addressees, but also of the novel's characters, the Old and the New People. In this way, Chernyshevskii's main preoccupation in the sphere of aesthetic theory — the ontology of literary fiction — found its way into his own literary practice.

The readers of thick journals would have been able to recognise the narrative voice of *Chto delat'?* as Chernyshevskii's familiar discursive manner, as practised in his role as *Sovremennik*'s leading literary critic. The interpretative rhetoric of journal articles is carried over into the literary text of Chernyshevskii's novel, offering a running commentary on the unfolding events of the plot. Ultimately, *Chto delat'?* provides the reader with the critical apparatus needed to decode its own text.

In *Chto delat'?*, the narrator engages with his addressees in various ways, from staging direct rhetorical confrontation in dialogue, to internalising their free indirect speech into his own statements. The novel's implied audience, broadly divided into supporters and adversaries, becomes the narrator's interlocutor, participating in the debates on the aesthetics of realist narrative. In my analysis, I have argued that the narrator's patronising attitude to his narratees owes more to Chernyshevskii's unease about the aesthetic compromise he had to resort to in his novel than to his actual contempt for his implied audience.

Since the narrator is constantly present in the text, the external focalisation of the third-person omniscient narrator (typical for realist prose of the period) is continuously compromised. Instead, Chernyshevskii imports into his novel the rhetorical type of internal focalisation that he used as a journalist and editor. Often, potentially metaleptic scenes, such as the narrator's direct appeals to his characters, are impossible to categorise in terms of focalisation because they have been dramatised as dialogues. The narrator's conversations with Vera, Maria Alekseevna or Rakhmetov, as well as his arguments with the perspicacious reader, are presented as dialogues — the ultimate dramatic symbiosis of showing through telling. Thus, the focalisation also reflects the merging of the literary and publicistic discourse.

Most of the narratorial asides in the novel explore issues of literary aesthetics, but it is the narrator's conversations with the adversarial perspicacious reader that demonstrate the novel's use of metanarrative at its best. The passages featuring the perspicacious reader established the function of this figure who went beyond his role as the narrator's addressee and a sounding board for his ideas. On several occasions, the perspicacious reader is addressed as if he were present during the act of the text's composition or were able to influence the development of the plot by voicing his opinion. These interactions transgress the barriers between the ontological levels of the text, shattering the novel's mimetic and diegetic unity.

With the help of metanarrative, *Chto delat'?* offered a general commentary not just on literary aesthetics but also on the ontology of novelistic form, testing out various types of relationship between literary fiction and objective reality.

Notes to Chapter 2

1. Demchenko and Pokusaev, *N. G. Chernyshevskii*, pp. 207–09.
2. *Sovremennik*, 1–2 (1862), cover. See Figure 2.1.
3. Aside from *Chto delat'?*, by 1863 Chernyshevskii had produced just two pieces of literary fiction, both unfinished: *Teoriia i praktika* [Theory and Practice] (1848) and *Poniman'e (Ne sudite)* [An Understanding (Do Not Judge)] (1848).
4. Gary Saul Morson, *The Boundaries of Genre: Dostoevsky's Diary of a Writer and the Traditions of Literary Utopia* (Austin: University of Texas Press, 1981), p. 99.
5. For more on the reception of the thesis, see Irina Paperno, *Chernyshevsky and the Age of Realism: A Study in the Semiotics of Behavior* (Stanford, CA: Stanford University Press, 1988), pp. 159–66.
6. The phenomenon of the Russian 'thick journals' is broadly covered in *Literary Journals in Imperial Russia*, ed. by Deborah A. Martinsen (Cambridge: Cambridge University Press, 1997). For the information on the particular journals, published in the 1860s, see one of the articles from the same collection by Robert L. Belknap, 'Survey of Russian Journals, 1840 — 80', ibid., pp. 91–117, as well as V. A. Alekseev, *Istoriia russkoi zhurnalistiki, 1860–1880* (Leningrad: Leningradskii gosudarstvennyi universitet, 1963); B. L. Koz'min, *Zhurnalistika 60-kh godov XIX veka* (Moscow: Vysshaia partiinaia shkola, 1948). For more specifically on *Sovremennik*, see V. E. Evgen'ev-Maksimov, *'Sovremennik' v 40–50 gg.: ot Belinskogo do Chernyshevskogo* (Leningrad: Izdatel'stvo pisatelia, 1934); V. E. Evgen'ev-Maksimov, *'Sovremennik' pri Chernyshevskom i Dobroliubove* (Leningrad: GIKHL, 1936); V. E. Evgen'ev-Maksimov, *Poslednie gody 'Sovremennika': 1863–1866* (Leningrad: GIKHL, 1939).
7. A. Ia. Panaeva, *Vospominaniia* (Moscow: GIKHL, 1956), pp. 324–27.
8. For more on this complicated relationship, see Iu. V. Nikulichev, 'Bog, mamona i obyknovennye novye liudi: ot "Kto vinovat?" k "Chto delat'?", *Voprosy literatury*, 2 (2014), 142–75. On Nekrasov's relationship with *Sovremennik*'s censor V. N. Beketov see ibid., p. 182.
9. On Vsevolod Kostomarov's involvement with Chernyshevskii over the years 1861–63, see Demchenko and Pokusaev, *N. G. Chernyshevskii*, pp. 223–25. Kostomarov's claim that Chernyshevskii was the author of the subversive proclamation *Barskim krest'ianam ot ikh dobrozhelatelei poklon* [To the Manorial Peasants from Their Well-Wishers, Greetings] has since been contested and is believed to have been fabricated. However, the question of the proclamation's authorship remains open. A. A. Demchenko, who believed that Chernyshevskii had no connection to the proclamation, wrote about his debate on the subject with an archive scholar M. I. Perper in A. A. Demchenko, 'Pamiati M. I. Perper', *Novoe literaturnoe obozrenie*, 53 (2002), 258–60.
10. In his memoirs, Chernyshevskii recalls a visit from Dostoevskii, who was convinced of Chernyshevskii's influence on the rioting students. See N. G. Chernyshevskii, 'Moi svidaniia s F. M. Dostoevskim', in *F. M. Dostoevskii v vospominaniiakh sovremennikov*, ed. by A. S. Dolinin, 2 vols (Moscow: Khudozhestvennaia literatura, 1990), I, 5–7 (p. 5). A historical, albeit ideologically biased, account of Chernyshevskii's involvement with the young radicals can be found in N. N. Novikova and B. M. Kloss, *N. G. Chernyshevskii vo glave revoliutsionerov 1861 goda* (Moscow: Nauka, 1981). For a more balanced view, see Paperno, *Chernyshevsky and the Age of Realism*, p. 21.
11. Even after his incarceration, Chernyshevskii remained a popular figure among the Russian radicals, as evidenced by their memoirs, summarised in *Spodvizhniki Chernyshevskogo*, ed. by V. A. Prokof'ev and others (Moscow: Molodaia gvardiia, 1961).
12. N. G. Valentinov, *Nedorisovannyi portret* (Moscow: Terra, 1993), p. 495. In his memoirs, Valentinov recalls a conversation with Lenin, when he mentioned the effect that *Chto delat'?* had on him. Lenin would later use Chernyshevskii's title for his own pamphlet *Chto delat'? Nabolevshie voprosy nashego dvizheniia* (Stuttgart: Verlag von J. H. W. Dietz, 1902). See also V. I. Lenin, *Lenin o literature i iskusstve* (Moscow: Khudozhestvennaia literatura, 1976), p. 647. Although this is not a direct quotation from Lenin's actual writings, its influence on the reception of Chernyshevskii's work in the Soviet times was long-lasting.
13. Even though the first negative review from the censorship committee was produced as early as 15

May 1862, V. N. Beketov still approved the publication of the issue of *Sovremennik* that contained the rest of the novel on 18 May 1863. For a detailed reconstruction of the circumstances of the novel's publication and its censorial history see Demchenko and Pokusaev, *N. G. Chernyshevskii: nauchnaia biografiia*, pp. 211–15; Evgen'ev-Maksimov, *Poslednie gody 'Sovremennika': 1863–1866*, pp. 54–66; S. A. Reiser, 'Nekotorye problemy izucheniia romana "Chto delat'?"', in *Chto delat'?* (Leningrad: Nauka, 1975), pp. 782–834.

14. Three subsequent editions of *Chto delat'?* were published in Geneva by M. K. Elpidin (1867, 1876, 1902), and a photo-reprint edition was published in Leipzig by E. L. Kasporovich in 1897. For more information on the circulation of illegal editions and hand-written copies see Reiser, pp. 788–89. Irina Paperno also offers statistics for handwritten illegal copies that acquired the status of a cultural artifact, see Paperno, *Chernyshevsky and the Age of Realism*, pp. 27–28.

15. Reiser, pp. 788–89.

16. The overall number of published editions was significantly higher since *Chto delat'?* was published in other languages of the constituent republics of the Soviet Union, to be circulated in the local libraries. How many of these volumes were printed to meet the actual demand and how many to meet the governmental quota remains a subject for further research. For a full bibliography of the translations up to 1975, see B. L. Kandel, 'Bibliografiia perevodov romana "Chto delat'?" na iazyki narodov SSSR i na inostrannye iazyki', in *Chto delat'?* (Leningrad: Nauka, 1975), pp. 862–69.

17. For a historical overview of secondary literature on Chernyshevskii see U. A. Gural'nik, *Nasledie N. G. Chernyshevskogo-pisatelia i sovetskoe literaturovedenie: itogi, zadachi, perspektivy izucheniia* (Moscow: Nauka, 1980). I have also written elsewhere on conceptual changes in Chernyshevskii studies over the years in M. I. Vaysman, 'Problemy osveshcheniia romana N. G. Chernyshevskogo "Chto delat'?" v nauchnoi i kriticheskoi literature (1863–2011)', *Vestnik Permskogo universiteta. Rossiiskaia i zarubezhnaia filologiia*, I (2011), 130–39; as well as in M. Vaysman, '"Unnecessary Melodrama": Ideology and Narrative Legacy in Nikolai Chernyshevskii's *What Is to Be Done?* (1863) and William Godwin's *Caleb Williams* (1794)', *Modern Language Review*, 112.1 (2017), 1–19. For the sake of brevity, the review offered in this chapter covers only the works that discuss the problem of metanarrative in Chernyshevskii's writings.

18. 'Obraz avtora' was a definition used in Soviet literary scholarship that was roughly equivalent to Wayne C. Booth's 'implied author'. For more on the Soviet conceptualisation of this narrative device, see William Mills Todd III, 'Discoveries and Advances in Literary Theory, 1960s–1980s: Neoformalism, the Linguistic Model, and Beyond', in *A History of Russian Literary Theory and Criticism: The Soviet Age and Beyond*, ed. by Evgenii Dobrenko and Galin Tihanov (Pittsburgh: University of Pittsburgh Press, 2011), pp. 230–49 (p. 233). Even though B. O. Korman's method can be seen as an original Soviet equivalent of Seymur Chatnam's and Wayne C. Booth's work on the idea 'implied author' and Wolfgang Iser's 'implied reader', the way it was put into practice by Korman's followers was not always as rigorous. For a representative example of the complete confusion between the historical author, implied author, narrator and implied reader, see M. V. Teplinskii, 'Avtor-povestvovatel' v romane N. G. Chernyshevskogo "Chto delat?"', *N. G. Chernyshevskii: stat'i, issledovaniia i materialy*, 8 (1978), 127–37. An impressive attempt to look at the autobiographical motives in Chernyshevskii's work from the point of view of narratology has been more recently undertaken by V. S. Vakhrushev. See V. S. Vakhrushev, '"Chto delat'?" i "Avtobiografia" N. G. Chernyshevskogo: igrovye khody avtorskoi mysli', *N. G. Chernyshevskii: stat'i, issledovania, materialy*, 13 (1999), 14–30.

19. G. E. Tamarchenko, '"Chto delat'?" i russkii roman shestidesiatykh godov', in *Chto delat'?* (Leningrad: Nauka, 1975), pp. 747–82 (p. 777).

20. Ibid., p. 761.

21. According to G. E. Tamarchenko, an author of a number of books and articles on *Chto delat'?*, the narrator of the novel mediated between the inner 'love plot' of Vera Pavlovna and the outer 'revolutionary plot' of Rakhmetov. Ibid., p. 755. Tamarchenko also elaborates on the same topic in his monograph on Chernyshevskii: G. E. Tamarchenko, *Chernyshevskii-romanist* (Leningrad: Khudozhestvennaia literatura, 1976), pp. 231–63. Another scholar, Iu. K. Rudenko, suggested a different division of plots: the inner plot of the new people's life featuring an extradiegetic

omniscient narrator and an outer plot of the author/reader polemic. Rudenko noted the constant crossings of ontological levels between those plots, acknowledging that the novel functioned simultaneously as a self-contained fictional model of reality as well as a part of the same model. Iu. K. Rudenko, *Chernyshevskii-romanist i literaturnye traditsii* (Leningrad: Izdatel'stvo Leningradskogo universiteta, 1989), pp. 81, 232.

22. The Soviet ideological bias had a remarkable effect on the scholars' investigations into the genealogy of Chernyshevskii's narrative strategies. Since Chernyshevskii's intellectual genealogy had to be strictly progressive, comparative studies were very selective and had a distinct preference for Laurence Sterne (N. L. Brodskii and N. P. Sidorov, *Kommentarii k romanu N. G. Chernyshevskogo 'Chto delat'?'* (Moscow: Mir, 1933), p. 57; Rudenko, *Chernyshevskii-romanist i literaturnye traditsii*, p. 136). Until the 1990s, the problem of literary influences on Chernyshevskii in terms of narrative strategies was addressed in a very specific way, reaffirming Chernyshevskii's absolute originality. In this spirit, N. A. Verderevskaia claimed in 1980 that 'the novel's main defining feature, the structural and compositional role of the author and the elements of framing' was absolutely unique to *Chto delat'?*. Along with the 'device of using the author as a character and a participant in the novel's events' it, according to this otherwise very astute scholar, had 'no analogues in the European novel of the nineteenth century or earlier periods' (N. A. Verderevskaia, *Russkii roman 40–60-kh godov XIX veka: tipologiia zhanrovykh form* (Kazan': Izdatel'stvo Kazanskogo universiteta, 1980), p. 107). I have written elsewhere on the problems of studying Chernyshevskii from a comparative point of view and in particular on the influence that eighteenth-century English literature and philosophy had on *Chto delat'?* (see Vaysman, ' "Unnecessary Melodrama" ').

23. For the history of the term and its use as a metastylistic device, see Lev Loseff, *On the Beneficence of Censorship: Aesopian Language in Modern Russian Literature* (Munich: Otto Sagner, 1984), pp. 23–29.

24. In 1979, Rudenko suggested that a division of two readerships into censors and appreciative readers was too simplistic. The critic argued that Chernyshevskii played the two types of implied readers off each other in order to emphasise the differences in their aesthetic rather than ideological preferences. Iu. K. Rudenko, *Roman N. G. Chernyshevskogo 'Chto delat'?': Esteticheskoe svoeobrazie i khudozhestvennyi metod* (Leningrad: Izdatel'stvo LGU, 1979), pp. 2, 8. In his study of Russian utopias, Morson also focuses on this division of readers in two groups. Ultimately, he traces it back to the general rhetoric of apocalyptic narratives, in which the reader has to either accept the view the narrator is advocating or face existential annihilation. Morson, *The Boundaries of Genre*, p. 99.

25. Rudenko, *Chernyshevskii-romanist i literaturnye traditsii*, pp. 20, 39, 19.

26. Morson, *The Boundaries of Genre*, p. 99. The tendency to analyse the poetics of *Chto delat'?* in terms of the binary 'author'/'reader' opposition was so persistent that it has been carried over into the few contemporary studies of Chernyshevskii's fiction. Tat'iana Metlasova's 2006's study of intertextuality in *Povesti v povesti* effectively analysed instances of metanarrative in Chernyshevskii's second novel, focusing particularly on the narratorial voice. And yet, using only of methodologies of B. O. Korman, K. V. Vinogradov and only marginally Roland Barthes, Metlasova defined the instability of the narratorial voice as a constant change of the 'author's masks', leaving the ontological implications of this strategy unexplored. T. M. Metlasova, *Intertekstual'nost', reministsentsii i avtorskie maski v romane N. G. Chernyshevskogo 'Povesti v povesti'. Avtoreferat dissertatsii na soiskanie uchenoi stepeni kandidata filologicheskikh nauk* (Saratov: Saratovskii gosudarstvennyi universitet, 2006).

27. Andrew M. Drozd, *Chernyshevskii's 'What Is to Be Done?': A Reevaluation* (Evanston: Northwestern University Press, 2001), p. 74.

28. Morson, *The Boundaries of Genre*, p. 99.

29. Moser, *Esthetics as Nightmare*, p. 143.

30. The parallax effect, or factor, is a physical distortion of the field of vision that occurs if an object is observed from two different points of view. It has been introduced to literary theory by the scholars of narrative and fictionality. For a discussion of a relationship between mimetic realism and the parallax factor as 'distortions inherent in perception', see Stephen G. Nichols, 'Foreword', in Riffaterre, *Fictional Truth*, pp. vi–x, viii–ix.

31. Aside from major revisionist studies by Andrew M. Drozd and Irina Paperno in English, a number of academic studies and works aimed at a general reader, written in the same spirit, have been published in Russia in the last thirty years. For Russian attempts at redefining Chernyshevskii's work and his place in the literary canon, see *'Chto delat'?' N. G. Chernyshevskogo: istoriko-funktsional'noe issledovanie*, ed. by K. N. Lomunov (Moscow: Nauka, 1990); P. Vail' and A. Genis, *Rodnaia rech'* (Moscow: Nezavisimaia gazeta, 1994), pp. 125–31; A. A. Demchenko, 'Nikolai Chernyshevskii: k 180-letiiu so dnia rozhdeniia', *Izvestiia Saratovskogo universiteta*, 9.1 (2009), 36–44; *N. G. Chernyshevskii: pro et contra*, ed. by A. A. Demchenko (St Petersburg: RGKhA, 2008); V. K. Kantor, 'Srublennoe derevo zhizni. Mozhno li segodnia razmyshliat' o Chernyshevskom?', *Oktiabr'*, 2 (2000), 157–80; I. V. Kondakov, 'Ot istorii literatury — k poetike kul'tury', *Voprosy literatury*, 2 (1997), 49–59. A recent colloquium at Princeton University 'Is This Not the Beginning of a Change? Chernyshevsky, His Time and His Legacy' (12 April 2019) brought together scholars working on various aspects of Chernyshevskii's legacy, from narrative dynamics to ethnography of the novel.
32. For more on the 1860s public debates in general and Chernyshevskii's contribution in particular, see either Egorov, *Izbrannoe*, pp. 140–58, or Moser, *Esthetics as Nightmare*, pp. 31–56, 43–45, 266–68.
33. Paperno, *Chernyshevsky and the Age of Realism*, pp. 159–73; B. F. Egorov, 'Filosofskie osnovy mirovozzreniia shestidesiatnikov', in *Izbrannoe. Esteticheskie idei v Rossii XIX veka*, pp. 308–21. For a recent discussion of erroneous academic assumptions about Chernyshevskii's intellectual development, see A. V. Vdovin, 'Chernyshevskii vs. Feierbakh: (psevdo)istochniki dissertatsii "Esteticheskie otnosheniia iskusstva k deistvitel'nosti"', *Zeitschrift für Slavische Philologie*, 68.1 (2011), 39–66; Irina Paperno, 'Russkie kritiki 1830–1860-kh godov v bor'be za vlast'', *Novoe literaturnoe obozrenie*, 6 (2011), 403–07.
34. Chernyshevskii discussed this approach in detail in his scathing review of Turgenev's novella *Asia* (1858). N. G. Chernyshevskii, 'Russkii chelovek na rendez-vous. Razmyshleniia po prochtenii povesti g. Turgeneva "Asia"', *Atenei*, 18 (1858), 65–89.
35. Paperno, *Chernyshevsky and the Age of Realism*, p. 8.
36. For more on Chernyshevskii's disciples, see Egorov, *Izbrannoe*, pp. 160–73, 366–83, 404–27.
37. Paperno, *Chernyshevsky and the Age of Realism*, pp. 8–9.
38. L. Ia. Ginzburg, *O literaturnom geroe* (Leningrad: Sovetskii pisatel', 1979), p. 52.
39. A function that Michael Finke credits as begetting metafictional narratives. Finke, *Metapoesis*, p. 2.
40. Paperno traces this approach to Chernyshevskii's work on Lessing in *Chernyshevsky and the Age of Realism*, p. 164.
41. Ibid., p. 11.
42. Finke, *Metapoesis*, p. 20.
43. N. P. Zhdanovskii, 'Osobennosti realizma pisatelei-demokratov 60-kh godov XIX v.', in *Problemy tipologii russkogo realizma*, ed. by N. L. Stepanov and U. R. Fokht (Moscow: Nauka, 1969), pp. 306–43 (p. 308).
44. Ibid., p. 321.
45. F. M. Tolstoi (Rostislav), 'Lzhemudrost' geroev g. Chernyshevskogo', *Severnaia pchela*, 27 May 1863, pp. 551–53; V. S. Kurochkin (Znamenskii), 'Pronitsatel'nye chitateli. (Iz rasskazov o starykh liudiakh)', *Iskra*, 32 (1863), 421–29.
46. N. N. Strakhov, 'Schastlivye liudi', in *N. G. Chernyshevskii: pro et contra*, pp. 555–77; D. I. Pisarev, 'Mysliashchii proletariat', ibid., pp. 436–86; N. S. Leskov, 'Nikolai Gavrilovich Chernyshevskii v ego romane "Chto delat'?"', ibid., pp. 427–36; V. P. Botkin and A. A. Fet, '"Chto delat'? Iz rasskazov o novykh liudiakh". Roman N. G. Chernyshevskogo', ibid., pp. 486–555. This is by no means a full account of the reviews that followed the publication of *Chto delat'?*. For comprehensive guides to contemporary reception of the novel, see 'Nikolai Chernyshevskii v rossiiskoi pamiati i kritike', ibid., pp. 7–51; G. E. Tamarchenko, *Romany N. G. Chernyshevskogo* (Saratov: Saratovskoe knizhnoe izdatel'stvo, 1954), pp. 134–44; A. P. Skaftymov, 'Kommentarii k zhurnal'noi redaktsii "Chto delat'?"', in Chernyshevskii, *PSS*, XI, 702–22 (pp. 706–11).
47. Leskov, 'Nikolai Gavrilovich Chernyshevskii v ego romane "Chto delat'?"', p. 428.
48. Ibid., p. 429.

49. N. S. Solov'ev, 'Teoriia bezobraziia', *Epokha*, 7 (1864), 1–16 (pp. 15–16).
50. Strakhov, 'Schastlivye liudi', p. 575. For more on Strakhov's views on *Chto delat'?* see G. N. Antonova, 'N. N. Strakhov o romane "Chto delat'?"', in *N. G. Chernyshevskii: Stat'i, issledovaniia i materialy*, ed. by E. I. Pokusaev (Saratov: Izdatel'stvo Saratovskogo gosudarstvennogo universiteta, 1978), pp. 148–61.
51. Botkin and Fet, '"Chto delat'? Iz rasskazov o novykh liudiakh". Roman N. G. Chernyshevskogo', pp. 491, 530.
52. M. E. Saltykov, 'Nasha obshchestvennaia zhizn'. X. Mart 1864 goda', in *Sobranie sochinenii*, 20 vols (Moscow: Khudozhestvennaia literatura, 1966–77), VI: *Stat'i 1863–1864* (1968), pp. 290–330 (p. 324).
53. V. A. Zaitsev, 'Glupovtsy, popavshie v "Sovremennik"', *Russkoe slovo*, 2 (1864), 34–42.
54. Explaining his attitude to Chernyshevskii's novel in a note, addressed to the journal *Epokha*, Saltykov wrote: 'First of all, what made him conclude that my attitude to this novel was negative? If he thought so because of my review that mentioned dog-eared readers and holy fools, then it must be said that the review addressed not the novel itself, but a well-known opinion about the novel and this opinion's influence on the kind of teachings that are derived from the novel.' M. E. Saltykov, 'GG. Semeistvu M. M. Dostoevskogo, izdaiushchemu zhurnal "Epokha"', in *Sobranie sochinenii*, VI, 524–31 (p. 527). For more on Saltykov's reflections on *Chto delat'?*, see P. S. Reifman, 'Shchedrin i Chernyshevskii (po materialam khronik "Nasha obshchestvennaia zhizn'")', *Uchenye zapiski Tartuskogo gosudarstvennogo universiteta. Trudy po russkoi i slavianskoi filologii. XI. Literaturovedenie*, 209 (1968), 109–12; E. I. Pokusaev, 'N. G. Chernyshevskii i M. E. Saltykov-Shchedrin', *Uchenye zapiski Saratovskogo gosudarstvennogo universiteta im. N. G. Chernyshevskogo*, 19 (1948), 35–101; I. P. Viduetskaia, 'Roman "Chto delat'?" v otsenke revoliutsionno-demokraticheskoi kritiki', in *'Chto delat'?' N. G. Chernyshevskogo: istoriko-funktsional'noe issledovanie*, pp. 78–107 (p. 82).
55. A. M. Bukharev, 'O romane g. Cheryshevskogo "Chto delat'?"', in *Chernyshevskii: Pro et contra*, pp. 577–616 (p. 579).
56. I. V. Kondakov, '"Chto delat'?" kak filosofsko-intellektual'nyi roman (k dialektike soznaniia i samosoznaniia stanoviashchegosia zhanra)', in *'Chto delat'?' N. G. Chernyshevskogo: istoriko-funktsional'noe issledovanie*, pp. 183–218 (p. 191).
57. Kurochkin (Znamenskii), 'Pronitsatel'nye chitateli. (Iz rasskazov o starykh liudiakh)', pp. 421–29.
58. For more on Chernyshevskii's trial and its day-by-day chronology, see *Delo Chernyshevskogo: sbornik dokumentov*, ed. by N. M. Chernyshevskaia and I. V. Porokh (Saratov: Privolzhskoe knizhnoe izdatel'stvo, 1968); for an overview of contemporary trials of other radicals see M. K. Lemke, *Politicheskie protsessy M. I. Mikhailova, D. I. Pisareva i N. G. Chernyshevskago: po neizdannym dokumentam* (St Petersburg: Izdatel'stvo O. N. Popovoi, 1907).
59. Reiser, p. 794.
60. N. G. Chernyshevskii, '"Chto delat'? Rasskazy o novykh liudiakh" (Chernovaia redaktsiia i varianty otdel'nykh glav)', in *Chto delat'?* (Leningrad: Nauka, 1975), pp. 345–715.
61. 'Zapiska ot 18 fevralia 1881', *Krasnyi Arkhiv*, 22 (1927), p. 226. Cited in Reiser, p. 783.
62. This is how Chernyshevskii referred to his writing project in the letter he submitted to the investigating committee to ask for permission to buy and start translating Friedrich Christoph Schlosser's *Weltgeschichte in zusammenhängender Erzählung* (1815–57). N. G. Chernyshevskii, 'Letter to the Superintendent of the Peter and Paul Fortress from 20 December 1862', cited in Demchenko and Pokusaev, *N. G. Chernyshevskii: nauchnaia biografiia*, p. 209. In the 1860s critical vocabulary, 'belletresticheskii' could refer to either a fictional piece, or a piece of genre fiction: both definitions were used to mark Chernyshevskii's proposed text as harmless, from the censors' point of view.
63. Demchenko and Pokusaev, *N. G. Chernyshevskii: nauchnaia biografiia*, p. 210.
64. Chernyshevskii, 'Letter to O. S. Chernyshevskaia from 5 October 1862', p. 456.
65. Ibid.
66. 'All the skills [...] that a good writer of fairy tales needs — a writer like Dickens or Fielding, or, among our writers, Pushkin or Lermontov (in their prose) — I have, too, and these are good enough skills, and I have plenty of them. Nature has not bestowed on me the gift of versification.

But my prose is like good poetry.' (N. G. Chernyshevskii, 'Letter to O. S. Chernyshevskaia from 10 March 1883', in *PSS*, xv: *Pis'ma 1877–1889 godov* (1950), pp. 388–90 (p. 390))

67. Chernyshevskii, 'Letter to O. S. Chernyshevskaia from 5 October 1862', p. 456.
68. Vinogradov and Elizavetina's article on the image of the reader contains a good exploration of Chernyshevskii's awareness of the contemporary public's literary tastes. See K. V. Vinogradov and G. G. Elizavetina, 'Predstavlenie o chitatele v demokraticheskoi kritike 'shestidesiatykh godov', in *'Chto delat'?' N. G. Chernyshevskogo: istoriko-funktsional'noe issledovanie*, pp. 14–37 (pp. 28–33).
69. For innovative interpretations of Lopukhov's travel to America see A. A. Arustamova, 'F. M. Dostoevski vs N. G. Chernyshevskii: polemika o Novom Svete i russkom cheloveke', in *Russko-amerikanskii dialog XIX veka: istoriko-literaturnyi aspekt* (Perm': Permskii gosudarstvennyi universitet, 2008), pp. 306–25; A. M. Etkind, *Tolkovanie Puteshestvii: Rossiia i Amerika v travelogakh i intertekstakh* (Moscow: Novoe literaturnoe obozrenie, 2001), pp. 79–81.
70. For an overview of the history of the chapter's interpretation see Michael R. Katz, 'The Conclusion of *What Is to Be Done?*', *Russian Review*, 41 (1982), 181–96. An authoritative attribution of characters has been carried out by B. Ia. Bukhshtab and published in B. Ia. Bukhshtab, 'Zapiska Chernyshevskogo o romane "Chto delat'?"', in *Bibliograficheskie razyskaniia po russkoi literature XIX veka* (Moscow: Kniga, 1966), pp. 117–32.
71. Rimmon-Kenan's description is an updated version of Genette's definition of the same narrative figure. Rimmon-Kenan, *Narrative Fiction*, p. 48. For Genette's original definition, see Gérard Genette, *Narrative Discourse: An Essay in Method*, trans. by Jane E. Lewin (Ithaca, NY: Cornell University Press, 1980), pp. 72–73. For a discussion of metadiegesis as a 'second-degree' narrative, see ibid., pp. 231–34.
72. Chernyshevsky, *What Is to Be Done?*, p. 40; Chernyshevskii, *Chto delat'?*, p. 7. The use of underscoring is mine throughout the book unless otherwise indicated. All further quotations in English from the novel are from this edition unless otherwise indicated.
73. The explanatory dictionary of Chernyshevskii's contemporary, Vladimir Dal''s *Tolkovyi slovar' zhivago Velikoruskago iazyka* (1861) lists the meaning of 'event' [происшествие, приключение, случай, встреча, неприятность] as a secondary one for 'history' [история]. 'Istoriia', in *Tolkovyi slovar' Dalia onlain* <http://slovardalja.net/word.php?wordid=12229> [accessed 18 August 2019]. The word retains the same homonymy in contemporary Russian: see 'istoriia' in *Slovar' Ozhegova: tolkovyi slovar' russkogo iazyka* <http://www.ozhegov.com/words/11435.shtml> [accessed 18 August 2019].
74. Chernyshevskii, *What Is to Be Done?*, p. 41; Russian: дух отрицания и прогресса побежден окончательно, Chernyshevskii, *Chto delat'?*, p. 8.
75. Note that Michael Katz's 1989 English translation offers different chapters division, in which the 'Preface' is a stand-alone piece. N. G. Chernyshevsky, *What Is to Be Done?*, pp. 47–49.
76. 'ты не вздумай заключить, что я так прямо и объясняю тебе, что я нисколько не похож на рассказчиков, которых ты считаешь великими художниками, что мой рассказ ты должна поставить ниже их повестей, — нет, он слишком слаб сравнительно с произведениями людей, действительно одаренных сильным талантом, например с "Мещанским счастьем", "Молотовым", с маленькими пьесками г. Успенского, — но ведь ты, моя добрейшая публика, еще не разобралась, что эти вещи разнятся, как небо от земли, от восхищающих тебя сочинений прославленных твоих художников, — с этими-то сочинениями ты смело ставь наряду мой рассказ по достоинству исполнения, а по содержанию он выше их.' [Don't you dare think that I am going to explain to you, just like that, that I am not at all like other narrators whom you consider to be great artists, that my story should be ranked lower than their novellas — no, it is too weak in comparison with works by people who possess a true, strong gift, for example with *Philistine's Happiness*, or *Molotov*, or with Mr Uspenskii's short plays, — but you, my kind audience, have not yet figured out that these works could not be more different from the texts produced by the 'artists' you admire. It is with these works that you should directly compare my story in the noble way in which it is presented, as well as in its more impressive content.] Chernyshevskii, *Chto delat'?*, p. 356.
77. Rimmon-Kenan, *Narrative Fiction*, p. 48.
78. On Chernyshevskii and Sterne see above, note 22; on Chernyshevskii and Fielding see Iu. K.

Rudenko, *Chernyshevskii-romanist i literaturnye traditsii. Avtoreferat dissertatsii na soiskanie uchenoi stepeni doktora filologicheskikh nauk* (Leningrad: Leningradskii gosudarstvennyi universitet, 1990), p. 27.
79. Pisemskii, *Vzbalamuchennoe more*, p. 429.
80. 'Я был тогда уже не молод, жил порядочно, потому ко мне собиралось по временам человек пять-шесть молодежи из моей провинции. Следовательно, я уже был для него человек драгоценный [...].' (Chernyshevskii, *Chto delat'?*, p. 208). [By that time I was no longer so young, and had already lived for quite a while; therefore, some five or six young people from my province would occasionally gather at my place. Consequently, I was already something of a valuable person for Rakhmetov [...]. (*What Is To Be Done*, p. 284)].
81. Chernyshevskii, *Chto delat'?*, p. 265.
82. Ibid., p. 345.
83. Chernyshevsky, *What Is to Be Done?*, p. 50, 76.
84. In Mieke Bal's classification, the narrator in *Chto delat'?* can be categorised as 'explicit': 'a story teller, a visible, fictive 'I' who interferes in his/her account as much as s/he likes, or even participates as a character in the action. Such an explicit narrator is a specific version of the narrator, one of the several different possibilities of manifestation.' (Mieke Bal, *Narratology: Introduction to the Theory of Narrative* (Toronto: University of Toronto Press, 2009), pp. 17–18).
85. Chernyshevskii, *Chto delat'?*, p. 37.
86. Chernyshevsky, *What Is to Be Done?*, p.87.
87. Chernyshevskii, *Chto delat'?*, p. 54.
88. Chernyshevsky, *What Is to Be Done?*, p. 97.
89. Ibid., p. 151.
90. Chernyshevskii, *Chto delat'?*, p. 99.
91. Chernyshevsky, *What Is to Be Done?*, p. 151.
92. H. Porter Abbott, *The Cambridge Introduction to Narrative* (Cambridge: Cambridge University Press, 2002), p. 69.
93. Chernyshevskii, *Chto delat'?*, p. 15.
94. Ibid., p. 210.
95. Chernyshevsky, *What Is to Be Done?*, p. 111; and similar throughout the novel.
96. N. M. Karamzin, 'Otchego v Rossii malo avtorskikh talantov?', in *Izbrannye sochineniia*, 2 vols (Moscow: Khudozhestvennaia literatura, 1964), II: *Stikhotvoreniia. Kritika. Publitsistika. Glavy iz "Istorii Gosudarstva Rossiiskogo"*, pp. 183–87. On Karamzin's ideas of language reform, see B. M. Uspenskii, 'Iazykovaia programma N. M. Karamzina i ego storonnikov', in *Kratkii ocherk istorii russkogo literaturnogo iazyka (XI–XIX vv.)* (Moscow: Gnozis, 1994), pp. 150–56.
97. For an overview of contemporary debates about the female readers and writers see Dmitrii Ravinskii, 'Pisatel'nitsy o chitatel'nitsakh: zhenskoe chtenie na stranitsakh russkoi zhenskoi prozy XIX veka', in *Zhenskii vyzov: russkie pisatel'nitsy XIX–nachala XX veka*, ed. by Elisabeth Cheauré and E. N. Stroganova (Tver': Liliia Print, 2006), pp. 51–61.
98. Chernyshevskii, *Chto delat'?*, p. 12.
99. Ibid.
100. Chernyshevskii, *What Is to Be Done?*, p. 47.
101. N. G. Chernyshevskii, 'Ocherki gogolevskogo perioda russkoi literatury', in *PSS*, III (1947), pp. 5–309 (p. 305). In the same article, Chernyshevskii elaborated: 'The conditions that will define the further development of Russian literature [...] depend on the reading public. [...] Literature can provoke the public to become intellectually active, but it can neither stand in for the public itself, nor can it exist without the public's support' (ibid., pp. 304–05); 'The public should know that it has a right for good literature, and this would make literature develop. Without the public, all literary success is a matter of chance and does not last long' (ibid., p. 306); 'The development of the Russian literature depends on you, reader: you need to express your unbending will for it to develop, and only then will it have an opportunity to do so' (ibid., p. 309).
102. Chernyshevskii, *Chto delat'?*, p. 14.
103. Chernyshevskii, *What Is to Be Done?*, p. 49.

104. For example, Lunacharskii's famous article on Chernyshevskii mentions the 'black bear of censorship', that made it impossible for Chernyshevskii to make his point directly. See A. V. Lunacharskii, 'Chernyshevskii kak pisatel'', in *Stat'i o literature* (Moscow: Khudozhestvennaia literatura, 1988), pp. 204–36 (p. 216).
105. For more on Chernyshevskii's ties to the European Enlightenment, see N. M. Belova, *Roman N. G. Chernyshevskogo 'Chto delat'?' i prosvetitel'skaia literatura XVIII veka* (Saratov: Izdatel'stvo Saratovskogo universiteta, 1994); V. F. Pustarnakov, 'N. G. Chernyshevskii kak vyrazitel' tipichno prosvetitel'skoi kontseptsii sootnosheniia poznavatel'nogo i tsennostno-otsenochnogo i prosvetitel'skogo antistsientizma', in *Filosofiia prosveshcheniia v Rossii i vo Frantsii: opyt sravnitel'nogo analiza* (Moscow: Rossiiskaia akademiia nauk, Institut filosofii, 2002), pp. 174–77; James P. Scanlan, 'Chernyshevskii and Rousseau', in *Western Philosophical Systems in Russian Literature: A Collection of Critical Studies*, ed. by Anthony M. Mlikotin (Los Angeles: University of Southern California Press, 1979), pp. 103–19.
106. Chernyshevskii, *Chto delat'?*, p. 13.
107. Chernyshevskii, *What Is to Be Done?*, p. 47.
108. Chernyshevskii, *Chto delat'?*, p. 13.
109. Chernyshevskii, *What Is to Be Done?*, p. 47.
110. Chernyshevskii, *Chto delat'?*, p. 13.
111. Chernyshevskii, *What Is to Be Done?*, p. 48.
112. Ibid., p. 307.
113. Peter Brooks, *The Melodramatic Imagination: Balzac, Henry James, Melodrama, and the Mode of Excess* (New Haven: Yale University Press, 1976), p. x.
114. Chernyshevskii, *What Is to Be Done?*, p. 306. I have written elsewhere on Chernyshevskii's adaptation of melodrama as genre and literary form: see M. I. Vaysman, *Melodramaticheskaia modal'nost v romane N. G. Chernyshevskogo "Chto delat'?": Avtoreferat dissertatsii na soiskanie uchenoi stepeni kandidata filologicheskikh nauk* (Perm': Permskii gosudarstvennyi natsional'nyi issledovatel'skii universitet, 2011); M. I. Vaysman, 'Melodramaticheskaia i ideologicheskaia modal'nost' v romane N.G. Chernyshevskogo "Chto delat'?"', *Vestnik Piatigorskogo gosudarstvennogo lingvisticheskogo universiteta*, 3.2 (2009), 193–96.
115. Chernyshevskii, *Chto delat'?*, pp. 77–78.
116. Ibid., p. 146.
117. Chernyshevskii, *What Is to Be Done?*, p. 271.
118. Ibid., p. 119.
119. Chernyshevskii, *Chto delat'?*, p.72.
120. Chernyshevskii, *What Is to Be Done?*, p. 119.
121. Ibid.
122. Ibid.
123. Ibid., p. 120.
124. Ibid., p. 149.
125. Ibid., p. 114.
126. Chernyshevskii, *What Is to Be Done?*, p. 169.
127. See, for example, the following passage: 'Они даже и не подумали того, что думают это; а вот это и есть самое лучшее, что они и не замечали, что думают это. А впрочем, не показывает ли это проницательному сорту читателей (большинству записных литературных судий показывает — ведь оно состоит из проницательных господ), не показывает ли это, говорю я, что Кирсанов и Лопухов были люди сухие, без эстетической жилки?.' (Chernyshevskii, *Chto Delat'?*, p. 77) [They were not even aware of the fact that they were thinking this. And that is precisely what's the best thing about it. They were not even aware that they were thinking this. However, doesn't this demonstrate to the perspicacious sort of reader (as it does to the majority of ordinary men of letters, consisting of the most perspicacious gentlemen), does this not demonstrate, I repeat, that Kirsanov and Lopukhov were both withered men, devoid of any 'aesthetic streak'?] (*What Is To Be Done?*, p. 125)
128. Chernyshevskii, *Chto delat'?*, p. 66–67.
129. Ibid., p. 213.

130. 'Воспитание Веры Павловны было очень обыкновенное. Жизнь ее [...] представляла кое-что замечательное, но не особенное. А в поступках ее уже и тогда было кое-что особенное' (ibid., p. 15); [Vera Pavlovna had a very ordinary upbringing. Her early life [...] contained a few noteworthy events, but nothing unusual. Even then, however, her behavior showed itself to be somewhat exceptional] (*What Is To Be Done?*, p. 50).
131. Ibid., p. 268.
132. Ibid.
133. Chernyshevskii, *Chto delat'?*, p. 200.
134. Chernyshevskii, *What Is to Be Done?*, p. 271.
135. Ibid., p. 307.
136. Ibid., p. 308.
137. Chernyshevskii, *Chto delat'?*, p. 243.
138. Chernyshevskii, *What Is to Be Done?*, p. 323.
139. Ibid., p. 328.
140. Chernyshevskii, *Chto delat'?*, p. 352.
141. 'Посвящается моему другу О.С.Ч.' Chernyshevskii, *Chto delat'?*, p. 7.
142. Ibid., p. 198.
143. Ibid., p. 228.
144. Ibid., p. 202.
145. Ibid., pp. 203–04.
146. Chernyshevskii, *What Is to Be Done?*, pp. 274–77.
147. Chernyshevskii, *Chto delat'?*, pp. 208–11.
148. Chernyshevskii, *What Is to Be Done?*, pp. 284–85.
149. Chernyshevskii often uses zeugmas for comic effect. For an analysis of a large array of rhetoric devices used in *Chto delat'?* for comic effect, see B. I. Lazerson, 'Ironiia v publitsistike N. G. Chernyshevskogo', in *N. G. Chernyshevskii: Stat'i, issledovaniia i materialy*, ed. by E. I. Pokusaev (Saratov: Izdatel'stvo Saratovskogo universiteta, 1958), pp. 272–335.
150. Chernyshevskii, *Chto delat'?*, p. 215.
151. Chernyshevskii, *What Is to Be Done?*, p. 293.
152. Chernyshevskii, *Chto delat'?*, pp. 215–16. The use of bold is mine.
153. Chernyshevskii, *What Is to Be Done?*, p. 294.
154. Ibid., p. 294.
155. For the same passage in the pre-publication draft, see Chernyshevskii, *Chto delat'?*, p. 585.
156. Ibid., p. 231.
157. Chernyshevskii, *What Is to Be Done?*, p. 311.
158. Chernyshevskii, *Chto delat'?*, p. 231.
159. Chernyshevskii, *What Is to Be Done?*, p. 311.
160. Ibid., p. 311.
161. Chernyshevskii, *Chto delat'?*, pp. 712–14. This piece of the novel's draft only became widely available to scholars after 1975, when it was published in the academic edition of the novel. This explains the fact that it is rarely referred to in the bulk of the literary criticism on the writer published before the mid-1970s.
162. Ibid., p. 334.
163. Chernyshevskii, *What Is to Be Done?*, p. 431.
164. Ibid.
165. Ibid., p. 713.
166. Ibid.
167. For more on this, see Reiser, pp. 819–33.
168. Ibid.
169. Chernyshevskii, *Chto delat'?*, p. 47.
170. Ibid., pp. 59–61.
171. Ibid., pp. 113–14.
172. Ibid., p. 61.
173. Ibid., p. 243.

174. Ibid., pp. 148–50; 202.
175. 'Таких людей, как Рахметов, мало: я встретил до сих пор только восемь образцов этой породы (в том числе двух женщин)' (ibid., p. 202); [Nowadays there are only a few people like Rakhmetov. Up to the present time I've met only eight examples of this breed (among them two women)] (*What Is To Be Done?*, p. 274).
176. For the exploration of a notion of a 'metadiegetic narrator' and other forms of second-degree narratives see Genette, *Narrative Discourse*, pp. 232–34.
177. Ibid., p. 232.

CHAPTER 3

An Author of a Different Kind

> Everyone thinks I am a Realist writer and this is, indeed, who I am. For years, however, I have had a deep and sincere sympathy for authors of a different kind...
>
> ALEXEI PISEMSKII. Letter to F.I. Buslaev, 4 November 1877[1]

Alexei Feofilaktovich Pisemskii, a writer who was once very popular with Russian readers, is now almost forgotten by the general public. In the modern Russian literary canon he occupies the position of a secondary playwright, not quite as prominent as his contemporary Aleksandr Ostrovskii.[2] And while Ostrovskii's literary fame is still sustained by the ubiquitous presence of his drama *Groza* [The Storm] (1859) in the Russian theatre repertoires,[3] Pisemskii's novels have mostly been out of print since the 1960s.[4] As a prose writer, he is seen as a marginal figure on the late nineteenth-century literary scene. This, however, was not always the case.

A sought-after writer during his lifetime, Pisemskii had the misfortune of having had such literary giants as Ivan Turgenev, Ivan Goncharov, Fedor Dostoevskii and Lev Tolstoi as his contemporaries. Nonetheless, Pisemskii's plays and novels enjoyed an unambiguous popularity and brought him financial stability at a time when only a handful of writers could support themselves solely through literature. As his friend and contemporary Petr Boborykin recalled,

> Pisemskii enjoyed the most extreme popularity for five or six years up to the beginning of the 1860s. He became the toast of St Petersburg society, the journal editors courted him, he was often seen in the fashionable salons, and was known as a public reader and even amateur actor.[5]

Pisemskii's literary achievements also paid off financially: the proceeds from his novels bought him a spacious house in Moscow, and parts of this house were named after the books that financed them: the house itself after *Vzbalamuchennoe more* (1863) and the two wings after *Liudi sorokovykh godov* [People of the Forties] (1869) and *V vodovorote* [In the Whirlpool] (1871).[6]

However, Pisemskii's fame proved to be great but fleeting, and when he died in 1881, interest in his work had been steadily declining for a decade. A number of biographical studies were published in the period 1884–95, and one more followed in 1909.[7] After a brief lull, a publication of Pisemskii's correspondence by M. K. Kleman and A. P. Mogilianskii in 1936 opened an era of Soviet scholarship on the writer.[8] But despite the work of a number Russian, Soviet and Western critics and scholars,[9] their critical output was still significantly smaller than that of Pisemskii's contemporaries. So central was his position on the literary scene in mid-nineteenth century Russia that critics of virtually every ideological and aesthetic persuasion left an account, note or review of one of Pisemskii's novels (including A. N. Ostrovskii, K. S. Aksakov, M. E. Saltykov-Shchedrin, A. V. Druzhinin, D. I. Pisarev, A. A. Grigor'ev and N. V. Shelgunov, to name a few). This has left the field of Pisemskii studies in a state of imbalance, where personal accounts and opinion pieces have traditionally prevailed over historical facts and academic expertise. Recent interest in the secondary figures of Russian Realism has brought Pisemskii's novels back into the orbit of academic attention,[10] drawing attention to his transitory status in the literary canon. It has also brought into focus the most interesting aspects of Pisemskii's style: his peculiar brand of literary realism and its manifestation in the unusual narrative structures of his prose pieces.[11]

The idiosyncratic meta-realism of Pisemskii's most scandalous novel, *Vzbalamuchennoe more*, was glossed over by the Soviet critics,[12] leading to a continued misinterpretation of Pisemskii's style in general and key aspects of *Vzbalamuchennoe more*'s narrative structure in particular. The double weight of the novel's reactionary political agenda and bared devices of realist narration ultimately almost obliterated it. *Vzbalamuchennoe more* was twice deemed ideologically unsound: first, by Pisemskii's contemporaries (it offended both the conservatives and the radicals since it depicted both groups in an unflattering light) and, the following century, by Soviet scholars, who thought it too reactionary and therefore harmful for Pisemskii's already shaky reputation.

Its place in the twentieth-century Russian literary canon was all but eliminated: for instance, the authoritative 1959 collection of Pisemskii's works did not include *Vzbalamuchennoe more*. Currently, it is out of print and only available as a print-on-demand edition from the Russian online platform *Ozon*.[13] As I will demonstrate in this chapter, the novel's overtly metafictional poetics was perceived as confusing but not unusual by contemporary critics. Later on, however, it did not fit in with the traditional reading of the Russian realist novel as aiming, above all, for mimetic illusion. This has kept the novel outside the group of texts usually considered to be the classic Russian novels, distorting our perception of Russian realist texts' capacity for narrative self-reflection. Aiming to address this problem, in this chapter I discuss the historical circumstances in which *Vzbalamuchennoe more* was written, analyse Pisemskii's aesthetic views and ideas on realism, and, finally, offer a close reading of the novel's metafictional chapters.

A Bitter Fate

Pisemskii's career was launched in 1850, when his first novella *Tiufiak* [Simpleton] (1850) was published in *Moskvitianin* [Muscovite], a Moscow-based, as the title suggested, conservative literary journal. It was an instant success. *Moskvitianin*'s editor Mikhail Pogodin signed Pisemskii up to publish all his further texts in the same journal and bought the rights to a future collected works. The editors Andrei

Kraevskii and Adal'bert Starchevskii invited him to publish in *Otechestvennye zapiski* and *Biblioteka dlia chteniia* [Library for Reading]. Soon afterwards, in 1851, Pisemskii published his next novel,[14] *Bogatyi zhenikh* [The Rich Fiancé], in *Sovremennik*. The year 1853 saw the publication of his collected works in three volumes, just three years after his debut, and by 1856, he was enough of an established writer to be invited to join an official expedition to the Caspian Sea organised by the Naval Ministry.

In 1857 he became an editor of *Biblioteka dlia chteniia*, *Sovremennik*'s closest rival, and his novella *Staraia barynia* [An Old Lady], published in the same year, drew Chernyshevskii's attention and praise. In 1858 Pisemskii published *Tysiacha dush* [A Thousand Souls], his most accomplished novel, to critical acclaim.[15] Finally, in the early 1860s, at the high point of his literary career, Pisemskii's play *Gor'kaia sud'bina* [Bitter Fate] won (jointly with Ostrovskii's *Groza*) the prestigious Uvarov drama prize[16] from the Academy of Sciences.

But Pisemskii's success did not last. When he started at *Biblioteka dlia chteniia* in 1857, he worked as an editor under Aleksandr Druzhinin and, when Druzhinin retired in 1860, Pisemskii gained full control of the journal. As a declaration of intent, he published an aesthetic and political programme, 'Ob izdanii zhurnala "Biblioteka dlia Chteniia" v 1861 godu' ['On Publishing the Journal *Library for Reading* in 1861']. He then illustrated it with a series of six feuilleton articles that were intended to promote the values of the 'pursuit of good', the 'unbiased examination of evil deeds' and the 'struggle for truth'.[17] In three articles signed by 'state councillor Salatushka' and another three signed by the 'old feuilleton horse Nikitushka Bezrylov',[18] Pisemskii attempted to launch a literary polemic with the major St Petersburg critics and publishers of the day. The articles managed to offend everyone, from Nikolai Chernyshevskii and Nikolai Nekrasov to Aleksandr Gertsen and Maksim Antonovich, through a series of highly insulting personal quips that had nothing to do with either aesthetics or politics.[19]

The first three pieces attacked bureaucracy and the radical intelligentsia, and the rest discussed questions of education for the poor, the emancipation of women and literary fundraisers. The scandal started in earnest in December 1861 and culminated in March 1862, when the editors of the St Petersburg satirical weekly *Iskra*, Vasilii S. Kurochkin and Nikolai Stepanov, challenged Pisemskii to a duel. He tried to arrange a public expression of support, but those he had considered his allies failed him and refused to help.[20] Disillusioned and hurt, Pisemskii left for Europe, officially to visit his son at the University of Heidelberg. Pisemskii returned to Russia early in the autumn of 1862 and moved to Moscow in either March or April 1863 to join Mikhail Katkov as a co-editor of the literary department at *Russkii vestnik*. A staunch conservative, Katkov was at that time slowly cultivating a circle of like-minded individuals around his Moscow journal.[21]

Pisemskii most likely did not anticipate how violent a reaction the articles would provoke, but his reputation nevertheless took a blow from which it never recovered. The aftershocks were felt for a few years: in 1863 there were still publications mocking him for his misstep, such as a descriptively titled dramatic parody *Gor'kaia sud'bina kota, ili legkaia boinia. Vzbalamuchennaia opera v neskol'kikh aktakh* [Cat's Bitter Fate, or Light Carnage: Troubled Opera in Several Acts] by G. N. Zhulev.[22]

These were the circumstances in which Pisemskii's next novel, *Vzbalamuchennoe more*, was produced. The novel was initially conceived as the coming-of-age story of a typical privileged Russian young man. Almost exactly as planned, *Vzbalamuchennoe more* ended up spanning nineteen years in the life of the main character, the 'regular' young gentleman Alexandr Baklanov.[23] Stretching roughly from 1843 to 1862, the novel ended in the immediate present of the author and the readers, offering Pisemskii's views on the reasons for the contemporary crisis in a society overrun by young 'empty-heads' [svishchi] with unsustainable political ideas. The novel also featured a metadiegetic narrator, who, for the duration of the six chapters in Part Five, turned into a character called 'Pisemskii', a 'realist writer',[24] who, in his turn, closely resembled Alexei Pisemskii himself and espoused views on 'subjective' and 'objective'[25] types of narration, and the importance of realism for contemporary society.

Pisemskii remained in Moscow for the rest of his life and, after his move, visited St Petersburg only briefly: it became 'absolutely repugnant' to him in the aftermath of the feuilleton scandal.[26] Pisemskii's trip to Europe, designed to take his mind off the scandal, was also not very enjoyable, as evidenced in the few letters he sent home.[27] This dissatisfaction would later find its expression in the chapters of *Vzbalamuchennoe more* dedicated to the characters' travels in Germany, Switzerland, France and England. Another biographical event that found its way into the novel was that of Pisemskii's meeting with Gertsen on 19 June 1862.[28] Pisemskii and Gertsen disagreed in their views on Russian politics, and the meeting was not a success. As with Pisemskii's disagreement with the Russian radicals at home, this disastrous meeting added insult to injury and further accelerated his fall from grace. Not surprisingly, Gertsen, who was satirised in the novel, referred to it as a 'stirred-up rubbish heap' [vzboltannaia pomoika] in his review.[29]

The publication of such an openly polemical work so soon after the scandal did not revive Pisemskii's reputation; it ruined it completely. After his 1860s feuilleton articles and *Vzbalamuchennoe more* had made Pisemskii's political views clear, the radical establishment turned on him, transforming his career, in the words of Charles Moser, into 'an unusually faithful microcosm of the nonradical writer's situation during these years'.[30] Indeed, Nikolai Leskov's career took a similar turn after Pisarev sharply criticised his novel *Nekuda* [Nowhere] (1864) in an article of 1865, 'Progulka po sadam russkoi slovesnosti' [A walk in the gardens of Russian literature]. The trajectory of Pisemskii's and Leskov's literary careers was part and parcel of the period of the long 1860s, when influential radical critics shaped the literary landscape. Despite his falling-out with the critics, Pisemskii remained a strong presence on the contemporary literary scene: an 1866 collection of critical articles by Dmitrii Pisarev (still one of the leading Russian critics at that stage) opened with a review of Pisemskii's work and featured two further articles, 'Pisemskii, Turgenev i Goncharov' [Pisemskii, Turgenev and Goncharov], and 'Zhenskie tipy v romanakh i povestiakh Goncharova, Pisemskogo i Turgeneva' [Female types in the novels and novellas by Goncharov, Pisemskii and Turgenev].[31] This was a clear indication of Pisemskii's literary status at the time, even if the overall tone in which some critics discussed his novels had changed from enthusiastic to mocking.

'This novel is my life's work: whether it comes out bad, or good, I will not be able to write anything better or more powerful',[32] Pisemskii wrote to his friend B. N. Almazov. Indeed, as Pisemskii predicted, *Vzbalamuchennoe more* became his magnum opus. *Vzbalamuchennoe more* thus signalled a pivotal point in Pisemskii's life and his ultimate fall from grace, marking him as an author of a kind that was very different from the literary establishment's idea of a progressive realist novelist. The novel's unusual metadiegetic narrator, who befriended his own characters, did not win it any admirers, either — the majority of Pisemskii's readers were as confused by the novel's metafictional poetics as they were outraged by its politics. Four more novels followed *Vzbalamuchennoe more* in 1869, 1871, 1877 and 1880, but none of them was as successful as Pisemskii's previous works.

Vzbalamuchennoe more as a Mirror of Russian Conservatism

On 8 October 1862, Pisemskii wrote to his friend and literary critic Pavel Annenkov, inviting him to a reading:

> Why don't you come and listen to a small part of the new novel, and bring along your ladies... [...] and when you decide when you can come, let me know — I will invite some others who could assist with my literary work...[33]

Pisemskii often arranged readings of his works-in-progress: as a passionate amateur actor, he liked holding his audience captive and enjoyed these occasions. In addition, readings served more utilitarian purposes, both as a part of his creative process (a way of getting direct feedback) and as a networking opportunity. It would take Pisemskii another year to complete the new novel he mentioned, *Vzbalamuchennoe more*, but during that time he would read excerpts from it to various audiences, testing out the new chapters. One such high-profile reading took place at the house of Minister of the Interior, P. A. Valuev, on 2 April 1863, when Pisemskii presented several chapters of *Vzbalamuchennoe more*, hoping to win the minister's support of the book pre-publication. Once the novel was published, Pisemskii also presented a signed copy of it to Tsar Alexander II, hoping to gain literary patronage of the highest order. This aspiration reflected not just his own political leanings but also the new professional allegiances Pisemskii was forging after his falling out with the radical critics and *Sovremennik*. In a neat *mise-en-abyme*, there is a scene of a public reading in the novel itself, featuring a character who can be seen as a representation of the conservative readership that Pisemskii was hoping would approve of his novel.

A little less than a month later, on 1 November of the same year, Pisemskii contacted another friend of his, Boris Almazov, to inform him that he was now working on something rather impressive: 'I am now writing a big novel, bigger than *Tysiacha dush*. Everyone who listened to it is full of praise, and it describes all of our Mother Russia; in other words, it is a serious undertaking.'[34] At the time of its composition and afterwards, Pisemskii saw the strengths and 'seriousness' of his novel in its epic sweep and specifically in its political impact. Indeed, despite the speed with which it was written ('none of my other things [...] have I written with such enthusiasm and as quickly as this novel'),[35] Pisemskii's 1863 piece had more of an epic scope than his 1858 triumph *Tysiacha dush*.

These two features — epic scope and a conservative political message — remained the two most important things about *Vzbalamuchennoe more* that Pisemskii would point out over and over, for years to come. In a letter to Turgenev of 1869, Pisemskii again emphasised the political message of the novel: he wanted *Vzbalamuchennoe more* to be translated so that it was available to European readers. Describing 'contemporary Russia', the novel exposed 'our revolutionary party, the vilest and the worst party that the world has ever imagined'.[36] Looking back on the composition of *Vzbalamuchennoe more* in 1878 in a letter to one of his translators, he would also recall writing a 'big novel' with a 'political meaning' that described the origins of nihilism in Russia.[37] At the time of its publication, the aim of the novel was made explicit in a note accompanying the copy given to the Tsar in 1864. Pisemskii stressed the fact that *Vzbalamuchennoe more* represented Russian society as truthfully as possible, including its 'false and fake' [lzhivye i fal'shivye] aspects. The novel, according to Pisemskii, was intended to appeal to the Tsar's mercy for those who were in charge of the 'pseudo-revolution' but were more interested in big pronouncements than actions.[38]

Pisemskii wrote the bulk of his 'serious' novel in 1862, while arranging his move to Moscow. The timing is significant, as Pisemskii was exploiting readers' current interest in politics, already piqued at it was by the country's domestic and international troubles: civil unrest in the capital, the consequences of the implementation of the new property laws for peasants, as well as rising tensions between Russia and Poland. At the same time, he was genuinely interested in making a political statement, and, since he has been compromised as a journalist in the course of the Nikita Bezrylov feuilleton affair, he turned to literary fiction as the next best medium to make his voice heard — a popular move at the time. After Pisemskii resigned as an editor of *Biblioteka dlia chteniia* in January 1863 and accepted the post of director of the literary section at *Russkii vestnik*, this newly forged affiliation with Katkov's conservative journal must have been another impetus to make his views public.

Russkii vestnik was Pisemskii's first choice for publication even before his move to Moscow (because, in his own words, it suited his novel 'in spirit'[39]), even though he had made an earlier promise to Mikhail Korsh at *Peterburgskie vedomosti* [St Petersburg Record], who intended to publish the novel as a supplement to his newspaper. After months of negotiations[40] (which included a bid from Nekrasov for *Sovremennik*) *Vzbalamuchennoe more* found its way back to Katkov's journal and was published there in instalments from March to August 1863. In addition to his ideological and aesthetic concerns, Pisemskii was keen to ensure the commercial success of his novel during this difficult period. The repeated references to the novel in his correspondence reveal more than a simple desire to share the agonies and ecstasies of the creative process. Rather, he was aiming to orchestrate the publication of the novel before it had even been finished.

Pisemskii was astute and even ruthless in handling the practical matters of getting his texts published, and, by this stage of his career, was not above selling his novel to the highest bidder. To this end, he was effectively publicizing the novel in his correspondence with editors and their de facto agents while still writing it.[41] It was in a similar spirit of practicality that Pisemskii referred to his text as 'big': he was not just warning his future readers about the epic scale of his work, but, on a rather mundane level, was also alerting the publishers to the fact that it would need to be published in instalments. Thus, the letters that started with an artistic discussion of the novel's scale often ended on a more practical note: 'I would ask you to reply to this letter after you have found out if they would like to buy such a big thing'.[42] The same applied to the way Pisemskii described his novel in a letter to Katkov, dispatched the same day: 'I am now writing a huge novel (up to 35 printer's sheets)'.[43] From the very inception of *Vzbalamuchennoe more*, Pisemskii was concerned with what we would now call his novel's extra-literary context, carefully considering its political, aesthetic, but also commercial impact.

Because of the novel's serialisation, the second half was still a work-in-progress by the time the first had been sent to press. This fact explains the sharp change of tone from the first to the second part of the novel, where the descriptive realism of the story following the life of the young gentleman Baklanov was suddenly infused with the denunciatory fervour. The repeated references to the novel in Pisemskii's correspondence reveal that Pisemskii adapted the novel as he went along, aiming to keep it relevant to contemporary public debates and his own personal circumstances. Including himself as a character in his own narrative, Pisemskii had transported these discussions into a metafictional setting that showcased the opposing sides in one of the significant literary debates of his time.

As well as coming out in monthly instalments in *Russkii vestnik*, *Vzbalamuchennoe more* was simultaneously published as a separate edition, and then reissued twice in 1868 and 1884–85 with minor changes.[44] Unlike the artistically more polished *Tysiacha dush*, *Vzbalamuchennoe more* was most representative of Pisemskii's original style. The novel showcased Pisemskii's artistic strengths, such as shrewd (if cynical) characterisation, sarcastic humour and naturalistic honesty, but also exposed his particular weaknesses: a lack of continuity in style, weak plotting, and sudden switches into moralising. These stylistic setbacks provided plenty of fodder for discussions in the press.

The critics reacted with a plethora of reviews, some of which were genuine discussions of the novel's literary qualities. Most, however, chose the publication of the novel as an opportunity for a public debate with a popular author, sometimes slipping into an outright condemnation of his character and writings.[45] Similarly to *Chto delat'?*, the publication of *Vzbalamuchennoe more* served as a chance to discuss the writer's politics and the effect they had on the novel's aesthetics — not an unusual occurrence in Russian literary criticism of the 1860s. But even though the novel was pilloried by the critics, it was widely read: as A. P. Miliukov noted in his memoires, 'the novel was, without a doubt, read by all our reading public'.[46] It must have attracted the readers with its masterful, if biased, representation of contemporary reality and a titillating, if improbable, plot. As another critic predicted disparagingly, 'dirty descriptions of scandals will make this novel very popular among old men and old maids'.[47]

The novel's popularity with readers could also be explained by the fact that *Vzbalamuchennoe more* acted as a foil for contemporary political and aesthetic discussions. To paraphrase the title of Lenin's 1908 essay on Tolstoi, it could be seen as a kind of a mirror of contemporary Russian conservatism, partly because of Pisemskii's own political inclinations and partly because of his affiliation with *Russkii vestnik* and Katkov's conservative milieu that was established when he was working on the last few chapters of his novel. Prior to the publication of Pisemskii's novel, Mikhail Katkov had already published a number of articles exposing what he saw as the evil of Russian nihilism. Most revealingly, one of Katkov's 1862 articles catalogued different types of nihilists, all of which were faithfully represented in Pisemskii's novel.[48]

This connection was noticed by contemporaries, who joked about the 'troubled way of thinking' [vzbalamuchennyi obraz myslei] that had taken hold of Pisemskii ever since he joined *Russkii vestnik*, with its propensity to 'hate and revile anything that is fresh, young and is starting a journey on the road of life'.[49] Pisemskii, on the contrary, felt at the time that Katkov was 'a hero [...] inspiring the country in these difficult times. In this case, we all want to help him in his sacred endeavors'.[50] (It is worth noting, though, that, like Pisemskii's other attempts at collaboration, their alliance did not last).[51]

Although in keeping with Katkov's political agenda, Pisemskii's novel stood out among other contemporary literary texts because it offered an unusually critical description of the young nihilists. Previous popular fictional representations, such as Turgenev's *Ottsy i deti* (1862) (also edited by Katkov), treated the issue gingerly but compassionately. Of course, none of the vitriol that Pisemskii espoused in *Vzbalamuchennoe more* came even close to the chilling portraits of devious youths that found their way onto the pages of Dostoevskii's *Besy* [Demons] (1871) a few years later. However, in 1863 it was still unusual for a writer as prominent as Pisemskii to viciously attack the young radicals who were gaining more and more prominence in society. This charge has earned *Vzbalamuchennoe more* the title of the first 'anti-nihilist novel' in the Soviet histories of nineteenth-century Russian literature, but recently this dated definition became an object of an academic debate on account of its politicised nature.[52] Whether *Vzbalamuchennoe more* was the original anti-nihilist novel or not, the nature of its polemical thrust was certainly anti-radical.

To build a comprehensive counter-argument to radical nihilism, Pisemskii aimed to analyse the social processes that produced such characters as Turgenev's Bazarov. In this new reality, where radical nihilists came to occupy positions of power, 'regular men' like Pisemskii's hero Baklanov found it difficult to fit in. For Pisemskii, this was a conflict of world-views rather than of generations, and in his novel, the old bureaucrats and moneylenders are in league with the young 'empty heads'. It is not certain whom Pisemskii hated more: the familiar old villains who wanted money and power, or the 'goalless' and rudderless youths. The radical critics, naturally, did not take kindly to such denunciations.

'What do you mean, Mr. Pisemskii?'

'There have been thousands of articles and all of them in a querulous tone, obviously',[53] Pisemskii wrote to Boris Almazov, trying to persuade him to publish a favourable review. In fact, not all the reviews were negative: E. N. Edel'son's article in *Biblioteka dlia chteniia* was encouraging, if not laudatory, but the majority of the critics indeed had nothing good to say about Pisemskii's work. This was partly a result of Pisemskii's already tarnished reputation: little things that would have been overlooked before were now pounced on and dissected. Hatred for *Vzbalamuchennoe more* united representatives of opposing literary camps and proponents of different political and aesthetic doctrines. One recent study identified a positive review in *Kievskii telegraf* [Kiev Telegraph], but even that review used the novel to prove its point about the positive effect of corporal punishment.[54] The other two laudatory references can be found in Turgenev's letter to the writer Nikolai Sherban' (Turgenev called the novel a 'great thing' [otlichnaia veshch'] that he 'really liked'),[55] and in the poet Nikolai Schcherbina's unpublished letter to Katkov.[56] In comparison, the range of negative, even scornful, reviews was impressive. The criticism did not abate with the passage of time: Pisarev referred to the numerous weaknesses of Pisemskii's style in 1864 and 1866, as did Miliukov in an article, reprinted as late as 1875.

Pisemskii's contemporary Nikolai Shelgunov believed that the main problem with *Vzbalamuchennoe more* was that it ended up being too epic for Pisemskii, a writer whose talent shone most in naturalist observations and folk-type anecdotes turned into short prose pieces. Essentially, Shelgunov's claim was that Pisemskii was not talented enough to create a sweeping panorama of Russian life. In a scathing description, he wrote:

> Mr. Pisemskii, with all his gifts, is far from being a thinker, and his attempt to paint wide, all-Russian pictures in no way corresponds to his force of analysis and his ability to understand correctly the historical meaning of events. Having been seduced by an idea to portray something grandiose and feeling in his memory a rich store of material, Mr. Pisemskii had revealed his constraints in an all-promising title, which ended up exposing his idea but also his incompetence when faced with this task.[57]

Pisemskii indeed aimed for an all-encompassing view of contemporary society, as is evidenced by his correspondence at the time. (Even if critics thought that his attempt had failed, he did not abandon this ambition. In a later novel, *Liudi sorokovykh godov* (1869), he would once again try to depict the life of a character who was a typical representative of his class, if not of his generation.) Generally, critics agreed that Pisemskii had bitten off more than he could chew: the epic sweep of a panoramic novel was too much for his talent. It is my suggestion that in a struggle to use his widely acknowledged gift for naturalist descriptions to convey an overtly polemic message, Pisemskii compromised the stylistic homogeneity of his text by introducing, among other things, overtly metafictional elements.

For the duration of the six chapters in Part Five, the previously omniscient narrator of the novel turned into a character called 'Pisemskii', who closely resembled the actual writer. This character assumed the duties of the first-person narrator, but also engaged with the other characters of the novel despite having claimed elsewhere that they were 'completely fictional figures'.[58] This created an ontologically confusing web of metafictional relations, not unlike those in typical twentieth-century metafictional texts such as John Fowles's *The French Lieutenant's Woman* (1969), a textbook example of the same device in a twentieth-century metafictional novel.[59]

Among Pisemskii's contemporaries, only a few noticed the irregular appearance of the author as a character in the fictional narrative. One of the most vocal critics of the novel, Nikolai Shelgunov, noted in his article on *Vzbalamuchennoe more*:

> Baklanov invited Mr Pisemskii to his house. 'What do you mean, Mr. Pisemskii?' asks the reader. Indeed, Mr Pisemskii; the author was personally acquainted not only with Baklanov, but also with Sofi, and had even read his texts at her literary evenings. It was with Mr Pisemskii that Baklanov had shared his unhappiness about the emancipation of the serfs.[60]

Another reviewer remarked that the appearance of the author himself was most likely 'a simple oversight that would be crossed out by the author in the second edition'.[61] Despite the critics' comments on their unorthodox nature, Pisemskii did not eliminate these metafictional elements. Far from crossing out the offending passages, in future revisions Pisemskii emphasised exactly this narrative trick.[62]

Until then, Pisemskii had never introduced himself as a fully-fledged character in his fiction or drama,[63] and has not left any overt clues as to why he would turn to this technique in his second novel. However, his attempt to merge real and fictional worlds in *Vzbalamuchennoe more* by means of introducing himself as a character was not arbitrary. An examination of Pisemskii's views on the nature of literary realism reveals the aesthetic reasons behind this particular narrative strategy. Pisemskii's interpretation of Belinskii's aesthetic legacy, his understanding of Gogol''s style and his fixation on the notions of 'true' and 'false' in realist fiction, explored below, all shed light onto his seemingly bizarre use of metafictional narrative in his novel.

True Lies of Mimesis

In addition to the essays, plays, novels and shorter fiction that comprise the nine volumes of the fullest edition of his collected works (1959), Pisemskii also left a substantial corpus of correspondence with the leading literary figures of his time. In between negotiations of acceptable fees with his publishers and bids for strategic literary support from his friends, a discerning reader finds in this corpus remarkable observations on the theory and practice of literary realism in Russian literature of the 1860s. Over the years, in a series of letters to his friends, Pisemskii consistently addressed an aesthetic issue that was most important for his own work: the conflict between realist representation and didactic impulse in fiction.

In 1877, Russian philologist and historian of folklore Fedor Buslaev sent Pisemskii his 'leaflet' [broshiurka] 'O znachenii sovremennogo romana i ego zadachakh' [On the meaning of the contemporary novel and on its goals] (1877). In his reply (Pisemskii would call it 'a confession of [his] thoughts and aesthetic views'), the writer shared his opinion of the article and his own views on the novel:

> You demand from the novel (which you justly consider to be the most common and hardy representative of contemporary imaginative literature) a certain didacticism, a lesson, since the novel can popularise the entire unbound mass of knowledge and age-old experience. Indeed, constrained by neither the difficulties of form, typical for the purely lyrical works, nor the strict adherence to the actual event, typical for historical narrative, nor the tight framework of drama, the novel is freer in its movement and can include a lot and explain a lot. But does it actually manage to do it in practice, as soon as an author takes on such a task?[64]

In Pisemskii's opinion, didacticism in a novel was a great idea that was usually poorly realised. Contemporary authors (including Chernyshevskii) who shared such ambitions were doomed to 'swift and eternal oblivion'. In contrast, 'the old big novelists' such as Cervantes, Smollett, Walter Scott and George Sand, as well as Pushkin and Lermontov, were 'poetic', and managed to influence their readers without even trying. Gogol', on the other hand, compromised himself by resorting to open lecturing in the form of lyrical digressions, because he was 'confused by the advice of his friends, who had no idea about aesthetics and no understanding of the character or limitations of this great writer's gift'.[65]

Pisemskii understood the novel differently from Buslaev:

> the novel, as much as any other work of art, needs to be born, and not composed; as a fruit of the author's material body and spirit, it should also represent distilled reality: its outer open surface or its psychological mysteries. Everyone thinks I am a realist writer, and that is who I am, although at the same time from very early on I have had a sincere and deep sympathy for authors of a different kind. I just would like them to be skilled at what they do.[66]

As these remarks show, Pisemskii was not against *romans à thèse* as such, but approached such texts according to primarily aesthetic criteria and had no sympathy for those in which 'there was no art, no artists, just rhetorical cries'.[67] Earlier, in a letter to A. N. Maikov, the writer complained about critics who were so preoccupied with their search for social messages in novels that they tended to overlook the aesthetic qualities of literary texts, 'failing to see art in art'.[68] Pisemskii felt, perhaps, that at this point he was one of the few people who gave preference to aesthetics over rhetoric.

Contemporary accounts show that Pisemskii held similar views throughout his career. The writer Petr Boborykin, who took over *Biblioteka dlia chteniia* after Pisemskii left, remembered that his predecessor preferred to avoid 'sharp tendentiousness in fiction, saturated with famous, albeit fashionable topics' and believed it to be detrimental to 'literary ideals'.[69] For Pisemskii, as he explained in a letter to Turgenev in 1855, the realist representation of 'truth' [pravda] ultimately constituted art itself:

> I'd like to recommend to young writers to write only about their own experiences, which they have lived through, even though it might be a bit tactless. But it would be definitely sincere and true. In order to assume, straightaway, a position of a spectator, and a humorous spectator at that, one needs to dive deeper into the well of life and to have definite powers of a talent, because otherwise instead of attacking reality he would swat only at phantoms in his own imagination and, like Don Quixote, fight the windmills.[70]

The concepts of the 'truth' [pravda] and the 'lie' [lozh'] formed the axis of Pisemskii's views on literature and art in general. 'Lie' is a recurrent motive in Pisemskii's correspondence in the 1860s, and in *Vzbalamuchennoe more*. The novel's final line described the text as 'a truthful, if not all-encompassing, picture of contemporary morals; and if it did not manage to represent all of Russia, it had at least carefully brought together all of its lies'.[71] Immediately after *Vzbalamuchennoe more*, Pisemskii started working on a cycle of stories entitled *Russkie lguny* [Russian Liars], in which he aimed to 'present Russian life through a typology of liars'.[72] The cycle was never completed, but Pisemskii's preoccupation with the 'lies' and 'truths' of contemporary life was clear. 'Lie' for Pisemskii came to mean both the falsehood of society's fads and an aesthetic failure, an inability to represent reality in its fullness.[73]

In Pisemskii's 1855 review of the second half of *Mertvye dushi*, another interesting, if brief, account of his aesthetic views, 'truth' and 'lies' become the most important criteria by which a literary work is judged. The article 'Sochineniia N. V. Gogolia, naidennye posle ego smerti. Pokhozhdeniia Chichikova, ili mertvye dushi. Chast' vtoraia' [Works by N. V. Gogol, found after his death. Adventures of Chichikov, or the Dead Souls. Part Two] came out in *Otechestvennye zapiski* in October. Pisemskii was determined to 'tell the truth' about Gogol', even if other critics would not agree with his vision. He firmly believed that 'the passage of time will show that my position was that of the truth'.[74] He characterised Gogol''s style as 'true to reality' [vernoe deistvitel'nosti],[75] 'breathing with truthfulness' [istinoi vse eto dyshit],[76] and, in the same vein, referred to Gogol''s mistakes as falsehoods, an inability to 'tell the truth' [govorit' pravdu].[77]

This review revealed how closely Pisemskii's idea of realism was related to his understanding of Gogol''s style. Pisemskii made a direct allusion to Gogol''s masterpiece in the title of his 1858 novel *Tysiacha dush* and his contemporaries often referred to him as Gogol''s literary successor.[78] It is worth noting, however, that literary criticism of the 1860s used this label widely, and often indiscriminately. The phrase 'Gogolian trend'[79] [gogolevskoe napravlenie] was adopted to replace the 'natural school' [natural'naia shkola], a term that had effectively been almost banned by the censors after Belinskii's death. The resulting hybrid, 'Gogolian school' [gogolevskaia shkola], conflated the actual traits of Gogol''s poetics with Belinskii's understanding of the goals of contemporary literature as formulated in his articles on Gogol'. When Pisemskii's contemporaries called him 'a writer in the Gogolian tradition', they generally implied that his style was similar to the other writers of the 'gogolevskoe napravlenie', that is, he was at the forefront of progressive literary development. Such writers had to conform to a set of rules: to set their story in contemporary Russia, preferably in the provinces, and to represent reality faithfully, but at the same time critically, through the prism of social satire.

When *Vzbalamuchennoe more* came out in 1863, Pisemskii still enjoyed the reputation of precisely this type of writer. In a way, this new novel seemed to be a stylistic setback: critics were most surprised by Pisemskii's reversion to the naturalist style of the 1840s and, more disturbingly, by an at times almost complete subjugation of the realist narrative to polemical outbursts. Considering Pisemskii's declared contempt for tendentiousness, his direct appeals to the reader in *Vzbalamuchennoe more* might seem out of character. However, in Pisemskii's opinion, he merely tried to present the facts in a way that would prove his overall argument. Unlike *Chto delat'?* (a novel destined for oblivion, in Pisemskii's opinion), his novel was not propelled by a utopian impulse. Neither did he aim for overt didacticism, as this would compromise his realist credentials, on which he kept insisting. It seems that the Bezrylov feuilleton affair had compromised Pisemskii's public persona to such an extent that he had to resort to a literary statement instead of an article or an open debate. As one of Pisemskii's biographers aptly noted, 'realising the futility of combatting radical ideas by upholding the principle of "art for art's sake", Pisemskii decided to face the radicals in a more militant fashion'.[80] On the one hand, Pisemskii sympathised with the proponents of 'pure art'; on the other, he shared Belinskii's idea 'that literature should not shun reality, no matter how ungainly this reality might appear'.[81] It is this intermediary aesthetic position between Belinskii and Druzhinin that made Pisemskii's struggle to find a balance (in theory and in practice) between realism and didacticism even more apparent.

Despite the lack of philosophical expertise on Pisemskii's side, the problem that he addressed was not trivial. The integration of didacticism and realist narration remains a recurrent issue in the theory of mimesis. According to the critic René Wellek, this is precisely the main contradiction of the theory of realism:

> in [the] original definition, 'the objective representation of contemporary social reality', didacticism is implied or concealed. In theory, a completely truthful representation of reality would exclude any social purpose or propaganda. Obviously, the theoretical difficulty of realism, its contradictoriness, lies in its very point. [...] there is a tension between description and prescription, truth and instruction, which cannot be resolved logically.[82]

Erich Auerbach's insistence that 'real realism [...] must not be comic, that it must not be didactic or ethical or rhetorical or idyllic'[83] led him to exclude Defoe, Richardson and Fielding (and by extension, George Eliot or Lev Tolstoi) from the ranks of realist writers.[84]

In the nineteenth century, this 'tension between description and prescription' was at the centre of the literary polemics of the 1860s. What contemporary scholar of mimesis Sarah Ruth Lorenz called the 'intersection of two aesthetic imperatives, that of imitation and that of visionary didacticism'[85] reached its height in the philosophy of the Russian utilitarian critics, such as Dobroliubov, and in literary texts of the period. It is precisely the examination of 'the conflicting underlying aesthetic imperatives of the texts [that] helps make sense of their volatility, instability and radicalism'.[86]

The transgression of the ontological levels of narrative in Pisemskii's text was a consequence of the specific literary climate of the 1860s, when, for a brief period, metafictional narratives became almost de rigueur. It seems that in the mid-1860s, addressing an ideological matter in a literary text also called for an explicit examination of the aesthetic assumptions behind the narrative process. The theory of realism that was outlined in Belinskii's articles two decades earlier was re-examined not just by critics, but also by the writers of the 1860s, who were struggling to adapt the narrative legacy of the natural school to the demands of the contemporary literary fashion for utilitarianism and radical aesthetics. One manifestation of Pisemskii's attempt to reconcile the two was the introduction of a self-conscious narrator who entered his own story.

Reader as Ally

As evidenced by his correspondence, Pisemskii had a clear idea of the novel's structure and composition for *Vzbalamuchennoe more* before he started writing. In a letter to A. A. Kraevskii of 17 August, 1851, he wrote:

> As a plot, I am going to choose the autobiography of an ordinary man: I'll start from his birth and will follow his continuous development. I will surround him with ordinary circumstances [...] and will follow him through the mistakes of his youth, bitter lessons, and finally the slow cooling of his senses, during which he would look back at his youth and write his memoirs.[87]

The finished novel consisted of six parts, and followed the life of its main character, Aleksandr Baklanov. At the beginning of the novel, Baklanov is an impressionable and immature nineteen-year-old heir to a prosperous estate; in the concluding chapters, he is a disillusioned, bankrupt middle-aged man with few if any prospects in life. Each part describes a stage in Baklanov's life: from *barchuk* (a young nobleman) to student, to civil servant, and ultimately to misguided radical. The central love plot serves as a metaphor for Baklanov's wasted life: he falls in and out of love with his cousin Sofi, who keeps leaving him for more suitable and usually wealthier suitors. A series of subplots (Baklanov's love affairs and civil service court cases, Sofi's post-emancipation battle for her estate, the adventures of Sofi's maid Irodiada and her lover Mikhailo, etc.) maintain the lively pace of the novel and present a broad picture of the Russian society of the 1850s–1860s.

Since Pisemskii chose to tell a story of an 'everyman', the first chapters of the novel introduced a typical landowner family, Baklanov's cousins, the Basardins. A summary of the family history offered readers a snapshot of the immediate social environment in which Baklanov's life was to unfold. Pisemskii described the last twenty years in the life of the declining Russian gentry, with their crumbling estates, boarding and military schools, petty scrambles for small governmental posts and the dependence of both masters and peasants on the effective management of the land. Here, Pisemskii's style was a curious mixture of Gogolian satire, Shchedrin's naturalism and Turgenev's lyricism, betraying his deep, if not uncritical, sympathy for the way of life he was depicting.

Aleksandr Baklanov, a 'young man wearing a student uniform',[88] first featured in the novel's fifth chapter, aptly entitled 'Young bucks'. Vain, weak and not particularly smart, he nonetheless won the reader's instant sympathy because of his sincere and ardent efforts to succeed in life and love. Baklanov's fate was supposed to serve as an example of failure that befalls 'a man of the forties' who is trying to build a life for himself in the new, post-reform Russia. First, with some help from a wealthy relative, he manages to get a small post in the civil service, but falls out with his superiors and is forced to quit. He then marries for money and attempts to manage his wife's estate but quickly grows bored, seduces his children's nanny and buys into a disastrous financial scheme with fake shares that leaves him almost bankrupt when it collapses. Fed up with family life, he gets back together with Sofi and leaves for St Petersburg.

The end of Part Four sees Pisemskii's hero fail at everything he previously cared for: career, family and fortune. This part of the novel, published in June 1863, puzzled Pisemskii's contemporaries. Suddenly retreating from Baklanov's story, Pisemskii offered his readers musings on recent events in Russian history. If previous chapters were written in a style that was recognisably Pisemskii's own, Part Four was more polemical and openly didactic than any fiction he had ever published. This marked a departure within the novel from a mode of realist narration to a new, hybrid type of narrative that resulted from Pisemskii's struggle to unite a didactic message with realist poetics.

But it is in the Part Five, when Baklanov and Sofi enjoy their glamorous life in the capital, that we finally meet the novel's metadiegetic narrator, 'Pisemskii'. At this point, the story catches up with recent times, and, to emphasise Baklanov's connection to immediate social reality, Pisemskii introduces himself as a character who befriends Baklanov and Sofi. He accompanies Baklanov to parties, flirts with Sofi at her soirées, discusses politics with the couple's friends and, finally, reads his own novella *Starcheskii grekh* [An Old Man's Sin] at one of Sofi's literary evenings. At the end of their stay, 'Pisemskii' sees Baklanov and Sofi off at the station. Thus, the story of their entire time in St Petersburg is narrated from both objective and subjective perspectives (Pisemskii-character merged with Pisemskii-narrator), allowing for multiple meta-observations.

The final part of the novel follows Baklanov's and Sofi's adventures in Europe and their return Russia. The novel concludes with Baklanov and his wife Evpraksia arriving in St Petersburg in May when the city was in chaos because of the disastrous 1862 fires. The final passage, driving the author's point home, discusses the necessity of the truthful representation of all the lies and troubles of contemporary society in literary fiction.

There are several instances of metafictional narration in *Vzbalamuchennoe more*, demonstrating a series of minor and major ontological frame-breaks, or metalepses. In addition to the five chapters in which the narrator features as a character, there are nine more minor metalepses in the text, often dramatised as conservations with an omniscient reader. As isolated occurrences, they strike neither the lay reader nor the literary critic as something out of the ordinary, but when viewed together, these narrative transgressions offer an insight into the literary realisation of Pisemskii's polemic argument about didacticism, politics and aesthetics. Their accumulation in the text suggests that sustained metafictionality in *Vzbalamuchennoe more* is more than a 'simple oversight', as it might have appeared to critics. Moreover, it exposes Pisemskii's practical understanding of the ontology of fiction, emerging in an attempt to produce a politically astute and at the same time aesthetically pleasing realist narrative.

Similarly to Chernyshevskii's continuous engagement with his perspicacious reader in *Chto delat'?*, Pisemskii, following nineteenth-century novel-writing conventions, also maintains a dialogue with a 'reader' [chitatel'] throughout his novel. However, unlike Chernyshevskii's reader-adversary, whom the narrator constantly outsmarts, Pisemskii's reader is his ally. Over the course of the novel the innocuous asides to this sympathetic reader build up to a fully established breaking of the novel's ontological frame, transforming the conventional reader-addressee into an agent of metafictionality in the novel. Pisemskii does not silence his readers by shoving napkins into their mouths but rather enlists their help in interpreting the characters, plot developments and political messages in the novel. Ultimately, in the novel's metaleptic chapters, the implied reader assumes an omniscience that not just rivals but exceeds that of the novel's narrator once he crosses the ontological border to enter his own narrative.

The appeals to the implied allied reader feature in various parts of the novel, continuing past the stylistic break in Part Four. Baklanov's character develops under the reader's close observation from the very first descriptions of his childhood and youth. In order to win the reader's sympathy, Pisemskii often uses a device that would later become Lev Tolstoi's trademark: attributing a universal emotion to particular character. For example, describing young Baklanov's circumstances at his parents' house, the narrator implores the reader to

> Припомните, читатель, ваше юношество, первое, раннее юношество! Вы живете с родителями. Вам все как-то неловко курить трубку или папироску в присутствии вашего отца. [...] То же, или почти то же самое, чувствовал и мой девятнадцатилетний герой.[89]

> [Remember, reader, the days of your youth, early, fresh youth! You still live at your parents' house. You are still feeling somewhat embarrassed to smoke your pipe or your cigarette in your father's presence. [...] The same, or almost the same, feelings were common for my nineteen-year-old hero.]

The reader cannot help but sympathise with the young Baklanov, emerging from under his parents' wing. Since the novel opens with a brief history of the Basardins, Baklanov is first introduced to the reader as their guest; straight away, the main character is represented as a member of a larger community of landed gentry. The reader is, therefore, invited to relate not only to Baklanov's forays into adult life, but also to his attempts to find a place for himself in the world of his ancestors.

Baklanov's quest for a suitable role in a rapidly changing world is the essence of the novel's plot, and this scene essentially foreshadows future plot developments and the reader's role in interpreting the rest of the novel.

The reader is also summoned at a pivotal moment when young Baklanov concocts his first big lie and claims to have seduced his cousin Sofi. He boasts to his friend Veniavin that he has slept with her, but the reader is invited to question such claims. The reader's omniscience is emphasised in the conventional metaphors of sight and vision, such as the narrator's claim that 'Читатель очень хорошо видит, что молодой человек тут лгал безбожно, немилосердно!' [The reader could very well see that our young man was telling an outrageous lie, a terrible lie!].[90] 'The reader' had indeed been offered a description of Baklanov's meeting with Sofi and knows his account to be false.

'The reader' here is invited to assume the position of the omniscient narrator: they share knowledge of what happened and both can 'see through' Baklanov's bluff. This passage proves to be highly significant in the overall context of the novel, since one of its goals is to expose Baklanov as a fake. In the microcosm of this scene, the reader is invited to use his advanced knowledge to see through Baklanov's lies, but also to validate Baklanov's actions through acknowledging his experience as universal — a mental process that the reader is supposed to employ throughout the novel.

Particularly revealing are the instances when the reader is summoned to judge the authenticity of the plot development and the degree of the characters' fictionality. In a curiously metaleptic scene, Baklanov, incensed by the news of Sofi's alleged affair with the Jewish usurer Galkin, loses his temper in an argument with the local governor. As a result of such insubordination, his career in the civil service is finished. This scene describes their argument and its aftermath, and finishes on the narrator's note that undermines the legitimacy of the narrative he had just offered to his readers:

> На другой день Бакланов был отозван из комиссии к другим занятиям, более подходящим, как сказано в предписании, к его образованному уму. 'Что это?.. Не может быть!' — восклицает, вероятно, и по преимуществу великосветский читатель. Что делать!.. — смиренно отвечаю я: — очень уж зафантазировался, написал то, чего никогда не бывает, — извините.[91]
>
> [On the next day, Baklanov was called away from the commission and given another job that was better suited to his educated mind. 'What is this? This can't be true!' a reader from a high society would probably ask. 'What to do?' I will answer modestly. 'My fantasy got out of control, I wrote something that could never be, excuse me!']

If previous references to 'the reader' in the text are conventional and do not break the narrative frame, this one introduces a notion of a fictional 'possible world', a discursive strategy typical of a metanarrative.[92] For a brief moment, Baklanov's story 'forks', allowing for an alternative course of events. Through asides such as this, Pisemskii makes sure his reader is aware that what is presented to him is fiction rather than studies from life. In a similar vein, after a description of the beginning of Baklanov's zealous service in chapter 11, the narrator explicitly states:

> Город, выбранный нами в настоящем случае, совершенно идеальный и несуществующий. Лица, в нем выведенные, тоже совершенно вымышленные, и мы только в них, по мере нашего понимания, старались выразить те явления, которые не совсем же неприсущи нашей жизни, а теперь, сообразно нашему плану, нам придется выдумать и целое уголовное дело [...] Бунтовщиков предали военно-судной комиссии. В комиссии этой предписали заседать и Бакланову.[93]

> [The city that we have chosen here is absolutely exemplary and does not exist in reality. The characters described here are also completely made up and we have only tried to express through them, as far as we understand, events that do really happen in our life, but now, to follow our own plan, we will need to make up an entire criminal case [...] The rebels were brought before the military court commission. Baklanov was supposed to be a member of this commission.]

Not only is Baklanov investigating a fictional murder in a non-existent town, but the entire story of his investigation can have alternative outcomes. The fictionality of the other characters is also repeatedly emphasised, and they are referred as to 'figures accidentally chosen to be portrayed' to illustrate contemporary mores of the 'Russian kingdom'.[94] Appealing to the readers' intertextual interpretative powers, this fictionality is established through references to their previous literary experiences.

One particular character seems to be lifted entirely out of a popular crime novel in the vein of Eugène Sue's *Les Mystères de Paris* (1842–43): the troublesome coachman Mikhailo, whose talent for disguises fools even the omniscient reader, who, as the narrator supposes, 'would not have been able to recognise him'.[95] This character has an intriguing meta-literary function. Mikhailo features in a mystery sub-plot that has self-consciously literary origins. The climax of this sub-plot occurs in Part Four, in a chapter called 'A scene that could have featured in a French novel'. Mikhailo and his lover Irodiada, Sofi's maid, hire a boat to escape with Sofi's jewels, and then kill the boatman and flee.

Just a few chapters later, 'Pisemskii' accompanies Baklanov on his visit to Irodiada in prison. 'Pisemskii' questions Irodiada and is present while she tells Baklanov the full story of her crimes. This becomes a point of convergence of two ontological levels within the fictional world of the novel. Irodiada is a fictional character, so much so that the sub-plot in which she features is stylistically different from the rest of the novel, and yet she meets the ostensibly 'real' 'Pisemskii'. This produces a confusion of ontological levels, which might not have been intended by the author, but appears to be a result of his struggles with the unyielding realist discourse. The effect it creates is similar to any metanarrative: unwittingly, it exposes the constructed nature of 'reality' as a concept.

As these passages demonstrate, Pisemskii intended this reader to become an active co-interpreter of the plot and the characters in the spirit of the eighteenth-century poetics of didacticism. Revealingly, the crucial description of Baklanov as a character in the polemical Part Four follows a direct appeal to the reader, who is supposed to have noticed that 'что герой мой, во-первых не герой, а обыкновенный смертный из нашей так называемой образованной среды' [my hero, is, first of all, not a hero but an ordinary mortal from our so-called educated society].⁹⁶

Here, Pisemskii addresses the discrepancy between the reader's expectations and the way in which Baklanov's story unfolds. This rhetorical figure is used throughout the novel: Baklanov's failures are examined against the reader's supposed understanding of his character. This allows Pisemskii to emphasise the difference between Baklanov's self-image and how the other characters, the readers and the narrator perceive him. However, in comparison to Chernyshevskii's use of the same strategy, Pisemskii's reader is in the right and Baklanov is in the wrong — he is, after all, an 'average man', and the readers are often asked to sympathise with him. When Baklanov invests all his money into shares that prove to be worthless, the narrator enquires: 'А сами вы лучше, благоразумнее, накупили акций, признайтесь-ка?' [And you think that you, better and more level-headed people, would not have bought the shares? Admit it!].⁹⁷

By the end of the novel Pisemskii fashions his readers into two groups, in much the same way as Chernyshevskii had in his novel. This categorisation was, of course, typical for the public rhetoric of the period and not exclusive to these two texts; a similar division of readers into progressive and conservative categories will be discussed in the following chapter on Panaeva. What is remarkable is that Pisemskii's demarcation of the two groups is carried out in the same rhetorical manner (through negation) and, most importantly, does not utilise the presumptions of gender that affect both Chernyshevskii and Panaeva. For Pisemskii, age, or maturity, is more important as a factor. The final paragraph of *Vzbalamuchennoe more* contrasts 'sixteen-year-old female readers' and 'weak-headed youths' (naïve readers) to 'future historians', 'attentive' and 'trusting' (ideal readers):

> Труд наш мы предпринимали вовсе не для образования ума и сердца шестнадцатилетних читательниц и не для услады задорного самолюбия разных слабоголовых юношей: им лучше даже не читать нас; мы имели совершенно иную (чтобы не сказать: высшую) цель и желаем гораздо большего: пусть будущий историк со вниманием и доверием прочтет наше сказание: мы представляем ему верную, хотя и не полную картину нравов нашего времени, и если в ней не отразилась вся Россия, то зато тщательно собрана вся ее ложь.⁹⁸

> [We have undertaken this labour not to educate the minds and hearts of sixteen-year-old female readers, and not to please the cocky self-esteem of weak-headed youths: they should not even bother reading this. We have a different, even noble, goal, and desire for much more: to let a future historian read our tale with attention and trust: we offer him a true, if incomplete, picture of the mores of our times, and if it does not reflect all of Russia, it certainly reflects all of its lies.]

Despite the fact that Pisemskii never used the word 'nihilist' in his novel, his barbs against the young radicals should be read in the context of Katkov's denunciatory publications in *Russkii vestnik*, mentioned above. Baklanov dismisses the young radicals as 'boys', a definition that is borrowed directly from Katkov's vocabulary, as well as 'empty-heads', 'seminarians-crammers' and 'chatterboxes'.[99] By denouncing the youngsters and the sentimental young ladies, he is reinforcing the bond with his ideal readers: inquisitive conservatives. Pisemskii is addressing those who already share his views, rather than the St Petersburg literary establishment, or, as he called them 'Petersburg literary bastards' [peterburgskaia literaturnaia svoloch']) with his expository tale.[100]

These minor frame-breaks, analysed above, establish the image of Pisemskii's implied and ideal readers and emphasise the fictionality of the narrated story. A major challenge to this perceived fictionality is launched in Part Five, the most metaleptic fragment of the novel. Grammatically, the third-person narration turns into a first-person one. Focalisation changes, as well: we no longer see the world through Baklanov's eyes; instead we are following 'Pisemskii'-character in his St Petersburg adventures.

The Paradox of Omniscience

Vzbalamuchennoe more presents its readers with a confusing array of several author-figures. First, there is the biographical author of the text, the actual historical figure Aleksei Pisemskii. Then there is 'Pisemskii'-character ('Pisemskii'), a fictional figure closely resembling the implied author Aleksei Pisemskii. They are, however, not identical. *Vzbalamuchennoe more* is not an autobiographical novel, and, although some of the events in the novel, like Baklanov's visit to London, are inspired by Pisemskii's actual travels, the accounts of these events are not historically accurate. Finally, there is the metadiegetic narrator of *Vzbalamuchennoe more*, who, at some point in the novel, switches from an 'objective' to a 'subjective' method of narration and enters his own story in Part Five. The ripple effects of the switches between these figures contribute to the ontological instability of the text.

By the time 'Pisemskii' enters the narrative in chapter 3 of Part Five, Baklanov has left his family, abandoned his career and moved to St Petersburg with Sofi. Baklanov, as usual following the latest fashion, now wants to publish an 'aesthetic journal'. 'Pisemskii' is a guest at Baklanov's soirée:

> На этот вечер, вместе с прочими гостями, был приглашен и автор сего рассказа. Извиняюсь перед читателем, что для лучшего разъяснения смысла событий я, по необходимости, должен ввести самого себя в мой роман: дело в том, что Бакланов был мой старый знакомый.[101]

> [The author of this tale has been invited to this soirée along with all the other guests. I offer the reader my apologies, since in order to better explain the meaning of the events I need to introduce myself into my own novel: actually, Baklanov was a good friend of mine.]

Aside from a faint echo of Pushkin's declaration of kinship with his character in *Evgenii Onegin*[102] in the announcement of the narrator's friendship with Baklanov, two things stand out in this explanation. Firstly, the fictionality of the narrated story and its characters is revoked. Someone who, a few chapters before, was an explicitly fictional character whose fate was subject to the narrator's whim is now characterised as the author's old acquaintance. Secondly, the narrator believes that the introduction of himself as a character requires an apology. This is not the first time he apologises to the reader: the previous instances all concerned the perceived gap between the reader's expectations and the actual narrative. Thus, we can assume that the apology indicated that the author believes that this narrative turn is unexpected and immodest and therefore might not please the reader. However, in the previous instances, it was only the naïve reader whom the narrator was afraid of upsetting, whereas the ideal reader has been sharing the narrator's omniscience. In consequence, the narrator seems to imply that for the discerning reader this turn of events should not be such a surprise.

The introduction of 'Pisemskii', who is acknowledged as the author of the unfolding narrative, is a major narrative frame-break. After the narrator and author merge, it turns out that 'Pisemskii' does not possess the advanced knowledge of the omniscient narrator. In fact, despite his promise to help 'explain the events', he seems to be at a disadvantage in relation to 'the reader'. When Sofi is introduced to 'Pisemskii' as Baklanov's cousin, he suspects that this is not the entire truth, exclaiming 'Я сейчас же понял, что тут было что-то такое, да не то!' [I immediately recognosed that something was amiss!].[103] 'The reader', on the other hand, knows perfectly well about the couple's affair. The character thus dissociates himself from the previously omniscient narrator, surrendering his advanced knowledge to the 'subjective method'. His role, it seems, is mainly functional — he facilitates scenes and steers the conversation to the topics that most expose Baklanov's pretence.

In the two chapters that follow Baklanov's intellectual development, 'Pisemskii' works towards exposing the falsity of his protagonist's aspirations. The first one, 'Baklanov-aesthetisist', describes Baklanov's plans to start an aesthetic journal. The opening statement of the second chapter of this kind, 'Baklanov-journalist', brings together fiction and reality: 'Очень невдолге герой мой начал на моих глазах переделываться' [It did not take long for my hero to start changing right in front of my eyes].[104] Baklanov becomes more than a mere character: he turns into the embodiment of his time. He 'endears' his creator, representing 'явление всей этой шумящей около меня, как пущенная шутиха, жизни!' [the presence of all the life, whirling around me like a just-released firework].[105] Sofi's fictional origins are also completely forgotten: upon meeting her, the author is infatuated with his own creation and is in the throes of 'indescribable pleasure'.[106] In the narrative space of Part Five of the novel, Baklanov and Sofi are paradoxically both fictional and real.

In his analysis of John Fowles's narrative technique in *The French Lieutenant's Woman*, Frederick M. Holmes calls this device 'a paradox of omniscience':

> the narrator identifies himself as the author [...] Consequently, he can periodically point out the artificial nature of his story without destroying it. Having momentarily dispelled the illusion that his characters have a reality apart from the book, he can continue to delineate the plot [...]. The reader, therefore, soon forgets the narrator's warning, once again becoming immersed in the verisimilitudinous account...'.[107]

At this point, the ontological levels in *Vzbalamuchennoe more* converge into a complex and not an entirely coherent structure. As a result, the reader remains in a state of mild confusion as to what is real and what is fictional in the novel, but also about the stability of the border between the two worlds. This creates an ontological uncertainty, which is exacerbated by the author's constant references to the concepts of truth and lies. Since one of the topics of the novel is Baklanov's susceptibility to fashionable ideas, the reader's confusion becomes in itself an almost accidental additional tool of interpretation. Baklanov has trouble identifying authentic ideas, and the reader in turn is forced by the narrative structure of the text to contemplate notions of authenticity, sincerity and verisimilitude, echoing the character's (and possibly the author's) musings.

Sincerity becomes an obsession for both Baklanov and 'Pisemskii'. When Baklanov's plans for the journal are met with the writer's disapproval, he rebukes him as 'a man from a different camp'. The point they most disagree on is sincerity: 'Искренности, искренности я больше желаю от вас, Бакланов! — сказал я ему однажды. — Я совершенно искренен, совершенно! — отвечал он мне. — Нет и нет! — кричал я ему' [Sincerity, I demand more sincerity from you, Baklanov! — I told him once. — I am absolutely sincere, absolutely! — was his reply. — No and no! — I shouted at him].[108]

Sincerity, alongside truth, is a key category in Pisemskii's understanding of literary aesthetics. Baklanov lacks sincerity and, therefore, substance: having no ideas of his own, he is forever following the latest ideological fashion. The same is the case with Sofi:

> Вы ужасная притворщица! — начал я прямо. — Не может быть, нет! — воскликнула она — У вас все только для наружности, и даже я знаю, что такое в вас искреннее. — Ну, что же во мне есть искреннего, что искреннего? Скажите! — пристала она ко мне. — Сколько могу отгадывать, так любовь к разнообразию.[109]

> [You are a terrible pretender! — I began directly. — No, that cannot be true, no! — she exclaimed. — Everything you do is just for show, I don't even know if there is anything sincere in you at all! — Well, tell, what is sincere, sincere in me? Tell me! — she demanded from me. — All I can guess at, it is your love for variety in life!]

The functional purpose of 'Pisemskii' is emphasised not only in the examples of dialogues above but even more directly in the scenes where he appears as a fully fledged character. Baklanov literally treats him like a puppet, manually turning 'Pisemskii' here and there to introduce him to new people: 'Бакланов прежде всего представил меня Софи [...] Бакланов между тем повернул меня и познакомил с другим молодым человеком. [...] Бакланов затем обернул меня в третью сторону' [Baklanov had first of all introduced me to Sophie [...] Baklanov had meanwhile turned me and introduced me to another young man [...] Baklanov had then turned me in a third direction].[110]

The guest of honour at Baklanov's party is his uncle Livanov, who, Baklanov hopes, will fund his future journal. In order to convince his uncle that such a journal would be a necessary addition to the contemporary intellectual debate, Baklanov discusses contemporary aesthetics and the nature of literary realism. Baklanov is worried about the intrusive poetics of the naturalist school ('and the filth and the fat of this "real school" is sticking out everywhere!') that he perceives to parade 'an excess of realism'. Irked by his uncle's insistence on the subversive nature of all contemporary art, Baklanov explains his view of realism in detail:

> По-вашему, значит, — начал он: — надо признать в искусстве совершеннейший реализм; рисовать, например, позволяется только вид фабрик, машин, ну, и, пожалуй, портреты с некоторых житейских сцен, а в гражданском порядке, разумеется, социализм: на полумере зачем уж останавливаться![111]

> ['You think, then,' said he, 'that we should acknowledge the most perfect realism in art; so it would only be allowed to paint factories, machines and, maybe, portrayal of some everyday scenes. That would mean, of course, socialism as the civil order: why stop halfway through!']

The discussion comes to nothing as the party disbands. Intriguingly, the writer in the room does not say a word — he is too distracted by Sofi's presence to pay any attention to abstract discussions.[112] 'Pisemskii' and Baklanov effectively change places: Baklanov discusses literature while 'Pisemskii' is preoccupied with Sofi — the physical 'turning' of his guest back and forth that Baklanov was doing at the beginning of the chapter realises its metaphorical potential. Sofi's company almost robs 'Pisemskii' of his function as witness: in her company, he keeps his eyes down so as not to be distracted from the sweet sound of her voice.

The 'Most Perfect' Meta-Realism

In these most metafictional chapters of the novel, Pisemskii-character is the star attraction at Sofi's party. She has arranged a literary reading at which he, a famous author, is presenting his latest work. The choice of a piece to read is not arbitrary: it is the actually existing Pisemskii's novella *Starcheskii grekh* (1860), and it is chosen to convey to Sofi his feelings for her.

> Бакланов между тем отнесся к Евсевию Осиповичу — Он будет нам читать свое произведение: 'Старческий грех'. Ливанов опять величественно склонил свою голову — Все, что вышло из под пера их, мне приятно, — сказал он ласково-обязательным тоном. — Господин Писемский реалист, — сказал Петцолов. Я ничего ему не возразил, а удивился только, что он знает это ученое слово. Читать меня Софи посадила против себя, и при этом я должен был сложить со столика 'Петербургские Ведомости', 'Современник' и 'Русский Вестник'. 'Странно что-то это', — думал я.[113]

> [Baklanov, meanwhile, addressed Evsevii Osipovich — He will read his own work to us: *An Old Man's Sin*. Livanov once again nodded magnanimously. — Anything that had come out from under their pen is pleasant to me, — he said in a tender-dutiful voice. — Mr Pisemskii is a realist, — said Petzolov. I did not contradict him, but was surprised that he knew such a learned word. Sofi made me sit in front of her for my reading, and I had to move several journals

such as *St Petersburg Record*, *Contemporary* and *Russian Herald* off the table. This is all very strange, — I thought.]

Sofi's display of the current periodicals demonstrates that she, following the St Petersburg fashion, pretends to be interested in current events. But Pisemskii-character, once again, sees right through this 'strange' arrangement: *Sovremennik* and *Russkii vestnik* are at the opposite ends of the ideological spectrum. *Peterburgskie vedomosti*, the oldest Russian newspaper, at that time offered a fairly liberal overview of current affairs in the capital, Russia and in the world. In a typical *mise-en-abyme*, *Russkii vestnik* is also the journal in which *Vzbalamuchennoe more* was eventually published. The incongruous mix of conservative and progressive journals further emphasises Sofi's hypocrisy: she clearly has no coherent views of her own but seeks to demonstrate her awareness of current issues to her guests. Among them, 'Pisemskii' has one ally. Livanov, an old conservative, likes anything Pisemskii has written, and is a personification of Pisemskii's ideal reader: intelligent, engaged, firmly backwards looking. 'Pisemskii' is here characterised as a 'realist-writer' — this seems to be how Pisemskii characterised himself as a writer, an observation also borne out by his correspondence.[114] His remark about 'learned words' shows, though, that he is aware of the differences in which writers and lay readers can use the same literary definitions.

The scenes of the reading can be interpreted as symbolic: in order to let Sofi know about his feelings, Pisemskii-character rushes through the novella to get to the love plot. Disappointingly, his audience constantly interrupts and gets excited at all the wrong moments: the depiction of the corrupted Russian school system, antisemitic caricatures of Jewish moneylenders, bullying by superiors in the army. The only member of the audience who is calm and unmoved is Livanov — he is, once again, an ideal reader (even if the character himself is portrayed as deplorable at times). If Baklanov, Sofi and their guests can only appreciate masterful descriptions of events that they can relate to, Livanov is capable of abstract thinking. Moreover, Livanov shares Pisemskii's understanding of 'pure realism' as a tool for interpreting reality. Livanov flatteringly assumes that a writer has a deeper knowledge of life than a regular person. 'Вот вы, как видно, наблюдали жизнь' [You, I see, have observed life'],[115] he says, addressing questions about contemporary society to 'Pisemskii'. Aside from being an ideal reader of Pisemskii's texts, Livanov here almost turns into his alter ego.

The two agree on philosophical, political and ethical matters, share a fascination with the culture of freemasonry, and articulate similar views on contemporary society and the younger generations. They both are captivated by Sofi, but both are too old for her — hence Pisemskii's choice of novella to read at her party. *Starcheskii grekh* follows the story of the middle-aged civil servant Ferapontov. Smitten with the young but devious maid by the name of Kostyreva, he embezzles government funds to help her out and, when caught, hangs himself. The fictional narrative of *Starcheskii grekh* here maps onto the events described in the scene of the reading, further undermining the text's ontological unity. Like Kostyreva, Sofi is manipulating her older admirers for her own gain: she is only interested in

Livanov because he is rich and in Pisemskii because he is famous. Another feature Livanov and Pisemskii-character share is a distaste for lies of any kind. Livanov's main problem with his nephew and Sofi is their shallowness and tendency to adopt fashionable ideas without digesting them: 'то, что есть в ней, она скрывает, а к чему участвует, то – лжет – того нет у ней в душе' [what she has, she conceals, and what she shows: that is a lie, it does not come from her soul].[116] The restrained praise Livanov bestows on 'Pisemskii' is also in agreement with Pisemskii's aesthetic preference for truth over style: 'ваш полет не высок, не орлиный, но не лживый' ['your flight is not very elevated', he said, addressing me, 'not that of an eagle, but you do not lie'].[117]

'Pisemskii' disappears at the end of chapter 8 and does not feature in rest of the novel. His final act is to see Baklanov and Sofi off at the railway station. The lovers are returning to Sofi's estate and 'Pisemskii' is there to witness their departure. Still an internal focaliser for now, he edges back to the omniscience of the extradiegetic narrator by eavesdropping on Sofi's conversation with her new conquest, young Petzolov. This final episode is a metaphor for the narrator's role in the text — he is literally retreating to a discreet presence behind his characters' backs and turning back to 'the objective method'.

The goodbyes between 'Pisemskii' and Baklanov are tender, as befits old friends — they part with tears in their eyes. The short period of Pisemskii-character's presence in the text of the novel ends with a passage that references the beginning of Part Four. The voice of the character merges with the voice of the narrator, lamenting the fate of his poor homeland, which is left in the hands of the new generation of 'lovers of progress' [progressisty] who cannot be trusted. These youngsters are not up to Pisemskii's exacting standards: they care for society and are happy to serve it, but, unfortunately, go about it the wrong way. Their heads are empty and ideas are abstract, their speeches are too contrived, and they treat their souls as commodities. The metafictional and ontologically heterogenic fragment of narrative finishes with a declared return to the 'objective' narrative mode: 'Возвращаюсь к объективному методу' [I am going back to the objective method again].[118] This declaration should be considered not just as a reference to the novel's fictionalised author-narrator, but also as a comment on realism. For Pisemskii, the word 'objective' had a precise meaning: not affected by personal opinion or impressions; reliable and devoid of interpretation. Thus, returning to external focalisation, he aims to reinforce the illusion of the author as a dispassionate chronicler of events, leaving the interpretation to the reader, as opposed to the narrator/character, who is an interpreter and a witness.

The six chapters in which the author features alongside his own characters show that his presence is highly metaphorical. In the scenes analysed above, Pisemskii-character has two distinct functions, and both are realised conceptually and discursively. His first function is that of interpreter. Because the 'objective method' does not allow for a narrator's interpretation of the events, he has to enter his own story in order to help the reader make sense of the events described. In his second role, he witnesses the events in order to give a first-hand account of plot developments. Pisemskii-character quietly observes the debates on aesthetics at Baklanov's house, accompanies Baklanov on his visit to Irodiada in prison, and eavesdrops at Sofi's parting with her young lover at the railway station. In order to achieve the multiple switches between 'subjective' and 'objective' methods, the novel employs a dynamic focalisation pattern. First, an external focaliser (an omniscient narrator) presents the story, and then, in Part Five, the external focaliser turns into an internal one when they merge into a character. The effect that these changes in the mode of narration have on the reader is twofold.

On the one hand, since this metalepsis is embedded in a realist narrative, the reader, as in the case of Fowles's paradox of omniscience, is comfortable enough not to let this brief deviation destroy the illusion of verisimilitude. On the other hand, the crossing of an ontological boundary creates a disturbing feeling of a lack of difference between the real world and the world of ideas. The main conceptual conflict of the novel is Baklanov's inability to see the difference between an abstract idea and its relevance to contemporary reality. Through the use of metalepsis in the six chapters of Part Five, the same issue is addressed at the structural level. Temporarily turning the external focaliser into an internal one crosses the boundaries between ontological levels in the text and shatters diegetic unity. A 'violation of the semantic threshold of representation',[119] it forces the reader to contemplate the relationship between fiction and reality. Despite the lack of consistency in the use of this narrative device, Pisemskii's decision to keep it in later editions of the novel suggests that its introduction was not arbitrary. In the six chapters of Part Five the main issues of the novel are brought together on the discursive, structural and metaphorical levels.

★ ★ ★ ★ ★

Despite the fact that *Vzbalamuchennoe more* is one of Pisemskii's most studied texts, it is often approached reductively, either as an example of the typical nineteenth-century realist novel, or as an anti-nihilist pamphlet. Both of these approaches prioritise proving that the text corresponds to the set of predetermined features, either stylistic or ideological. My hope is that the analysis presented above demonstrates that the novel holds an intrinsic interest as a representative example of nineteenth-century Russian metafiction. Created in a period that has been consistently praised as the Golden Age of the Realist novel, this text in fact questions the basic aesthetic assumptions of the realist narrative practice. In these chapters, Pisemskii was not only putting his theory into practice as he was composing the novel, but also self-reflexively meditated on the process. Symbolically, the majority of conversations between characters in these chapters centre on problems of aesthetics and literary styles, the role of literature and criticism in society, and misunderstandings about the nature of literary realism.

The dialogue with the reader that Pisemskii maintained throughout the novel culminated not only in the personification of the author who entered his own narrative, but also in bestowing on a character, who previously featured only in a supporting role, all the attributes of an ideal reader. The old conservative Livanov is attentive, insightful, self-aware, and, most importantly, shares Pisemskii's views and sentiments on progress, history, contemporary society, and the younger generation. The notions of falsehood and truth, sincerity and pretentiousness, were discussed in *Vzbalamuchennoe more* as both social and aesthetic problems. Pisemskii's political views were thus projected onto his aesthetic theory, which, despite its acknowledged incoherence, can be pieced together not only from his correspondence, articles, and comments on his novels recounted by contemporaries, but also from the use of narrative figures such as metalepsis in his fiction.

Tracing Pisemskii's influence beyond the early twentieth century is problematic, largely due to the restricted access to his texts during the Soviet period.[120] Like Ostrovskii, Pisemskii is acknowledged as a pioneer of Russian realist drama. His other legacy is *Tysiacha dush*, an innovative novel that introduced a new type of character — a man of business [delovoi chelovek][121] — to nineteenth-century Russian fiction. However, *Vzbalamuchennoe more* left a certain mark, too: even if it was not the first anti-nihilist novel, it defined the genre for years to come, both for writers and for critics. I would argue that the main reason why *Vzbalamuchennoe more* was widely read was not just because it provided a conservative alternative to the aesthetic and political radicalism of Pisemskii's contemporary Nikolai Chernyshevskii. It was precisely the uncanny fusion of aesthetic theory and ideology, exemplified in the novel's metafictional elements, which granted it a short-lived success and long-lasting significance.

Notes to Chapter 3

1. A. F. Pisemskii, *Pis'ma*, ed. by A. P. Mogilianskii and M. K. Kleman (Moscow: Izdatel'stvo Akademii nauk SSSR, 1936), p. 367. Translation from letters, articles and fiction in this chapter are mine unless otherwise indicated.
2. See, for example, L. A. Anninskii, *Tri eretika, Pisateli o pisateliakh* (Moscow: Kniga, 1988), p. 14: 'Broken, torn down from his pedestal, forgotten, he stepped back into the second row of the Russian classics', as well as A. V. Timofeev, 'Aleksei Feofilaktovich Pisemskii', in *Istoriia russkoi literatury XIX veka. 70–90-e gody*, ed. by L. D. Gromova, V. N. Anoshkina and V. B. Kataev (Moscow: Izdatel'stvo MGU, 2001), pp. 216–46; or Victor Terras, 'The Realist Tradition', in *The Cambridge Companion to the Classic Russian Novel*, ed. by Malcolm V. Jones and Robin Feuer Miller (Cambridge: Cambridge University Press, 1998), pp. 190–210 (p. 208).
3. Ostrovskii's plays remained in the Russian school curriculum even after the post-Soviet revisions of the school canon. For a recent discussion of Ostrovskii's relevance in an influential (if determinedly conservative) publication, see Olga Soboleva, 'Ostrovskii v sovremennoi shkole', *Literaturnaia gazeta*, 36 (2014), p. 4. *Groza* often features in permanent repertoires of regional state children's theatres but also in the most prestigious drama theatres like Evgenii Mironov's *Teatr Natsii*. Recent productions of *Groza* had been nominated for the Golden Mask, Russia's premier theatre award, in 2019, 2018 and 2017 <http://m.goldenmask.ru/spect.php?id=1682> [accessed 11 June 2019].
4. With the exception of *Tysiacha dush*, which remains Pisemskii's most popular novel even in the twenty-first century. Its most recent reprint is a part of a popular *Literaturnoe prilozheniie Istoriia Rossii v romanakh* series to *Komsomolskaiia pravda*, a Soviet newspaper that was reborn as a tabloid after 1991 (A. F. Pisemskii, *Tysiacha dush* (Moscow: Komsomolskaia pravda, 2016)).
5. P. D. Boborykin, 'Pamiati Pisemskogo', in *Literatura i zhizn'* <http://dugward.ru/library/pisemskiy/boborykin_pamyati_pisemsk.html> [accessed 7 August 2019].
6. For more on Pisemskii's finances, see S. N. Plekhanov, *Pisemskii* (Moscow: Molodaia gvardiia,

1986), p. 222. Plekhanov's account of Pisemskii's life is largely fictionalised but still contains valuable details from the writer's life.

7. S. A. Vengerov, *Aleksei Feofilaktovich Pisemskii: Kritiko-biograficheskii ocherk* (Moscow: Tovarishchestvo M. O. Vol'f, 1884); A. M. Skabichevskii, *A. F. Pisemskii, ego zhizn' i literaturnaia deiatel'nost* (St Petersburg: Tipografiia tovarishchestva 'Obshchestvennaia pol'za', 1894); V. V. Zelinskii, 'Aleksei Feofilaktovich Pisemskii, ego zhizn', literaturnaia deiatel'nost' i znachenie ego v istorii russkoi pis'mennosti: kritiko-biograficheskii ocherk', in A. F. Pisemskii, *Polnoe sobranie sochinenii*, 24 vols (St Petersburg: Tovarishchestvo M. O. Vol'f, 1885), I, 15–107; O. F. Miller, 'A. F. Pisemskii', in *Russkie pisateli posle Gogolia: chteniia, rechi i stat'i*, 3 vols (St Petersburg: Izdatel'stvo tovarishchestva M. O. Vol'f, 1890–1906), I (1890), 35–76; V. E. Cheshikhin-Vetrinskii, 'Aleksei Feofilaktovich Pisemskii', in *Istoriia russkoi literatury*, ed. by D. N. Ovsianiko-Kulikovskii (Moscow: Mir, 1909), pp. 232–52.

8. Since studying ideologically unsound writers required justification, Soviet scholars developed strategies to integrate Pisemskii into the canon. A common technique in Soviet criticism was to claim that he was in fact not as conservative as he might have appeared to his contemporaries, see, for example, P. G. Pustovoit, *A. F. Pisemskii v istorii russkogo romana* (Moscow: Izdatel'stvo Moskovskogo universiteta, 1969), pp. 3–4. See also A. A. Roshal', *Pisemskii i revoliutsionnaia demokratiia* (Baku: Azerbaidzhanskoe gosudarstevennoe izdatel'stvo, 1971), pp. 5–6. This position was so well argued that it was adopted by critics outside of the USSR: see Jenny Woodhouse, 'A Realist in a Changing Reality: A. F. Pisemsky and *Vzbalamuchennoye more*', *The Slavonic and East European Review*, 64 (1986), 489–505.

9. For an overview of early Soviet studies, see M. K. Kleman, 'Sud'ba literaturnogo naslediia Pisemskogo', in *Pis'ma*, pp. 3–20; as well as works such as Roshal', *Pisemskii i revoliutsionnaia demokratiia*; Pustovoit, *A. F. Pisemskii v istorii russkogo romana*; L. M. Lotman, 'A. F. Pisemskii', in *Istoriia russkoi literatury*, ed. by N. I. Prutskov and others (Leningrad: Nauka, 1982), pp. 203–31. Outside of Russia, Charles A. Moser's biography *Pisemsky: A Provincial Realist* (1969) and Maya Jenkins's 'A Study of A. F. Pisemsky and his Fate in Russian Literature' (unpublished doctoral thesis, University of London, University College, 1977) remain the two most authoritative works on Pisemskii. A comprehensive bibliography of secondary literature on Pisemskii is available in Jenkins, pp. 401–32.

10. A number of theses on Pisemskii have been defended in the last two decades. For a representative selection, see: K. Iu. Zubkov, 'Povesti i romany A. F. Pisemskogo 1850-kh godov: povestvovanie, kontekst, traditsiia' (unpublished doctoral thesis, SPbGU, 2011), Iu. Iu. Frolova, 'Poetika romana A. F. Pisemskogo "Tysiacha dush": khudozhestvennyi sintez realizma i sentimentalizma' (unpublished doctoral thesis, Voronezhskii gosudarstvennyi pedagogocheskii universitet, 2009); E. L. Zaitseva, 'Poetika psikhologizma v romanakh A. F. Pisemskogo' (unpublished doctoral thesis, Rossiiskii Universitet Druzhby Narodov, 2008); E. N. Kruglova, 'Khudozhestvennaia pozitsiia A. F. Pisemskogo v literaturnom protsesse 1840–60-kh godov' (unpublished doctoral thesis, Ivanovskii gosudarstvennyi universitet, 2008); E. V. Pavlova, Belletristika A. F. Pisemskogo 1840–1850-kh gg. i problema khudozhestvennogo metoda' (unpublished doctoral thesis, Pskovskii gosudarstvennyi universitet, 2007).

11. See E. N. Kruglova, *Khudozhestvennaia pozitsiia A. F. Pisemskogo v literaturnom protsesse 1840–60-kh godov: Avtoreferat dissertatsii na soiskanie uchenoi stepeni kandidata filologicheskikh nauk* (Kostroma: Ivanovskii gosudarstvennyi universitet, 2008), p. 17; E. V. Pavlova, *Belletristika A. F. Pisemskogo 1840–1850-kh gg. i problema khudozhestvennogo metoda: Avtoreferat dissertatsii na soiskanie uchenoi stepeni kandidata filologicheskikh nauk* (Cherepovets: Pskovskii gosudarstvennyi universitet, 2007), pp. 4, 5, 9.

12. A typical Soviet critical reading of Pisemskii's metanarrative can be found in Pustovoit's 1969 study, where the use of this technique was explained through Pisemskii's 'pamphlet narrative intention' that ultimately led the author to the 'complete loss of objectivity [...] and even hysterical cries and exclamations instead of a calm artistic representation of reality' (Pustovoit, *A. F. Pisemskii v istorii russkogo romana*, p. 167). For recent readings of Pisemskii's metanarrative as 'objectivisation of the author' and an authentication device, see L. N. Siniakova, *Kontseptsiia cheloveka v romanakh A. F. Pisemskogo 1860–1870-kh gg.* (Novosibirsk: Novosibirskii gosudarstvennyi universitet, 2007), pp. 70–72.

13. The 1959 edition follows the other two posthumous editions of Pisemskii's collected works, A. F. Pisemskii, *Polnoe sobranie sochinenii*, 24 vols (St Petersburg: Vol'f, 1895); A. F. Pisemskii, *Polnoe sobranie sochinenii*, 8 vols (St Petersburg: Izdatel'stvo tovarishchestva A. F. Marks, 1910–11). *Vzbalamuchennoe more* is Pisemskii's only major prose text that is excluded from the 1959 Soviet edition (A. F. Pisemskii, *Sobranie sochinenii*, 9 vols (Moscow: Pravda, 1959)). Currently, the novel is available as a print-on-demand book (<http://www.ozon.ru/context/detail/id/6595184/> [accessed 5 August 2019]). An academic edition of the text is currently in progress at IRLI RAN.
14. Pisemskii's early prose exercises approached a novelistic form, at least in length, in *Bogatyi zhenikh* (1851–52) or *Boiarshchina* (1844). However, *Tysiacha dush* has traditionally been identified as his first full-length novel. For more on the suggested periodisation of Pisemskii's prose see: Pustovoit, *A. F. Pisemskii v istorii russkogo romana*, pp. 7–9; Roshal', *Pisemskii i revoliutsionnaia demokratiia*, pp. 5, 73; Zubkov, 'Povesti i romany A. F. Pisemskogo 1850-kh godov', pp. 92–94.
15. D. I. Pisarev, 'Pisemskii, Turgenev i Goncharov (Sochineniia A. F. Pisemskogo, t. I i II. Sochineniia I. S. Turgeneva)', in *Polnoe sobranie sochinenii*, 10 vols (St Petersburg: Izdatel'stvo F. Pavlenkova, 1894–1904), I (1894), pp. 437–80 (p. 480).
16. For recent research on the prize, contextualising Pisemskii's win, see K. Iu. Zubkov, 'Ekspertnyi korpus Uvarovskoi premii dlia dramaturgov: sostav i evoliutsiia', *Karabikha: Istoriko-literaturnyi sbornik*, 10 (2018), 92–118.
17. These were outlined later, on the back of the first editorial, published at the end of the year. See A. F. Pisemskii, 'Ob izdanii v 1862 godu zhurnala "Biblioteka dlia chteniia" v 1861 godu', in *Pis'ma*, pp. 557–58.
18. 'Zapiski Salatushki. Mysli, chuvstva, vozrreniia, naruzhnost'i kratkaia biografiia statskogo sovetnika Salatushki' (1861); 'Fel'etony Nikity Bezrylova' (1861–62); 'Oblichitel'noe pis'mo iz ada', 'Zaveshchanie moim detiam Vasiliiu i Nikolaiu' (1862).
19. For more on this conflict see Charles A. Moser, 'Pisemskii's Literary Protest: An Episode from the Polemics of the 1860s in Russia', *Études slaves et est-européennes*, 8.1–2 (1963), 60–72, as well as Jenkins, pp. 160–72; Pustovoit, *A. F. Pisemskii v istorii russkogo romana*, pp. 146–47.
20. Pisemskii described this traumatic experience in one of his letters to I. S. Turgenev from February 1862. See *Literaturnoe nasledstvo*, 73 (1964), 177.
21. Fusso, *Editing Turgenev, Dostoevsky and Tolstoy*, p. 142.
22. G. N. Zhulev, 'Gor'kaia sud'bina kota, ili legkaia boinia. Vzbalamuchennaia opera v neskol'kikh aktakh', *Iskra*, 4 (1863), 583. The main character in this parody on Pisemskii's award-winning play is called Nikitushka Bezrylov.
23. Pisemskii's plan was to 'use an autobiography of a regular man as a plot'. 'Letter of 17 August 1851 to A. A. Kraevskii', in *Pis'ma*, p. 42.
24. Pisemskii, 'Letter of 4 November 1877 to F. I. Buslaev', in *Pis'ma*, p. 367; Pisemskii, *Vzbalamuchennoe more*, p. 434.
25. Ibid., p. 441.
26. Pisemskii, 'Letter of 19 February/3 March 1863 to I. S. Turgenev', *Literaturnoe nasledstvo*, 73 (1964), 177.
27. 'I have been dragging myself through Europe, and have not experienced any pleasures along the way, just troubles' (Pisemskii, 'Letter of 10 May 1863 to A. A. Kraevskii', in *Pis'ma*, p. 150).
28. For more on this meeting, see Charles A. Moser, *Pisemsky: A Provincial Realist* (Cambridge, MA: Harvard University Press, 1969), p. 120.
29. A. I. Gertsen, 'Vvoz nechistot v London', *Kolokol*, 15 December 1863, p. 1442.
30. Moser, *Pisemsky*, pp. 93–94.
31. D. I. Pisarev, *Sochineniia*, 10 vols (St Petersburg: Izdatel'stvo F. Pavlenkova, 1866–69), I (1866), pp. 3–80, 80–125.
32. Pisemkii, 'Letter of 15 November 1862 to B. N. Almazov', in *Pis'ma*, p. 153.
33. Pisemskii, 'Letter of 8 October 1862 to P. V. Annenkov', ibid., pp. 150–51.
34. Pisemskii, 'Letter of 1 November 1862 to B. N. Almazov', ibid., p. 151.
35. Pisemskii, 'Letter of 12/24 January 1863 to I. S. Turgenev', *Literaturnoe nasledstvo*, 73 (1964), 176.
36. Pisemskii, 'Letter of end of November/beginning of December 1869', *Literaturnoe nasledstvo*, 73 (1964), 183–84 (p. 184).

37. Pisemskii, 'Letter of 3 November 1878 to A. de Gubernatis', in *Pis'ma*, p. 765.
38. Pisemskii, 'Letter of 10 January 1864 to P. A. Valuev', ibid., pp. 164–65.
39. Pisemskii, 'Letter of 19 February/3 1863 March to I. S. Turgenev', *Literaturnoe nasledstvo*, 73 (1964), 177.
40. Pisemskii was an astute literary entrepreneur and his letters show evidence of negotiations with several bidders at the same time. In 1862, he wrote to B. N. Almazov (Pisemskii, 'Letter of 1 November 1862 to B. N. Almazov', in *Pis'ma*, p. 151), while dispatching a letter to Katkov (Pisemskii, 'Letter of 1 November 1862 to M. N. Katkov', ibid.).
41. Pisemskii, 'Letter of 8 October 1862 to P. V. Annenkov', in *Pis'ma*, p. 150; 'so you can see that I cannot treat the fruit of so much labour in haste and without consideration' (Pisemskii, 'Letter of 15 November 1862 to B. N. Almazov', ibid., p. 153).
42. Pisemskii, 'Letter of 1 November 1862 to B. N. Almazov', ibid., p. 151.
43. Pisemskii, 'Letter of 1 November 1862 to M. N. Katkov', ibid.
44. Zubkov traces these changes in K. Iu. Zubkov, 'Roman A. F. Pisemskogo "Vzbalamuchennoe more": vospriiatie sovremennikov i istoriia teksta', in *Ozernaia tekstologiia: trudy IV letnei shkoly na karel''skom peresheike po tekstologii i istochnikovedeniiu russkoi literatury* (Poselok Poliany (Uusikirko) Leningradskoi oblasti: St. Petersburgskii institut iudaiki, 2007), pp. 97–109.
45. For a full bibliography of reviews, see *Pis'ma*, pp. 653–54.
46. A. P. Miliukov, 'Mertvoe i vzbalamachennoe more', in *Otgoloski na literaturnye i obshhestvennye iavleniia* (St Petersburg: Tipografia F. S. Sushchinskago, 1875), pp. 188–203 (p. 195).
47. V. A. Zaitsev, 'Vzbalamuchennyi romanist', *Russkoe slovo*, 10 (1863), 23–44 (p. 30).
48. Katkov published six articles on nihilism in *Russkii vestnik* throughout 1862 and 1863. See M. N. Katkov, 'K kakoi my prinadlezhim partii' (*Russkii vestnik*, 37 (1862), 832–44), 'Neskol'ko slov po povodu odnogo ironicheskogo slova' (*Russkii vestnik*, 38 (1862), 463–81), 'Roman Turgeneva i ego kritiki' (*Russkii vestnik*, 39 (1862), 393–424), 'Zametka dlia izdatelia Kolokola' (*Russkii vestnik*, 39 (1862), 834–52), 'O nashem nigilizme (po povodu romana Turgeneva)' (*Russkii vestnik*, 40 (1862), 402–26), 'Po povodu stat'i "Rokovoi vopros"' (*Russkii vestnik*, 45 (1862), 398–418).
49. Zaitsev, 'Vzbalamuchennyi romanist', p. 34.
50. Pisemskii, 'Letter of 4/15 June 1863 to I. S. Turgenev', *Literaturnoe nasledstvo*, 73 (1964), 177.
51. For a more detailed explanation, see Pisemskii, 'Letter of 8 May 1866 to I. S. Turgenev', in *Pis'ma*, p. 203.
52. Both Pustovoit and L. M. Lotman believed that *Vzbalamuchennoe more* should be considered as the first anti-nihilist novel (Pustovoit, *A. F. Pisemskii v istorii russkogo romana*, pp. 169, 72 and Lotman, 'A. F. Pisemskii', p. 229). Contemporary scholarship is wary of this approach: both Siniakova and Zubkov question the entire idea of the validity of the definition of the 'antihilist novel' as introduced by A. G. Tsetlin in 1929 (A. G. Tseitlin, 'Siuzhetika antinigilisticheskogo romana', *Literatura i marksizm*, 2 (1929), 33–74). For more on this controversy see K. Iu. Zubkov, 'Antinigilisticheskii roman kak polemicheskii konstrukt radikal'noi kritiki', *Vestnik MGU. Seriia 9. Filologiia*, 4 (2005), 122–40; Siniakova, *Kontseptsiia cheloveka v romanakh A. F. Pisemskogo 1860–1870-kh gg.*, pp. 5, 6, 55.
53. Pisemskii, 'Letter of 29 January 1864 to B. N. Almazov', in *Pis'ma*, p. 166.
54. I. K., 'Mysli o "Vzbalamuchennom more"', *Kievskii telegraf*, 3 July 1864, p. 379; *Kievskii telegraf*, 5 July 1864, p. 383, as cited in Zubkov, 'Roman A. F. Pisemskogo "Vzbalamuchennoe more"', p. 97.
55. Pisemskii, 'Letter of 4/15 June 1863 to I. S. Turgenev', *Literaturnoe nasledstvo*, 73 (1964), 178.
56. Identified by A. V. Listratova in 1967. See A. V. Listratova, 'O literaturno-obschestvennoi positsii A. F. Pisemskogo 60-kh godov', *Uchenye zapiski Ivanovskogo gosudarstvennogo pedagogicheskogo instituta*, 38 (1967), 48–49. Cited in Jenkins, p. 187.
57. N. V. Shelgunov, *Literaturnaia kritika* (Leningrad: Khudozhestvennaia literatura, 1974), p. 49.
58. Pisemskii, *Vzbalamuchennoe more*, p. 304.
59. Waugh cites Fowles's novel as a typical example of metafiction throughout her theoretical study. See Waugh, *Metafiction*, pp. 4, 13, 22, 32–34.
60. Shelgunov, *Literaturnaia kritika*, p. 167.
61. N. B., 'Tekuchaia belletristika', *Den'*, 32 (1864), 18. Cited in Zubkov, 'Roman A. F. Pisemskogo "Vzbalamuchennoe more"', p. 103.

62. Ibid.
63. Pisemskii's novella *Plotnich'ia artel'* [The Company of Carpenters] (1855) also featured a first-person narrator seemingly identical to the implied biographical author; however, his ontological status remained unquestioned in this piece. I am grateful to Gabriella Safran and Alexei Vdovin to drawing my attention to this earlier text.
64. Pisemskii, 'Letter of 4 November 1877 to F. I. Buslaev', in *Pis'ma*, pp. 364–67 (p. 364).
65. Ibid., p. 365.
66. Ibid., p. 366.
67. Ibid.
68. Pisemskii, 'Letter of 12 March 1854 to A. N. Maikov', in *Pis'ma*, pp. 63–64.
69. P. D. Boborykin, *Za polveka: vospominaniia* (Moscow: Zakharov, 2003), p. 172.
70. Pisemskii, 'Letter of 30 May/11 June 1855 to I. S. Turgenev', *Literaturnoe Nasledstvo*, 73 (1964), 140.
71. Pisemskii, *Vzbalamuchennoe more*, p. 549.
72. Lotman, 'A. F. Pisemskii', p. 229.
73. For more on this dichotomy see Pavlova, *Belletristika A. F. Pisemskogo 1840–1850-kh gg. i problema khudozhestvennogo metoda*, pp. 9–10, 15.
74. Pisemskii, 'Letter of 26 October 1855 to M. P. Pogodin', in *Pis'ma*, p. 98.
75. A. F. Pisemskii, 'Sochineniia N.V. Gogolia, naidennye posle ego smerti. Pokhozhdeniia Chichikova, ili mertvye dushi. Chast' vtoraia', in *Sobranie sochinenii* (Moscow: Pravda, 1959), pp. 523–46 (p. 534).
76. Ibid., p. 532.
77. Ibid., p. 546.
78. Chernyshevskii, among others, designated Pisemskii a 'Gogolian writer' and approached him as such in his analysis of Pisemskii's peasant stories (N. G. Chernyshevskii, 'Ocherki iz krest'ianskogo byta A. F. Pisemskogo', *PSS*, IV (1948), pp. 567–72). V. G. Avseenko's 1881 obituary noted that Pisemskii was closer to Gogol' than to any other writer of the 1840s and called him 'an immediate heir to Gogol'' (V. G. Avseenko, 'Pamiati A. F. Pisemskogo', *Moskovskie vedomosti*, 26 (1881) (as cited in Pustovoit, *A. F. Pisemskii v istorii russkogo romana*, p. 73)), and Skabichevskii counted Pisemskii among the writers of the 1850s whose genealogy went back to Gogol' (Skabichevskii, *A. F. Pisemskii, ego zhizn' i literaturnaia deiatel'nost'*, p. 1). Soviet scholars followed suit: M. P. Eremin called Pisemskii 'an artist of Gogol''s school' (M. P. Eremin, *A. F. Pisemskii* (Moscow: Znanie, 1956), p. 7) and Pustovoit referred to the writer's attempts at 'Gogol''s realist method' (Pustovoit, *A. F. Pisemskii v istorii russkogo romana*, p. 79). Lotman discussed Belinskii's influence on Pisemskii's ideas about Gogol', as well as his view of Gogol' chiefly as a satirist (Lotman, 'A. F. Pisemskii', p. 204).
79. This translation of the term is offered in Terras, *Handbook of Russian Literature*, p. 366.
80. Jenkins, p. 186.
81. Ibid., p. 93.
82. Wellek, *Concepts of Criticism*, p. 242.
83. René Wellek, 'Auerbach's Special Realism', *The Kenyon Review*, 16 (1954), 299–307 (at p. 303).
84. Wellek, *Concepts of Criticism*, p. 242.
85. Sarah Ruth Lorenz, 'Visionary Mimesis: Imitation and Transformation in the German Enlightenment and Russian Realism' (unpublished doctoral thesis, University of California, Berkeley, 2012), p. 1.
86. Ibid., p. 6.
87. Pisemskii, 'Letter from 7 December 1851 to S. P. Shevyrev', in *Pis'ma*, pp. 41–42 (p. 41).
88. Pisemskii, *Vzbalamuchennoe more*, pp. 130–31.
89. Ibid., p. 147.
90. Ibid., p. 149.
91. Ibid., p. 317.
92. For more on the semiotics of 'possible worlds' in metanarrative see Eco, *The Role of the Reader*, p. 217.
93. Pisemskii, *Vzbalamuchennoe more*, pp. 304–05.

94. Ibid., pp. 343–44. I am grateful to Kirill Zubkov for pointing out that Pisemskii here is also clearly referencing the obsession with 'factual' information, typical for poetics of 'denunciatory' 1850s texts.
95. Ibid., p. 395.
96. Ibid.
97. Ibid., p. 359.
98. Ibid., p. 549.
99. Ibid., pp. 416–17.
100. Pisemskii, 'Letter to I. S. Turgenev from 19 February/3 March 1863', *Literaturnoe nasledstvo*, 73 (1964), 177.
101. Pisemskii, *Vzbalamuchennoe more*, p. 418.
102. A. S. Pushkin, *Evgenii Onegin*, in *Polnoe sobranie sochinenii*, 10 vols (Moscow and Leningrad: Izdatel'stvo Akademii nauk SSSR, 1949), v, p. 10.
103. Pisemskii, *Vzbalamuchennoe more*, p. 418.
104. Ibid., p. 428.
105. Ibid.
106. Ibid.
107. Frederick M. Holmes, 'The Novel, Illusion, and Reality: The Paradox of Omniscience in *The French Lieutenant's Woman*', in *Metafiction*, ed. by Mark Currie (London: Longman, 2001), pp. 206–21 (p. 207).
108. Pisemskii, *Vzbalamuchennoe more*, p. 451.
109. Ibid., p. 440.
110. Ibid., pp. 418–19.
111. Ibid., p. 423.
112. Ibid., p. 422.
113. Ibid., p. 434.
114. Ibid., p. 366.
115. Ibid.
116. Ibid., p. 438.
117. Ibid.
118. Ibid., p. 441.
119. John Pier, 'Metalepsis', in *living handbook of narratology* <http://wikis.sub.uni-hamburg.de/lhn/index.php/Metalepsis> [accessed 13 August 2019].
120. For a comprehensive account of Pisemskii's fortunes on the Soviet book market see Jenkins, p. 332.
121. P. V. Annenkov, *Kriticheskie ocherki* (St Petersburg: Izdatel'stvo RKhGI, 2000), pp. 179–201.

CHAPTER 4

A Woman's Answer

In March 1862, the first part of a novel titled *Zhenskaia dolia* appeared in *Sovremennik*. The publication was signed 'N. Stanitskii' and loyal readers would have been able to recognise a name that had appeared in nearly every issue of the journal for the last fifteen years. Not many of *Sovremennik*'s subscribers knew, however, that 'N. Stanitskii' was in fact a woman, for whom the issues addressed in the novel were a matter not merely of rhetoric but of personal experience.

Avdot'ia Panaeva's (1819–93) career at *Sovremennik* officially began in 1848 with the publication of a short story *Neostorozhnoe slovo* [Careless Word] already under her chosen pen name 'N. Stanitskii'.[1] Unofficially, she had been contributing to the journal ever since its new editorial team had taken over: the January 1847 volume featured a fashion column that Panaeva wrote together with her husband, Ivan Panaev. *Mody* [Fashions] remained a standing co-authored column in *Sovremennik* until 1857, except for the summer months when Panaev took sole responsibility for it while his wife was away in the country. As recent research shows, Panaeva also assisted the editors with the daily business of running the journal by reviewing and proofreading submitted manuscripts, as well as dealing with financial matters.[2] From 1847 to 1864, Panaeva became an in-house writer and in practice an editorial assistant at *Sovremennik*. In the course of her career she published short stories, novellas and novels (two of which, *Tri strany sveta* [Three Countries of the World] (1848) and *Mertvoe ozero* [Dead Lake] (1851), were co-authored with Nekrasov) and a few anonymous literary reviews printed in *Sovremennik*.[3]

From the beginning, the revived *Sovremennik* published a mix of critical articles and reviews, as well as Russian and translated fiction: under new leadership, the journal declared itself to be ready to 'tackle social questions not with sleep-inducing pedantry but with fire, so that it would electrify the readers and awaken in them a thirst for action'.[4] It was understood that the fictional narratives that were published in *Sovremennik* would align themselves with the general radically progressive ideology of the editorial team. Chernyshevskii had not considered offering *Chto delat'?* to any other journal except the one he used to work for, and similarly, Nekrasov stayed true to the journal's radical politics by swiftly withdrawing his offer to publish *Vzbalamuchennoe more* as soon as the anti-radical nature of Pisemskii's novel became apparent. In this way, Panaeva's prose, regularly appearing in *Sovremennik* alongside its major publishing coups such as Ivan Turgenev's *Zapiski okhotnika* [Hunter's Sketches] (1849) or Lev Tolstoi's *Sevastopol'skie rasskazy* [Sevastopol Sketches] (1855), had to be relevant to the issues covered in the 'serious',[5] to use Dmitrii Pisarev's definition, departments of the journal.

Together with her husband and Nekrasov, Panaeva was responsible for providing a steady stream of prose to fill the empty pages appearing in the journal sometimes as late as a few days before it went to press. Because of Russian censorship regulations, every issue of the journal had to be put together and then submitted to a censor for preliminary examination. Often, censors would release the issue too late for the editor to commission new pieces instead of those that had been removed. As a result, editorial boards of popular thick journals had to maintain in-house staff of 'little literary brothers' who could be asked to supply texts at short notice.[6]

As an in-house writer rather than just a contributing author, Panaeva had particular responsibilities: making sure her texts pleased the readers and, perhaps even more importantly, the censors. Panaeva's very first (and some argue, the best) piece of prose, *Semeistvo Tal'nikovykh* [The Talnikov Family] (1848),[7] was banned for 'undermining parental authority', and general 'cynicism, improbability and immorality', and as a result was not published until 1928.[8] Subsequently, her novellas continued to centre on the problems of women's emancipation but shied away from graphic descriptions of the victim's sufferings that made *Semeistvo Tal'nikovykh* such a powerful work. The in-house writers pledged to write suitable works officially: for example, in order to be able to publish *Tri strany sveta*, Panaeva and Nekrasov had to submit a written promise to the censorship committee, stating that there would be no 'victory of vice' in their 'generally cheerful and uplifting novel'.[9]

Zhenskaia dolia was written, much like Panaeva's earlier prose pieces, to be published in *Sovremennik* both as a gap-filler and as a crowd-pleaser. Addressing a burning question of female emancipation, the novel would have already attracted the readers' attention on account of its topic, but Panaeva's style was a distinct advantage. Although ridiculed by contemporary critics as 'heart-rending' [razdiratel'nyi],[10] it was very popular with the readers. Most of Panaeva's texts were favoured enough to be reissued as stand-alone editions soon after they appeared in *Sovremennik* in serialised form.

Panaeva's success with her contemporaries was not surprising: her novels and shorter pieces were written in a lively, accessible language, dealt with topical and sensationalist themes, and touched upon subjects of sex, incest and madness. Panaeva's emphatic narrators engaged the readers in an almost direct polemic. Even though they patronised the readers slightly, Panaeva's narrators assumed a shared understanding of the troubles of contemporary society, compassion to the sufferings of women and other vulnerable members of society, and a certain degree of progressiveness that was to be expected from *Sovremennik*'s audience.

Since the Russian reading public was already receptive to ideas and arguments about the situation of contemporary women from their readings of George Sand — a novelist much admired in Russia of both the 1840s and 1860s — Panaeva's popularity did not emerge from a vacuum.[11] All three writers discussed in this study had been influenced by George Sand,[12] but Panaeva's novels would have come the closest to the readers' expectations of who could be George Sand's Russian equivalent. Even though Panaeva's views on emancipation were far less progressive than Sand's, the general public's appetite for fiction about the 'woman question' (reflected also in the popularity of another woman writer, Charlotte Brontë, in the 1840s and 1850s[13]) would have guaranteed the reader's initial interest. Another reason behind Panaeva's success was *Sovremennik*'s clever literary marketing. Considering the journal's radical credentials and its capital of the readers' trust, Panaeva had an opportunity to pitch her texts to a like-minded audience. As a result, publishing her texts was a safe bet for *Sovremennik*'s editors, in terms of their potential popularity and ideological compatibility. In 1862, the censorship committee had once again threatened the journal with closure and the editors were counting on the expertise of their in-house writers to produce texts that would be approved by the censors.[14]

Like narrators of Chernyshevskii's *Chto delat'?* and Pisemskii's *Vzbalamuchennoe more*, the narrator of *Zhenskaia dolia* offered the readers self-conscious asides on the nature of literary fiction as art and political weapon. However, the way Panaeva's metanarrative introduced those issues was markedly different. Aside from the usual difficulties of navigating between the reader's expectations and the censor's restrictions, Panaeva was faced with another problem that was not an issue for the other two writers. One of the very few women playing an important role on the literary scene of the 1860s, she had to present a convincing literary contribution to contemporary debates in which usually only her male colleagues participated.

With its narratorial voice constantly questioning the dominant conventions of realist narrative, as well as women's representation in it, Panaeva's novel could be approached as an example of the nineteenth-century feminist metafiction. A woman writer's metafictional discourse traditionally relied on a particular set of narratological devices to communicate their message. The message — in this case, an ideological one — could often resemble that of her male colleagues, but would be delivered in a way that was different from that used by male writers. As Joan Douglas Peters has pointed out in her study *Feminist Metafiction and the Evolution of the British Novel* (2002), the authors of feminist metafiction write generic theory directly into the discourse of their fiction to produce ongoing 'underarguments' concerning the novel as a literary genre. These underarguments are performed through women's narrations that are simultaneously and explicitly set off against discursive presentations of existing patriarchal conventions of narrative, objectified textually in the form of literary parody. What results are dialogical discussions of the subject of narration conducted entirely on the level of text.[15]

Panaeva's underarguments concerned the most pressing issues of the day such as the utilitarian uses of literature and the political power of fictional narratives. In addition, they addressed the problems contemporary critics specifically identified with women's writing, such as excessive attention to detail, character description and weak plotting. Literary parody, a basic device of metafiction, dominated the second half of Panaeva's novel, juxtaposing the narratives of her female characters Sofiia and Anna to the Gogolesque satirical descriptions of male characters.

The ideological positioning of the narrator in Panaeva's text, delivering these underarguments, is performed through a complex rhetorical strategy of merging the identity of the narrator with that of his addressees. The narratorial voice in the novel explicitly identifies itself as male and maintains that his text is intended for 'young men's education'.[16] Rhetorically, however, the narrator keeps addressing 'the poor women' suffering from their hard lots in life as well as referring to his addressees as 'we'. This narrative transvestism[17] undermines the established narratorial voice of an objective male observer, as it simultaneously borrows the voice of authority while indirectly exposing its limitations. Throughout the novel, the subject and practice of narration are discussed by this unusual narratorial voice, through appeals to its multiple male and female addressees.

Panaeva's text serves as a third case study in my exploration of metafictional narrative strategies in a contained but representative sample of Russian novels of 1862–63. Offering a reading of *Zhenskaia dolia* as feminist metafiction that aimed to 'undermine established discourse within the novel's narrative text',[18] I explore the similarities in the universal strategies of metanarrative that featured in the works of writers of varying ideological persuasion and literary skill. This chapter offers a brief discussion of Panaeva's position in the Russian literary canon and some notes on the contemporary reception of her work in Russia and abroad. Following that, it reconstructs the historical and political context of the novel's publication in 1862 and provides a close reading of *Zhenskaia dolia* as feminist metafiction with a narrative voice that transgresses the boundaries of gender.

The Poet's Biographer versus the Poet's Wife

Avdot'ia Panaeva's literary fate — a successful and popular female writer demoted to the status of the 'muse' of her more successful male partner — is hardly unique.[19] It could even be considered perversely fortunate: many key female players of the mid-nineteenth-century Russian literary scene such as Evgeniia Tur, the Khvoschchinskaia sisters, or Maria Zhukova, are only now being reintroduced to Russian literary history and contemporary readers.[20] However, Panaeva's fall from literary grace also offers an insight into the history of the reception of Russian nineteenth-century metafiction in the twentieth and twenty-first centuries. The heightened self-reflexivity of her texts, notably *Zhenskaia dolia*, did not conform to the generally held perceptions of how a realist novel should function discursively and had therefore sped up her disappearance from the canon.

Panaeva's texts were first examined as facts of Russian literary history in the 1920s. In 1927–28, two of her most popular works, *Vospominaniia* [Memoirs] (1889) and *Semeistvo Tal'nikovykh*, were reissued by Akademiia, an early Soviet publishing house famous for its historical fiction series. Kornei Chukovskii, the literary critic and a popular children's writer, produced a scholarly edition of *Vospominaniia* for Akademiia, and it was so popular with the readers that *Academia* reissued it four times in the period 1927–33. Even though Chukovskii later claimed he had only spent an hour editing Panaeva's manuscript,[21] he must have undertaken a considerable amount of archival research to make these edits. Not only did he identify the real historical personalities behind the initials Panaeva used (made more confusing by the fact that she attached the same initials to different people), he also verified and corrected her multiple chronological errors. Chukovskii first wrote a short essay accompanying the reissued text and then revised it into a larger piece on Panaeva's relationship with Nekrasov for his book on the poet that came out the same year. In 1922, Chukovskii published an essay specifically on Panaeva as Nekrasov's common law wife, titled *Zhena poeta* [The Poet's Wife],[22] and published it as part of his series *Nekrasovskaia biblioteka* [Nekrasov's library].

Chukovskii's treatment of Panaeva is suggestive in many ways. Employing the early Soviet strategy of rehabilitating ideologically unsound texts by ascribing 'progressive' tendencies to their authors, Chukovskii did an admirable job of whitewashing Panaeva's questionable class credentials (coming from a family of successful actors, she was hardly a member of the proletariat). The critic praised 'her democratic way of thinking'[23] and argued that her texts, accessible even for the most unprepared reader, could function as an introduction to the mid-nineteenth-century Russian literary scene. Chukovskii's article, despite its scholarly expertise and lively style, was a typical response to nineteenth-century women's writing in early twentieth-century literary criticism: he saw Panaeva as a secondary historical and literary figure, only as interesting as the men she knew and too concerned with the trivialities of life to have produced anything of value.[24] Even though Panaeva was a published and popular writer, according to the critic, Panaeva's major claim to fame rested on her status as Nekrasov's lover and muse: Chukovskii calls the poems Nekrasov had dedicated to Panaeva 'the best monument to her life' and notes that 'her place on the pages of Nekrasov's works earns her the memory of posterity'.[25] Finally, in the critic's opinion, Panaeva was first a woman and only then — coincidentally — a writer: 'Charming, universally admired, she was also a novelist, a writer!'[26] Chukovskii suggested, erroneously, that Nekrasov did most of the writing of their co-authored texts and argued that Panaeva became an established writer almost by chance and would have preferred a more traditional womanly occupation.

Chukovskii's patronising assessment of Panaeva's career had a great influence on how Soviet literary studies approached her work. From the 1920s onwards, scholars have mostly treated Panaeva as a writer whose main contribution to Russian literature consisted of providing invaluable information about her male contemporaries. Chukovskii's dismissive attitude and his scathing remarks (he called Panaeva 'simple-minded' [prostodushnaia] as well as 'trivial and shallow' [obyvatel'ski-poverkhnostna][27] among other things) stuck, and the image of her primarily as a hostess of *Sovremennik*'s salon and Nekrasov's 'angry muse' rather than a novelist in her own right was perpetuated by generations of scholars.[28]

The interest in Panaeva's work in present-day Russian academia remains marginal. A number of joint Russian–German research projects in the 1990s introduced post-Soviet literary scholars to current methodology of women studies.[29] However, Panaeva and her contemporaries attract less scholarly attention than the authors of the twentieth-century 'zhenskaia prosa', or 'women's prose', partly because basic historiographic and bibliographic data on nineteenth-century Russian women writers is still lacking.[30] In the West, Panaeva studies are a minor but lively field. One of the first article-length studies on Panaeva in English was published by Marina Ledkovsky in 1974.[31] In 1998, Barbara Heldt chose Panaeva's *Semeistvo Tal'nikovykh* as one of the case studies in her chapter on gender in *The Cambridge Companion to the Classic Russian Novel*.[32] Panaeva's texts, Heldt argued, belonged to the alternative Russian novelistic tradition established by women writers. In their narratives, women employed modes of irony and lament, directly opposed to the male tendency to prophesise and preach. What was previously perceived by scholars as a narrative deficiency or a conscious choice on behalf of the women writers, Heldt saw as an inevitable consequence of the unequal distribution of power between men and women in the mid-nineteenth-century Russian literary scene.

In a similar vein, Panaeva featured in Jane Costlow's study of the way that female emancipation was represented in women writers' texts. Costlow discussed the male critics' dismissive attitude to the women writers' efforts to write about emancipation and offered a new reading of Dmitrii Pisarev's review of *Zhenskaia dolia*.[33] The leading contemporary Panaeva scholar, Jehanne Gheith, used archival documents to reconstruct Panaeva's exact involvement in the daily running of *Sovremennik* in her essay 'Redefining the Perceptible: The Journalism(s) of Evgeniia Tur and Avdot'ia Panaeva', as well as her work on Panaeva's *Vospominaniia*, jointly with Beth Holmgren.

From the 1920s onwards, scholars have explored Avdot'ia Panaeva's 1862 novel primarily in the historical context of her career: in her role as a hostess of *Sovremennik*'s salon and, more recently, as a celebrated woman writer. Her autobiographical texts, *Vospominaniia* and *Semeistvo Tal'nikovykh*, remain Panaeva's most studied pieces. However, the previously overlooked poetics and narrative mode of *Zhenskaia dolia*, the most resonant 1862 political novel by a woman writer,[34] also have a lot to tell about Panaeva's metaliterary contribution to the contemporary debates on literary realism.

'A Puppet Tragedy with a Bouquet of Civic Concerns'

Zhenskaia dolia was published in *Sovremennik* in three instalments, from March through to May 1862. Like the rest of Panaeva's fiction, this novel was explicitly concerned with what in Russia since 1855 has been referred to as 'The Woman Question'. Reflecting their readers' concerns, the thick journals of the 1860s offered an array of non-fictional texts about women's rights as well as fiction on the same topic,[35] and *Zhenskaia dolia* was precisely the kind of politically engaged literary text *Sovremennik* usually published. The novel was popular with the readers and was soon published in a stand-alone edition in 1864.

Typically for a popular novelist, success among readers did not guarantee Panaeva the critics' favour. A fellow woman writer, Nadezhda Khvoschchinskaia, commended the author for her 'passion' and her almost 'painful feeling of empathy', but characterised the style of *Zhenskaia dolia* as 'rude', 'abrupt' and 'full of caricatures'.[36] One of the most critical reviews was published by Dmitrii Pisarev in *Russkoe slovo* in 1864, and its opening paragraph is worth quoting at length:

> In every one of our journal parties there are incorrigible show-offs, who have never in their life managed to produce a single original thought. These people support in their work, most diligently and conscientiously, the very idea that gives them their daily bread — but this is not all that they do. Because of their vanity, typical for all mediocrities, they always want to express their guiding idea 'in their own words', and invent themselves various additions and embellishments, embody this idea in caricature-like images and finally reduce it to such pitiful impotence... [...] We have a lot of fiction writers of this type, and great are their achievements, but, it seems to me, in this sense no one can compete with Mr Stanitskii, thanks to whom respectable *Sovremennik* is so often burdened with heart-breaking novels. [...] Studying Mr Stanitskii is of great interest for us especially because this writer is working for *Sovremennik* on a permanent basis and, on a permanent basis, he denigrates with his showing-off the fair and wide ideas that were previously developed in this journal by people who actually think and act.[37]

Here, Pisarev criticises the absence of logic in Panaeva's political arguments, but his most vicious attack is directed at her style: she is too effusive ('a show-off, masking his intellectual poverty with shouts and wild gestures'), too concerned with inconsequential details ('in developing the details Mr Stanitskii is even more lovely, than in the general idea behind his works'), and too fiery ('the thoughts are not very well tied together, but there is a lot of fiery temperament'[38]).

Pisarev and Panaeva were personally acquainted and he was fully aware of the real personality of mysterious Stanitskii. Pisarev's attack on the in-house writer of a leading radical journal reflects the uneasy relationship between *Sovremennik* and *Russkoe slovo*, further complicated by Pisarev's personal ambition to be considered Dobroliubov's intellectual heir. However, a close reading of this passage shows that Pisarev was questioning more than Panaeva's literary skills and radical credentials. His problem with her was more fundamental — not only was she working for *Sovremennik* (often an object of Pisemskii's criticism), she was also a woman and, as such, unable to offer a worthy contribution to either realist fiction or to the ongoing debates on the woman question.

Pisarev's article 'Kukol'naia tragediia s buketom grazhdanskoi skorbi' [A Puppet Tragedy with a Bouquet of Civic Concerns] (1864) was representative of the general reaction of the male critics.[39] Ironically, they maintained that women did not contribute as much as they should to the discussion of the woman question, and when they did, they did not do it properly. Pisarev's and later Nikolai Shelgunov's problem with women writers was that none of them had created a character as vocal or liberated as Chernyshevskii's Vera Pavlovna.[40] One of the reasons why women writers did not succeed in this undertaking was the style of their prose, which differed from the narrative modes chosen by their male counterparts. In his article, Pisarev essentially accused Panaeva of writing a wrong kind of realist fiction: overwrought, 'over-salted realism' [peresolennyi realizm] and therefore 'not successful'.[41]

Pisarev does not explicitly state that the author is a woman and not all of his readers would have been aware of Stanitskii's actual identity, but many of those he was attacking in this polemical article — other critics — would have known

Panaeva personally through their dealings with *Sovremennik* or her literary salon. As Jane Costlow noted in her analysis of the review, even if Pisarev's judgement was fair in terms of aesthetics, it was still 'suspiciously gendered':[42] throughout the article his criticism of Panaeva was couched in derogatory terms traditionally used to denigrate feminine writing as irrational and too concerned with details of everyday life. Moreover, Costlow points out that 'the metaphors he uses to describe the "debasement" of lofty ideas are all associated either with the domestic realm or with (purported) feminine aesthetics: "[second-rate authors'] novels are usually sewn with living threads according to the latest fashionable patterns"; people and events are reflected in a "cheap mirror"; Dobroliubov's ideas are distorted with "innocent gossip"'.[43] Among Panaeva's supposed transgressions, according to Pisarev, was that she debased the serious arguments of her male colleagues. Even the title of his review pointed out Panaeva's unsuitability to discussions of serious matters: the tragedy of Panaeva's characters is 'doll-like' and her political arguments are referred to as a 'bouquet of civic concerns'. The critic compared Panaeva's writing to works by 'actually intelligent and worthwhile individuals' and declared it unworthy of *Sovremennik*.

Indeed, the constrained social experience of mid-nineteenth-century Russian women writers (as with many of their European counterparts) limited the number of topics they could comfortably address in their work. It affected the choice of subjects, characters, setting and style that often emphasised the need to escape from confined surroundings.[44] As Mary Zirin noted, this 'intimate focus was increasingly regarded by prescriptive critics as a retrograde clinging to Romantic egocentrism when the times called for scientifically based, objective — "masculine", "realistic" — depictions of broad cross-sections of life'.[45] The debates around the Woman Question in the Russian press had been conducted mostly by men such as radical critics Nikolai Shelgunov, Nikolai Dobroliubov, Dmitrii Pisarev, Nikolai Mikhailkovskii and Nikolai Chernyshevskii. At the same time, the number of women writers in mid nineteenth-century Russia was higher than ever before. Because of the commercialisation and further professionalisation of literature in this period, there was a viable market for fiction to which women contributed as authors of novellas, novels and short stories. This lucrative market depended on them, and the advances paid to writers such as Nadezhda Khvoschchinskaia or Evgeniia Tur equalled and sometimes exceeded the hefty sums paid to their male colleagues.[46]

Most women writers, however, lived in the provinces and were not a part of the literary establishment of the two capitals. Historically, it was also uncommon for women to engage in contemporary debates on social and aesthetic issues directly since formal polemic was seen as a male domain. As a result, their literary texts 'functioned as a channel for female intellectual expression' as well as a means of joining 'the debate on the destiny [prednaznachenie] of the new woman'.[47] Questioning the constrained role of women in society and the rhetoric of dominance, these texts also tested the boundaries of realist narrative. In these cases, metanarrative served as a rhetorical means for women writers to integrate their political or aesthetic argument into a fictional narrative. An example of such integration can be seen, for instance, in the texts of Maria Zhukova, a prolific writer of the 1840s. As Zhukova scholars have pointed out, her novellas created a 'narrutopia' — a kind of narrative which solipsistically offers a model of the world as a whole within a literary text.[48] Zhukova's 'metaliterary concerns'[49] found their expression in her fiction and functioned as an indirect contribution to contemporary polemics about literary language and narrative form.

As recent research indicates, there were indeed women journalists, reporters and editors in mid-nineteenth-century Russia who ran their own journals and contributed to the leading publications of the time.[50] However, only a very small number of these women were able to overcome the (sometimes self-imposed) barrier between them and open forums of public debate on pressing political, social and aesthetic issues. English literature scholar Naomi Schor's observation that 'there exists as yet no clearly constructed and readily available corpus of female-authored aesthetic discourse to read in conjunction with the male'[51] is in this case also applicable to Russian literary history. Women's aesthetic discourse traditionally had other outlets such as discussions in salons and private correspondence — a limitation that feminist metafiction was set to challenge in Britain, but also in Russia.

Ivan Panaev held a literary salon prior to his marriage and his wife assumed the duties of its hostess once they had moved to St Petersburg.[52] It was noted by the salon's guests and reflected in her memoirs that Panaeva actively participated in the literary debates that took place there. Topics discussed at the salon ranged from practical issues of literary production to the nature of realism and Romanticism.[53] However, her thoughts on these subjects can be reconstructed only by analysing her fiction and select passages of her memoirs that were composed and published decades after the events they described. Equally, even though most of Panaeva's texts are explicitly concerned with the problem of female emancipation, her interest in the topic was never expressed in a non-fictional form. Despite the fact that she was passionate about this issue, her access to formal outlets for her opinions was narrower than that of her male colleagues. Panaeva worked at *Sovremennik* alongside Chernyshevskii and was involved in the discussions of the journal's political stance. Like Pisemskii, by 1862 she was an established writer with a certain confidence in handling her audience, as well as a recognisable style and name. Panaeva burned most of her correspondence,[54] but it seems that the absence of any other secondary texts in her oeuvre is a result of historical circumstances rather than personal choice.

Zhenskaia dolia contains elements of metanarrative similar to those found in *Chto delat'?* and *Vzbalamuchennoe more*: authorial asides debating the nature of realism, literary language and form, the use of detail and character descriptions. The ontological shift between fiction and reality is not questioned as explicitly as in the other two novels, but the self-conscious narrator's constantly verbalised preoccupation with the power of fictional narrative and its influence on politics and everyday life is a clear indication of the presence of metafictional elements in the novel's poetics. The use of literary parody as a means of metanarrative in *Zhenskaia dolia* highlights how questioning the place of women in society was fused with challenging the premises of the dominant style of contemporary realist fiction.

This challenge was not specific to the Russian literary scene of the 1860s. In her study *The Sentimental Education of the Novel* (1999), Margaret Cohen convincingly argues that realism as a style and the realist novel as a genre had been intentionally 'masculinised' in the French debates on the validity of various literary methods in the 1840s–1850s. In these debates, Realism was opposed to Sentimentalism and the sentimental novel that had been reframed as a feminine genre. When attacked, Cohen claimed, 'realist works assert their claims to literary importance by identifying the novel with men, by forging a poetics associated with masculine forms of knowledge, and by undercutting the authority of the woman writer along with sentimental codes'.[55] In a later study, Cohen 'excavated', as she put it, a particular novelistic form that flourished in France during the July Monarchy but was not recognised as a part of the French realist canon alongside the texts by Balzac and Stendhal. Cohen identified this form as a 'feminine social novel', not necessarily written by women but thematically concerned with socially induced female suffering. Counteracting the masculine realist tradition, these novels relied on a different narrative dynamic and introduced a particular plot structure. A few of the Russian novels dealing with the woman question, including *Zhenskaia dolia*, closely resembled Cohen's 'feminine social novels' in their narrative dynamic and plot structure.[56]

In *Zhenskaia dolia* Panaeva created a particular type of feminist metafiction that owed its existence only partly to her writing style and largely to historical circumstances. Like other women writers of the period, she was 'finding a way as a woman to negotiate the particular nature of the Russian literary political scene'[57] — a strategy that emphasises the universal character of the narrative structure featured in *Zhenskaia dolia*.

'Oversalted' Meta-Realism of a Feminine Novel

A novel in two parts, *Zhenskaia dolia* tells the story of the equally unhappy fates of several women of different ages, classes, backgrounds and dispositions. What unites these women are the tragedies inflicted on them by the men in their lives: treacherous and abusive lovers, husbands, fathers, grandfathers, employers and even evil travel-companions.

The novel's 'thematic attention to the feminine condition as a social problematic'[58] and 'women's "sufferings" wreaked by all manner of social pressures'[59] is immediately apparent from its title. 'Dolia' in Russian is rarely used to describe a happy fate, and mostly refers to 'heavy lots' [tiazhelaia dolia]. The expression also presupposes certain fatalism — 'dolia' cannot be chosen, it is something one has to bear. Panaeva's title lets readers know that this is a text about the tragedy of a Russian woman's lot. Most of Panaeva's texts tell stories of victims: of parental tyranny in *Semeistvo Tal'nikovykh* and then the tyranny of men in *Bezobraznyi muzh* [Ugly Husband], *Neobdumannyi shag* [Reckless Step], *Stepnaya baryshnia* [Lady of the Steppes], *Domashnii ad* [Domestic Hell], *Sashka* and other novellas, and *Zhenskaia dolia* is no exception. The plot and narrative dynamics of the feminine social novel in *Zhenskaia dolia* function as a narrative structure for Panaeva's feminist metafiction, exploring the issues of female emancipation in society and testing the boundaries of the literary aesthetics of realism. As much as her novel debates the issues of women's emancipation as defined by men, the metanarrative in the novel questions the nature of realism as defined by male writers.

According to Margaret Cohen, a typical feminine social novel was deliberately constructed in opposition to the popular male-authored texts of the period and employed 'alternative narrative strategies'.[60] If novels by male authors relied on a conventional narrative dynamic outlined by Roland Barthes ('to narrate (in the classic fashion) is to raise the question as if it were a subject which one delays predicating; and when the predicate (truth) arrives, the sentence, the narrative, are over, the world is adjectivized'), the feminine social novel exposed the truth of the matter at the beginning. In the feminine social novel, 'the origin of the narrative is a pronouncement of women's social situation as it should and should not be. The novels proclaim this truth from their opening words, inscribing it on their covers, in titles [...] where the narrator addresses the reader directly and/or uses scenes peopled by recognizable social types to do the didactic work'.[61]

The opening scene in *Zhenskaia dolia* offers the readers just such a tableau of female types: a loving mother, neglected by her philandering husband, her innocent daughter, and a busy-body nosy neighbour. The 'novelistic universe [is called] into being with a minimum of physical details'[62] from which the location and social standing of the protagonists are immediately apparent. Most importantly, the company we are introduced to is exclusively female:

> В полдень жаркого, летнего дня, в селе Григорьевке, в барском саду, в густой аллее из акации, укрывалось от зноя небольшое дамское общество.[63]
>
> [At midday, one hot summer day, in the village of Grigor'evka, in the landowner's garden, in an alley densely planted with acacia trees, a small group of ladies was taking shelter from the heat.]

The typical conflict of a feminine social novel is often sparked by a collision of the social and the private spheres of a character's life. Exactly this kind of conflict germinates in chapter 1 of *Zhenskaia dolia*. The introduction is followed by a discussion between the ladies, in which the guest, Varvara Karpovna, functions as the agent of the social sphere, insisting that her host's daughter should be married and soon. The host, Anna Antonovna, on the other hand, is guarding her private values: she wants to educate her daughter before marrying her off. The social here intrudes into the private female world, producing a conflict of opinions: the progressive feminist ideas of the private and the exploitative traditions of the social. Further contrast between those two worlds is exemplified in the apparent differences between the two arguing ladies: 'the two ladies', we are told, 'could not have looked more different in their appearance'.[64] Anna Antonovna is, naturally, beautiful and noble even though the suffering she has experienced has left its mark. Her adversary is healthy and untroubled by worries, which gives her an almost animal look of 'limited intelligence and oxen nerves'.[65] The host is 'simply' dressed and wrapped in a shawl, as if it were autumn, whereas her guest is bothered by the heat despite wearing just a crumpled blouse and no bonnet. Panaeva's heavy-handed symbolism leaves her readers in no doubt of who of these two characters deserves their sympathy and attention.

The first chapter introduces the lead character, Anna Antonovna's young daughter Sofiia. As befits the heroine of the feminine social novel, Sofiia is set up to experience a traumatic event resulting from the further collision of the social and the private. The reader first meets her while she sits quietly, reading, and staring into the distance with her 'blue eyes full of some kind of anxious longing'[66] in the company of her mother. The mother–daughter dyad, a typical character unit of this genre, is opposed to the figure of the antagonistic father, who had abandoned his family. Panaeva's plotting is not sophisticated but her eye for psychological detail helps her to create complex and compelling characters, demonstrating her expertise as an author of popular novellas.

The plot of *Zhenskaia dolia* follows the breaking up of the feminine idyll showcased in the opening scenes. Sofiia is soon married off by her father to Petr, a young man with progressive pretensions; he praises female emancipation and promises Sofiia a life of enlightened happiness. But not long after their marriage and a move to Petr's estate, Sofiia realises that his progressiveness was just a fad. Petr's tyrannical grandfather runs the estate with an iron hand and is determined to break up the two lovers. As Sofiia gets to know her new family, new victims of the traditional women's lot appear: young 'prizhivalka' [a dependent female relative] Olimpiada is gradually revealed to be the grandfather's illegitimate daughter and the old house servant turns out to be his former lover. Petr's sometime serf mistress, who has born him an illegitimate son, also resides on the estate. Sofiia tries to keep her faith in her young husband and make a life for herself in these new circumstances. But, when Petr moves to the city to be with his new mistresses and abandons her in the country with his mentally ill nephew as her only friend, Sofiia gives up all hope. Later, in the second part of the novel, we learn that she has left her husband for a wealthy landowner Lakotnikov. At the beginning of Part Two, she has born Lakotnikov illegitimate children and lives with him in the country as his mistress.

The second part of the novel offers an urban parallel to Sofiia's nightmarish rural existence, introducing another set of characters. Anna, the second part's leading character, is the illegitimate daughter of a young woman seduced and abandoned by her treacherous lover. The readers meet Anna *in medias res*, in a travelling carriage: Anna, returning from abroad where she had been working as a lady's companion, is going to the country to join her godfather. At the coaching inn, an old lecherous general is offering her unwanted attentions but Anna is saved by the novel's single positive male hero, Aleksandr Snegov.

The Anna and Sofiia plots soon merge: the young woman's destination is Lakotnikov's estate where her godfather is employed as a manager. The two women become friends, but Lakotnikov soon starts pursuing Anna and casts Sofiia out. After that, both plot lines resolve swiftly: Sofiia, abandoned both by her husband

and by Lakotnikov, dies in poverty and Anna follows Snegov to Siberia where he has been exiled for opposing Lakotnikov and the old general. They open a school in Irkutsk and live an 'active life'.[67] The resolution is abrupt: typically for the feminine social novel, the absence of the tension between the two narrative codes (the proairetic one of the story and the hermeneutic one of its interpretation) produces an ending in which the conflict is not resolved but is made irrelevant.

The novel's setting falls into two parts, rural and urban. Sofiia inhabits the world of country estates, whereas Anna comes from a Dostoevskian world of urban poverty. The contrast between the two showcases Panaeva's skill in creating idyllic backdrops for society tales (honed while working on her earlier novellas) as well as her ability to follow the period's fashion for naturalist descriptions of city life. Similarly in keeping with the literary fashion is the way in which Petr's estate, run by his maniacal grandfather, is described as a locus of novelistic gothic.[68] The house is juxtaposed with the estate's gardens as the only place of calm. The daunting, menacing atmosphere of this secluded space is created through the use of narrative ellipses: sexual deviations and violence, such as incest and rape, are hinted at but never confirmed; the nature of the horrific events at a distant farm where Petr's serf mistress dies in exile is never named.

With its gothic gloom and a terrifying villain, Panaeva's description of Petr's estate foreshadows the later gothic nightmare of Saltykov-Shchedrin's *Gospoda Golovlevy* [The Golovlev Family] (1875–80). As a household run by a tyrannical man, it is contrasted with the idyllic picture of an estate run by Sofiia's mother, described in the opening chapters of the novel. Through a symbolic metonymy, Panaeva is making a statement about women's ability to manage not just households but profitable country estates. Even though at the time it was not uncommon for women in Russia to own and manage large estates, they were often legally more vulnerable than men.[69] Sofiia's mother attempts to reform her estate and liberate the serfs but her husband puts a quick end to it by declaring her insane and therefore legally incapable. Panaeva takes issue with this illusion of legal power as much as with the notion of 'fake' emancipation that liberates women but offers them no protection. As Belinskii's letters suggest, Panaeva herself had progressive ideas about estate management and was eager to put them into practice.[70]

The description of Anna's dwellings in St Petersburg emphasises the boundaries between the two worlds: not just those which divide the rich from the poor, but those which women cross when they behave in a way that society does not condone. When Anna's mother falls pregnant, she becomes a stranger in the world she had previously inhabited. Later on, her illegitimate child also struggles to fit in and only finds peace at the end of the novel in Siberia, alongside other outcasts. The issue of illegitimacy is a constant concern voiced by the novel's narrator and could be seen almost as a metaphoric manifestation of a woman writer's concern of venturing onto her male colleagues' territory.

The male characters in *Zhenskaia dolia* have almost unlimited control over all of the female characters. From the direct legal powers of a father, husband or serf-owner, to subtler ways of influence available to employers and leaders of society, what distinguishes a positive hero (in this and many other feminine social novels) from a negative one is the way they use their power. Remarkably, all non-villainous male characters in the novel are symbolically or actually incapacitated. Sofiia's mentally ill brother-in-law or the helpful military invalid at the coaching inn are portrayed as non-threatening because of their disabilities whereas Snegov's exile effectively removes him from the active life. Together with a lurking female villain/victim, the symbolic incapacity of the male hero is a classic trope of the nineteenth-century European novel written by women.[71] Its appearance in Panaeva's narrative puts *Zhenskaia dolia* in the context of an established literary tradition picking up plot elements from a shared pool of tropes and loaded metaphors.

It is obvious from the most dramatic scenes of the novel that Panaeva considers the power of love to be most destructive. The strongest hold male characters have on their lovers is emotional: Panaeva's heroines long for the love and approval of their fathers, lovers and husbands, and are unable to shake off this need. Sofiia's unfailing faith in her philandering husband or the grandfather's older mistress's heart-breaking story of their romance tell a story of psychological rather than social or even financial dependency. The author steers clear of the essentialist explanation that it is in the female nature to submit to such feelings. Instead, she explores the complex circumstances behind this imbalance such as the traditional ways in which societies function, the psychological (it is difficult to say no to love, she maintains), biological (women are perceived to age faster than men and lose their attractiveness) and cultural (men are perceived as sophisticated creatures of thought and women as basic beings) reasons behind the ease with which such power is exercised. The novel exposes the inadequacy of a female education that deliberately keeps women ignorant so that they are easier to control: 'everything crashes onto one woman, who is often brought up in such a way that she has no idea about the frightful consequences of love',[72] notes the narrator; 'from our childhood onwards they have put lead compresses onto our heads, so that no rational thought would get in',[73] laments Anna. The only women in control of their lives are those without social or financial constraints, such as the demimonde mistresses, *loretki*, of Sofiia's husband and father. The mercantile nature of their relationship with men gives them an ultimate privilege in Panaeva's world of emotional torment: they seem to have no feelings for the men with whom they are involved.

In contrast to the complex characters of society's female victims, the male characters in *Zhenskaia dolia* are developed only as far as they need to be in order to act as 'foils' for the heroines. Panaeva's heroes correspond to the character types 'imbued with fixed moral value' described by Cohen: the ideal man (Snegov) is opposed to a 'cold materialistic older man [...] skilled in the ways of *le monde*' (Sofiia's father, Petr's grandfather) and a 'frankly corrupt seducer' (Petr, Lakotnikov), or a mix of the two (the old general).[74] In addition, Panaeva's novel showcases two particular types of villains. It contrasts a traditional figure of the tyrannical male who revels in the power granted to him by society and personal wealth, such as Petr's grandfather or Snegov's employer, the old general, to the new type of villain — a fake progressist.

Sofiia's husband Petr and her lover Lakotnikov are exposed as covert enemies of female emancipation. Frightening caricatures of modern enlightened men, these characters masquerade as progressive men only to use recent social advances in women's rights to their advantage. The character of Petr's aunt is an interesting amalgam of a typical female villain of the feminine social novel ('an older, corrupt woman embodying all that is shallow and empty')[75] and a female version of a fake progressive, Panaeva's personal bête noire. The novel's major rhetorical thrust is aimed precisely against this type of contemporary villain. Panaeva's use of a term that is so integral for Chernyshevskii's theories (she calls these villains 'egoists') has produced a certain confusion, inspiring critics to claim that *Zhenskaia dolia* was influenced by Chernyshevskii's characters of the 'new people'. In fact, it would be difficult to argue the case for direct 'inspiration': chronologically, Panaeva's novel came out before Chernyshevskii's text was published. As a member of *Sovremennik*'s editorial board Panaeva might have had an opportunity to see the text before its publication, but the dates still indicate that her novel would have been completed earlier. *Zhenskaia dolia* did not polemicise with or put forward arguments in support of Chernyshevskii's ideas. Rather, the fact that Panaeva tackled the same problematic issues indicates her immersion in the discourse of contemporary political and social debates. The way Panaeva approached these issues in *Zhenskaia dolia* — through metafictional underarguments rather than direct metaleptic frame-breaks — was markedly different from Chernyshevskii's direct addresses to his reader, or Pisemskii's boundary-crossing narrator. Her first-hand experience of working as a female realist writer suggested that another, subtler but at the same time more subversive, approach might work just as well.

Her Master's Voice

Like the other two writers discussed in this study, Panaeva addressed 'a reader' throughout her novel. However, her 'reader' is not obviously marked as either an ally or an adversary, as was the case in *Vzbalamuchennoe more* and *Chto delat'*? Her reader is fashioned both as a victim of the traditional woman's lot, and, at the same time, a potential force for changing this unfair status quo.

The narrator's first direct appeal to their readers follows soon after the opening scenes of the novel. The narrator proclaims the novel's projected 'socio-moral truth':

> Чего же вы можете ждать, бедные, честные женщины, в жизни? [...] И не ждите ничего пока от эмансипации женщин! — Это проповедование также бесплодно, как и сострадание к человечеству, о котором так долго и бесплодно толкуют! И разве вы не видите, что женщина увлекавшаяся эмансипацией и отдавшаяся мужчине без всяких гражданских условий, — разве она не гибнет также в унизительном рабстве — и в придачу еще опозоренная! Поверьте, при разврате в обществе вам дают настолько свободы, чтобы без всяких жертв со стороны мужчин, вы служили бы минутным прихотям, а потом — также без всяких жертв — легко было и развязаться с вами![76]

[What can you expect from life, poor, honest women? [...] Do not expect anything to come from the emancipation of women for now! — This proselytising is as fruitless, as the general compassion to humanity, of which they have been talking for so long and to no result! And can you not see, that a woman, who was seduced by emancipation and had given herself to a man without any civic arrangements, would die in humiliating servitude and in addition also in shame! Believe me, it is the debauchery in the society that allows you so much freedom so that with no sacrifice on the men's part you could serve their smallest whim, and so that after — also with no sacrifices — it was easy for them to abandon you!]

As *Zhenskaia dolia* posits, female emancipation is necessary but essentially useless until it is fully acknowledged by society and codified in law. The ensuing tragic stories of women whose lives are ruined by uncritically accepting false emancipation illustrate this thesis. The problem with the type of emancipation that makes victims out of the novel's characters is that it is defined by men. After Sofiia's marriage, she becomes a member of an 'enlightened' household that is run according to ideas of progress and emancipation that, instead of liberating women, create another set of criteria by which to judge them. Jane Costlow maintains that *Zhenskaia dolia* is concerned with 'women's victimization in upper-class marriage',[77] but the array of victimised female characters, including peasant women and house servants, as well as urban female professionals, suggests that the novel's spectrum is wider than that.

The victimisation of the novel's heroines, and, through the tricks of Panaeva's self-conscious narrator, also of the addressees, has 'determining value' for the remainder of the plot. The proclamation of the socio-moral truth at the very beginning of the novel determines the narrative dynamic that tests the boundaries of the 'classic' realist narrative. Cohen, following Barthes, defines 'classic narrative' as a text where the hermeneutic and proairetic codes are 'in opposition, creating a tense forcefield where readerly suspense is produced and maintained', 'interpellat[ing] the reader through suspense and seduction'.[78] In the feminine social novel, instead of contrasting, the two codes reinforce each other. The function normally fulfilled by a hermeneutic code is transferred to the narratorial voice, which creates ample opportunities for metanarrative to emerge almost spontaneously.

This change significantly affects the novel's plot structure: 'rather than delays, jamming, and revelation, the privileged hermeneutic gestures in the feminine social novel are annunciation, emphasis, and repetition, sometimes with variation. Instantiating hermeneutic truth, the proairetic code is ruled by gesture of emphasis as well'.[79] Indeed, the stories of suffering women all resemble each other; the repetition is sometimes almost comical: most women are seduced/betrayed by the same man: Sofiia, Olimpiada and the young serf woman by Petr; Sofiia and Anna by Lakotnikov; and so on. The emphasis is achieved through both symbolic imagery and the narrator's emphatic rhetoric.

The narrative suspense in the generic feminine social novel and *Zhenskaia dolia* in particular, is created through the heroines' attempts at 'modify[ing] the truth of women's suffering as she struggles against her victimized lot'.[80] Sofiia's attempt to find 'enlightened love' and Anna's stubborn defence of her independence are 'resistant actions', providing 'the closest equivalent in the feminine social novel to the paradoxical overcoding of the classic text'. The stories of Sofiia, Anna and the other victims 'constitute concrete examples proving the opening kernel of narrative truth'.[81] The effect these stories have on the reader is both emphatic and didactic.

This type of 'emphatic narrative overcoding' requires the author to construct a particular type of narrator, who assumes the function of a 'hermeneutic guide'. The similarities between Panaeva's narrator in *Zhenskaia dolia* and the typical narrator of the feminine social novel, described by Cohen, are so striking that it is helpful to reproduce Cohen's definition at length. Such novels feature an

> omniscient, sentimental, voluble, moralizing, and exclamatory third-person narrator who [...] is above all occupied with reiterating the content and the significance of the actions depicted, employing a variety of tropes of hyperbole, emphasis, and foreshadowing. [...] Such foreshadowing helps generate the weak suspense previously described. How, the reader wonders, can the action to come possibly justify the hermeneutic build up it has received?[82]

In keeping with this tradition, the narratorial voice in *Zhenskaia dolia* often manifests itself as a separate rhetorical entity when it personally bemoans the lot of the characters:

> Все три женщины одинаково были несчастны. [...] Зачем они так унижены, между тем как лицемерие и преступление окружены уважением и спокойствием? В этих случаях, у меня ум за разум заходит.[83]
>
> [All three women were equally unhappy. [...] Why were they humiliated to this degree, while hypocrisy and crime enjoyed respect and calm acceptance? Such cases boggle my mind.]

Panaeva's narrator delivers the thesis of socio-moral truth through a dialogue with a constructed 'reader', narrator's addressee:

> И знаете почему? [...] Чего же вы можете ждать, бедные, честные женщины в жизни? [...] И не ждите ничего.... И разве вы не видите... Поверьте! [...] ... Но долго-долго еще придется тебе, любящая и честная женщина, лить слезы отчаяния... [...] Долго придется вам, бедняжки-младенцы, умирать тысячами... да и что за жизнь ваша! Сколько оскорблений вы вытерпите! И неужели эти страдалицы не дождутся никогда от цивилизованного общества лучшей участи? [...] Гордитесь же вы прогрессом в человечестве! Неужели вы не перестанете клеймить невинных детей позором их родителей![84]
>
> [And do you know why? [...] What else can you expect, poor, honest women, from your life? [...] And do not expect anything... Can you not see? ... Trust me! [...] But for a long time would you, loving and honest woman, have to pour your tears of despair... [...] For a long time would you, poor babies, die in your thousands... And what kind of life do you have! How many insults do you have to suffer! And will these suffering creatures never be handed a better fate from civilised society? [...] And you, so proud of progress in humanity! When will you stop to brand the innocent babies with the shame of their parents!]

Here, the addressee changes as the speech progresses: first, the narrator appeals to the loving, honest and, necessarily, weepy women, who need to see and believe his arguments (the invective 'Trust me!' features four times in one passage). Then, it is their illegitimate children, condemned to a life of misery because of the notional character of the emancipation that gave women freedom but no protection. These 'poor babies' are warned that they will have to wait for a long time before civilised society will accept them. Then the narrator addresses society itself, which mistakenly identifies progress with exhibitions of well-fed pets and artificial mushrooms. In a full rhetorical circle, the passage ends with a final appeal to the victims of society: vulnerable women and children.

Throughout the passage, the persona of the narrator becomes more defined: he is male, as Panaeva's chosen pen name 'N. Stanitskii' suggests, but very concerned with the issue of female emancipation. From the very beginning of her career as a published author, Panaeva adopted a male pen name. This meant, among other things, that she was a female writer whose narrators had an almost exclusively a male voice. This was by no means uncommon: as Mary Zirin has noted, in the 1860s 'the use of masculine, or gender-neutral, pseudonyms became common'.[85] Women writers in mid-nineteenth-century Russia tended to publish their works under male pseudonyms and were prepared to go to great lengths in order not to be exposed: a popular literary anecdote featured Nadezhda Khvoschinskaia asking Dmitrii Pisarev not to publish a review of her works in *Rassvet* [Dawn], a journal for women, in order to keep her identity as 'V. Krestovskii' secret. Male pseudonyms created 'a barrier between private identity and public discourse'[86] and allowed women to be seen as writers rather than women writers specifically.

In the previous chapters, I have discussed the strategies used to construct a self-conscious narrator in Chernyshevskii's and Pisemskii's texts. Here, the transgressive narratorial voice in *Zhenskaia dolia* is examined with reference to the specifics of the narrator-formation in the works of the women writers of the period. The type of transgression of gender boundaries in fiction that Panaeva has achieved in *Zhenskaia dolia* has been identified by scholars as 'narrative transvestism'. This term refers to narrative strategies aiming at gaining access to a voice on the other side of the structural divide between genders'[87] in order to overcome the 'constraints of gendered imaginations and gendered voices'.[88]

Remarkably, this type of narrator was already formed in Panaeva's earlier texts, particularly in her 1848 debut *Semeistvo Tal'nikovykh*. Natasha, the young protagonist of the novel, which relates the horrors of growing up in a physically and psychologically abusive household, has a fluid individual identity. As one Panaeva scholar noted, this identity freely merges with that of her siblings and 'anyone [...] who suffers neglect and abuse in their household. The self Natasha intimates [...] is fused with an abused, resourceful collective and keenly attuned to power relations and survival skills, not individual ambition and moral development'.[89] As Panaeva's writing matured, so did this strategy: the 'I' of the narrator in *Zhenskaia dolia* merges with 'we' of the oppressed women at addressed. Grammatically, the author remained male and addressed male readers (as the gendered verb flexes indicate) but rhetorically he was aligning himself with the women whose cause he is advocating. At the same time, the narrator wanted to make sure he is not perceived as someone who 'sees all men as villains'. His text is intended for the 'young men':

> И чтобы не приписали мне такого же взгляда, я должен оговориться, что я пишу этот роман для **юношей,** которые вступают только в общество, а потому, по неопытности, часто увлекаются рутинными, вредными понятиями о многих вещах, — тем более вредными, что эти понятия усвоены большинством. [...] Живя с честным человеком, женщина не нуждается ни в каких законных правах, она под защитой его; но чуть она очутилась в руках **эгоиста,** она — жертва его прихотей и раба общественных условий. Чтобы окончательно оградить себя от нареканий **пристрастного защитника женщин,** я должен сказать, что **знаю** слишком много также страшных семейных драм, где страдают жестоко отцы во имя любви к детям... И все это честные люди, все это вам, бедным, надо выносить на своих плечах, чтоб легче было жить грязным, развратным **эгоистам,** которые готовы побить каменьями каждого отца, если он захочет воспитать свою дочь не куклой, а матерью будущих граждан.[90]

> [And so that you do no ascribe to me the same views, I need to make clear, that I am writing this novel for the **young men,** who are only entering society, and so, because of their lack of experience, they often get carried away with routine, harmful ideas about many things, and even more harmful because these ideas are assimilated by a majority. [...] Living with an honest man, a woman does not need any rights guaranteed by law, she is under his protection; but the second she is in the hands of an **egoist,** she becomes a victim of his whims and a slave of social circumstances. In order to finally protect myself from the accusations of being a *biased protector of women,* I need to say, that I also *know* too many horrible family dramas, where the fathers suffer in the name of their love for their children... And all of them are honest people, and you, poor people, have to bear this weight on your shoulders, to ensure an easy life for those dirty, lascivious *egoists,* who are ready to throw stones at any father who wants to bring his daughter up not as a doll but as a mother of future citizens.]

Defending the narrator's 'objective' position, this passage effectively places him/her in an undefined gender space. Panaeva's choice of a male pen name and a male narrative voice put her in a vulnerable position as a realist narrator. On the one hand, adopting a male narratorial voice, she, as a woman, was 'borrowing the voice of authority'.[91] As Zirin noted, 'the identity of these authors might be an open secret in literary circles, but the names gave them an official male viewpoint from which to treat the broader society without being accused of infringing on a sphere beyond their ken'.[92] A reference to a doll here is also a clear indication of the author's awareness of the kind of attacks her text would provoke from the critics.

On the other hand, if the narrator was authenticating the events of the narrative by claiming first-hand knowledge of same events, then the non-gendered narrative voice could invalidate this strategy. The unavoidable division of readers into those who know the writer was a woman and those who do not created a space of gender ambivalence,[93] in which the same statements could be in interpreted in at least two different ways. Are we to trust the narrator because, as a woman, she has herself experienced the kind of suffering she portrays, or are we to respect the narrator's opinion because he is a man and, therefore, an objective distanced observer?

This ambivalence creates a certain sense of anxiety and provokes narrative self-reflection. In the passage quoted above, men and women (appealed to as a collective entity of 'poor, honest people') both suffer from a common enemy: 'dirty lascivious egoists'. The appeals to the egoists' victims, both male and female, would continue throughout the novel as will the narrator's need to constantly clarify what he is saying ('должен оговориться'; 'Чтобы читатель не составил себе преждевременно невыгодного мнения [...], я поспешу предупредить его...' ['I need to explain myself'; 'So that the reader does not form a prematurely negative opinion [...], I hasten to warn him ...']). The same gender ambivalence that defines the persona of the narrator is extrapolated onto the image of the implied reader. The ostensibly male narrator addresses ostensibly male readers: 'the young men'. At the same time, the addressee of the rhetorical appeals in the novel is often 'a poor woman' or a combined male/female victim. This raises the question of why the narrator opts not to address the female reader directly.

The problem with the female reader as an implied addressee is well illustrated by our previous case studies. The female reader is traditionally disparaged as emotional rather than rational, not interested in the serious implications of the text and, on the contrary, excited by cheap thrills. Most importantly, the female reader is portrayed as gullible. Chernyshevskii splits his audience into male and female and addresses them separately on the very first pages of his novel. Pisemskii reminds his readers what he expects from them in the last few lines of *Vzbalamuchennoe more*, which, he claimed, was written 'not for sixteen-year-old female readers and feeble-minded young men'.[94]

Moreover, the mid-nineteenth-century Russian novels that deal with the woman question specifically reinforce the stereotype of the female reader as inferior.[95] Women writers 'happily reproduced patronizing stereotypes',[96] and exposing female readers as inadequate became common in Russian women's writing in the mid-nineteenth century. Emphasizing the maleness of his intended audience, Panaeva's narrator constructed an ideal reader: a young, impressionable man for whom this story can serve as a revelation and a call to action.

This supposed power of fictional narrative is a constant concern of Panaeva's narrator, who often addresses its influence on 'real life' [deistvitel'naia zhizn']. Sofiia, we are told, loved 'fairytales' [volshebnye skazki], so much so that it was very difficult to persuade her that her nanny's stories were not real. But why tell children that 'magic oddities don't exist in real life' if they could explain the ills of contemporary society, asks the narrator? He then re-imagines social evils as something that could be explained by evil magic: money functioning as a magic wand, vanity having the same effect as 'dead' and 'alive' water, people becoming mute and dumb as fishes in the face of unfairness and the pain of others, and so on.

Later on in the novel, the explanatory potential of fairy tales is put to use in the scene of Anna's sojourn at a coaching inn:

> Путешественницу смотритель ввел в комнату с ковром, с шелковой мебелью, с теплым и чистым воздухом. Когда смотритель ушел, то путешественница уселась на диван и разглядывая комнату, думала, что

она теперь походит на сказочную героиню, которая по щучьему веленью, из хижины переносится во дворец. Ну, а в действительной жизни, на станциях, только генеральское приказание творит такие чудеса.[97]

[The innkeeper led the female traveller into a room with a carpet, silk-covered furniture, and warm and clean air. When the innkeeper left, the traveller sat on the sofa and looked around the room, thinking that now she resembles a fairy-tale character, who, by the order of a magic pike, was transferred from a hut to a palace. Well, in real life, at coaching inns, only the general's order makes such miracles happen.]

These passages showcase Panaeva's underargument concerning the relative validity of different types of realist narration. In the scene at the coaching inn, Anna as a focaliser is interpreting reality in terms of 'magic oddities', recalling modes of narrative that are not reliant on credibility and authentication. The narratorial voice, however, re-conceptualises the same events in the framework of 'real life', governed by issues of class, power and social order, as behoves a realist narrative. This contrast creates a particular type of metafictional tension, not immediately apparent at other points of the narrative.

Together with the inadequate education, it is literary fiction that is responsible for propagating harmful illusions: 'У нас в голове все романы да рыцари!'[98] [We only have novels and knights in our heads!], the narrator accuses his readers. The contrast between the 'novels' and 'actual life' is constantly emphasised: 'В романах можно так рассуждать, но не в жизни...'[99] [In the novel you can reason like that, but not in real life...];[100] Sofia, though well-read, 'многого еще не понимала в этой действительной, грязной жизни'[101] [did not yet understand many things in this real, dirty life].

Panaeva's narrator reflects on several aspects of realist narratives that have been specifically criticised as typical defects of women's writing. One of them is character description and her focus on this particular feature is not arbitrary. The nature of realist description, including the description of characters, is a problematic aspect of women's writing: for instance, it forms a basis of Khvoshchinskaia's reflections on realism as well as featuring in Cohen's examination of the problem of a 'light touch' characterisation, typical for the feminine social novel.[102]

The narrator in *Zhenskaia dolia* often uses a particular rhetorical strategy: he admits to not having done something that should be accomplished in a realist narrative, but then, as if pressured by readers, does it in the end:

Однако, я ничего не сказал о наружности Григория Андреевича, ни о его госте. Признаюсь, я не мастер списывать паспортные портреты моих героев и героинь. Пожалуй, можно описать каждую морщинку на лице Григория Андреевича, — но что толку, если для читателя он все-таки останется выцветшим дагерротипным портретом? Но так и быть: скажу кратко об их наружности.[103]

[I have, however, not said anything about what Grigorii Andreevich and his guest look like. I confess, I am not a master of copying passport-like portraits of my heroes and heroines. I can, I guess, describe every wrinkle on Grigorii Andreevich's face — but what would be the point if for the readers he will remain a faded daguerreotype portrait? But fine, I will say something very briefly about their appearance.]

Or, later on: 'О наружности Лакотникова могу сказать определительно только, что это был видный мужчина...'[104] [In regard to Lakotnikov's appearance, the only definitive thing that I can say is that he was a handsome man...]. This 'descriptive restraint', featured in *Zhenskaia dolia*, serves a particular function in the feminine social novel: it directs the reader's attention from the character's outer appearance to the workings of his/her heart. In this passage, the issue of over-doing or under-doing detailed descriptions — often featured in discussions and value judgements on women's prose — is debated.

This direct answer to criticism is not the only form of engagement with contemporary literary and critical paratexts in *Zhenskaia dolia* — literary parody is used throughout the novel as a form of metanarrative. Panaeva often veers into a narrative mode that parodies Gogolesque satire. For example, in Part One, Panaeva's narrator paints a parodic picture of alternative 'golden times' and then returns to 'realistic' description. The narrator starts his monologue with a question: 'Случалось ли моему читателю встречаться с художественными натурами?'[105] [Has my reader ever had a chance to meet artistic persons?]. He then paints a sarcastic picture of the artistic people exemplified in Sofiia's dissipated husband Petr, and how they are underestimated by everyone except impressionable self-educated youths [*iunoshi-samouchki*].[106] A 'golden time of true appreciation' will come for them, predicts the narrator, and describes this alternative golden future, in which these artistic natures are revered: 'Я замечтался о золотом времени!'[107] [I have lost myself in the dreams of this golden time!].

Panaeva's treatment of this alternative development, is, typically for feminist metafiction, completely different from the rest of the text, as a 'textual parod[y] of conventional literary discourses' that 'is recognizably out of place'.[108] The stylistic reference could not be clearer: the paragraph ends with a direct mention of Gogol''s play, *Revizor* [The Government Inspector]: 'Это все так приятно, так трогательно, что в то время, как я пишу эти строки, сам не знаю отчего — но слезы так вот рекой и льются [...] [как] у жены смотрителя в "Ревизоре"'[109] [All of this is so nice, so touching, that while I am writing these lines, I don't know why, but my tears flow freely, like a river [... like] the innkeeper's wife in *The Government Inspector*]. Equally, the narrator's self-consciousness often manifests in satirical asides: 'Однако что я делаю! — передаю грубое воззрение злого лакея на жизнь благороднейших людей!'[110] ['But what am I doing! — I am passing on an angry servant's opinion about the lives of the most noble people!]. Such remarks explicitly use the mode's performative potential.[111]

In another example, the satirical narrator styles himself as a voice of reason and a speaker for the underprivileged, in a parodic reference to Pushkin's poetic descriptions of Russian winter:

> ...мороз заметно усиливался. Наши поэты вообще часто воспевали прелесть русской зимы; а наши патриоты, проживающие в Италии или в Париже большую часть своей жизни, восторгаются трескучими

морозами, которым мудрые мужи приписывают мощь тела и духа русского человека. Я согласен, что мороз придает бодрость тому, что, целую ночь просидев за ужином, на другое утро встал с туманной головой, — он, разумеется, пройдясь по морозу освежится настолько, что почувствует силу снова провести также и следующую ночь. Поверю также, что русская зима имеет приятность для тех, кто, закутавшись в собольи и медвежьи шубы, промчится на рысаках после длинного обеда в оперу. Согласен, что может быть есть поэзия в морозе и для того, кто скачет на лихой тройке с сотенного пикника. Но сомневаюсь, чтобы мороз придавал бодрость духа и тела ямщику, сидящему на козлах.[112]

[...the frost was getting visibly stronger. Our poets in general have often sung the beauty of the Russian winter; and our patriots, living in Italy and Paris for the most part of their lives, admire the crackling frosts, to which the wise men ascribe the strength of the body and spirit of a Russian person. I agree, that the frost gives energy to the man who, having sat down for an entire night to have dinner, next morning gets up with a foggy head. He, of course, having gone for a walk in the frost, would be refreshed so much that he will feel enough strength to spend the next night in the same way. I can also believe that the Russian winter is also pleasant for those who, enveloped in sable and bear furs, will dash to the opera by fast horses after a long dinner. I agree there is poetry in frost also for those who are racing back in a fast carriage from their hundredth picnic. But I doubt that the frost gives any energy to the coachman, outside on his seat.]

Here, the narrator wants his readers to visualise a specific coachman ('посмотрите, как он съежился в своем дырявом армячишке'[113] [look, how he shivers in his coat, full of holes]). The miserable conditions in which the coachmen have to work are shocking, but the only passenger who is appalled is a young woman — sarcastically, the narrator notes that the only reason why she is bothered is her female sentimentality ('она только по женской чувствительности не разделяла того мудро-спокойного мнения, что все нипочем русскому мужику'[114] [it was only because of her female sensibility that she did not share that quietly wise opinion that a Russian muzhik can take anything]). Here, in a rhetorical trick, privileged appreciation of the Russian winter, gentle to the rich and cruel to the poor, is contrasted with a female sensibility, thus equating male sensibility with cruelty. Panaeva's satire is aimed at multiple targets: on the one hand, it attacks the narrative of social privilege. On the other, through equating privilege with masculinity, it highlights the similarities between victims of social and gender discrimination.

Sometimes a sarcastic reverie or a genuine alarmist monologue is checked by the narrator's self-awareness:

Достаточные столичные жители, как мне кажется, вместо сердца, имеют кусочки мамонтовой кожи... Впрочем я увлекся, осуждая равнодушие столичных жителей к беззащитным женщинам и детям. Они иногда бывают очень чувствительны в театрах и проливают обильные слезы...[115]

[Wealthy inhabitants of the capital have, I think, pieces of mammoth skin instead of a heart... However, I got carried away condemning the indifference

of the people from the capital to vulnerable women and children. They can sometimes be very sensitive in the theatres and their tears flow voluminously...]
or: 'Надеюсь, читатель не осудит [Лакотникова] за такую невинную слабость, особенно когда видит, что в этом человеке соединялось столько замечательных добродетелей...'[116] [I hope the reader will not judge [Lakotnikov] for such an innocent whim, especially when he sees that so many remarkable virtues have come together in this man]; or, for example: 'Ведь в самом деле читатель, молодость, положим, вещь хорошая, но зрелые года, согласитесь сами, все-таки лучше'[117] [Indeed, dear reader, youth is a good thing but mature years, you will agree, is after all a bit better]. This type of self-aware sarcastic narrative commentary actively involves the reader in the process of interpreting the text and establishes a shared experience of narration by using metafictional cues.

The boundaries of realist discourse and the structure of narrative are debated in the concluding chapter of the novel: 'Если так принято, чтобы автор заканчивал свой роман подробным отчетом, что и как продолжают существовать главные лица, то я должен это сделать'[118] [If it is common for an author to end his novel with a detailed report about what has happened to the main characters, then I am obliged to do this, too], reflects the narrator of Panaeva's novel. In a final reflection on the accepted structures of realistic narrative, the narrator once again conceives of himself as a rhetorical entity capable of objectively evaluating his own narrative. Carrying on with the rhetorical strategy he initiated earlier in the novel, he first questions but then ultimately follows the realist tradition of narrative closure, providing the account of Anna's, Snegov's, Sofiia's and Lakotnikov's lives.

This employment of rhetorical underarguments with realist poetics, carried out throughout the novel, becomes its major metafictional preoccupation. Panaeva's narrator reflects on his own struggles to accommodate his style to the demands of contemporary realist prose. As a result, the reader is often offered a running commentary on the issue the narrator is trying to solve: over/under descriptions of characters, the constraints of gendered narrative voices, realistic authentication of the events of the plot, the creation of narrative suspense and the dialogue with ideologically divided audiences.

The struggle against the dominant literary aesthetics is manifested on the structural and discursive levels of the text. As a subject of metanarrative, it mirrors the novel's ideological preoccupation with the woman question and the problems of female emancipation. The narrative voice in *Zhenskaia dolia* challenges the constraints of dominant contemporary aesthetic and political narratives, testing their boundaries and looking for opportunities for those brave enough to explore them.

★ ★ ★ ★

Zhenskaia dolia had been previously defined primarily as a novel on the subject of 'the woman question' and read in the historical and ideological context of the political debates of the 1860s. A focus on the novel's narrative voice, which self-consciously tested the aesthetic, ideological and gender boundaries of contemporary literary discourse, illuminates the place Panaeva's novel occupies in the transnational tradition of feminist metafiction.

The close reading offered in this chapter draws attention to the rhetoric of narrative self-consciousness in *Zhenskaia dolia*, showcasing the transgressive nature of the novel's narrative voice. Panaeva's narrator occupies an ambivalent position and, oscillating between the male voice of authority and female voice of empathy, utilises the narrative potential of both. The presumed reader's gender identity is equally fluid and inclusive: the text proclaims itself to be intended for the moral improvement of young men, and yet addresses all victims of life's unfair lot irrespective of their gender.

This ambivalence generates instances of narratorial self-reflection, questioning traditional principles of realist narration and the constraints they place on the writers depending on their gender. The structural and stylistic elements of narrative which are traditionally associated with women's writing, such as characterisation, plotting, imagery and the rhetoric of empathy, are transformed in *Zhenskaia dolia* 'into subversive and interactive forms that contest [...] historical convention'.[119]

The comparison with the French feminine social novel exposes the basic narrative structure of *Zhenskaia dolia*, which allows for the introduction of metafictional elements into the novel's ostensibly realist poetics. What seems unusual in the context of the Russian literary scene of the 1860s appears as a shared narrative strategy of a particular type of women's writing. Similar across European national literary traditions, it appears in women's novelistic fiction when the debates on realist aesthetics become fused with the discourse of gender dominance and submission.

As a text of the woman question with overt instances of metanarrative, *Zhenskaia dolia* is a case of Russian feminist metafiction of the 1860s. Imbued with the literary concerns of the period, *Zhenskaia dolia* addresses the same questions of the realist aesthetics and ideological potential of literary fiction as the other two novels discussed in this study but approaches them through a different type of narrative strategy. By following the rhetorical thrusts of the novel's narrative voice, we can retrace Panaeva's strategy of negotiating a literary 'realist position without losing whatever benefits her gender might confer'.[120]

Notes to Chapter 4

Part of this chapter was published also as 'A Woman's Lot: Realism and Gendered Narration in Russian Women's Writing of the 1860s', *Russian Review*, 80.2 (2021), 229–245. I am grateful to the publishers for their permission to reproduce it here.

1. *Sovremennik*, 3 (1848), 65–76. *Neostorozhnoe slovo* was almost immediately followed by the publication of an epistolary novella, inspired by George Sand, *Bezobraznyi muzh. Povest' v pis'makh* in the next issue of *Sovremennik*, 4 (1848), 131–58.
2. 'Mody' was published anonymously throughout the years but the Panaevs have been identified as its authors by V. E. Bograd. V. E. Bograd, *Zhurnal 'Sovremennik', 1847–1866: Ukazatel' soderzhaniia* (Moscow: GIKHL, 1959), p. 515. For more on Panaeva's editorial work see Jehanne M. Gheith, 'Redefining the Perceptible: The Journalism(s) of Evgeniia Tur and Avdot'ia Panaeva', in *An Improper Profession: Women, Gender, and Journalism in Late Imperial Russia*, ed. by Barbara T. Norton and Jehanne M. Gheith (Durham, NC: Duke University Press, 2001),

pp. 51–73; Marina Ledkovsky, 'Avdotya Panaeva: Her Salon and Her Life', *Russian Literature Triquarterly*, 9 (1974), 426–32 (p. 429), see also Panaeva's *Vospominaniia* (Moscow: GIKHL, 1956), pp. 186, 89–90, 252–56, 294, 350. Pisarev's negative review of *Zhenskaia dolia* referred to Panaeva as *Sovremennik*'s 'старый и постоянный сподвижник'. D. I. Pisarev, 'Kukol'naia tragediia s buketom grazhdanskoi skorbi', in *Polnoe sobranie sochinenii*, 6 vols (St Petersburg: Izdatel'stvo F. Pavlenkova, 1894–1907), IV (1894), pp. 147–96 (p. 148).
3. A significant amount of research has been done on the co-authored works, establishing exactly which chapters were written by Panaeva and which by Nekrasov. For more on the attribution of these texts, see B. L. Bessonov, 'Ob avtorskoi prinadlezhnosti romana "Tri strany sveta"', *Nekrasovskii sbornik*, 6 (1978), 111–30; M. A. Marusenko, 'Atributsiia romanov "Tri strany sveta" i "Mertvoe ozero"', *Vestnik SPbGU*, 1 (1997), 37–52; B. V. Mel'gunov, 'O novykh atributsiiakh romanov "Tri strany sveta" i "Mertvoe ozero"', *Russkaia literatura*, 3 (1998), 98–103.
4. Panaeva, *Vospominaniia*, p. 153. For a detailed discussion of the journal's first months under Panaev and Nekrasov's management see V. E. Evgen'ev-Maksimov, *'Sovremennik' v 40–50 gg.: ot Belinskogo do Chernyshevskogo* (Leningrad: Izdatel'stvo pisatelia, 1934), pp. 29–41. For a not entirely historically accurate but first-hand account of the journal's founding see Panaeva, *Vospominaniia*, pp. 151–60.
5. Pisarev, 'Kukol'naia tragediia s buketom grazhdanskoi skorbi', p. 151.
6. There is a wealth of sources on Russian censorship regulations of the second half of the nineteenth century. For a descriptions of the rules and regulations specifically in the 1860s see: Robert L. Belknap, 'Survey of Russian Journals, 1840 — 80', in *Literary Journals in Imperial Russia*, ed. by Deborah A. Martinsen (Cambridge: Cambridge University Press, 1997), pp. 91–117 (pp. 101–04, 113–14); M. K. Lemke, *Epokha tsenzurnykh reform 1859–1865 godov* (St Petersburg: Gerold, 1904); A. M. Skabichevskii, *Ocherkii istorii russkoi tsenzury, 1700–1863 g.* (St Petersburg: Tipografiia tovarishchestva 'Obshchestvennaia pol'za', 1892), pp. 445–71; Charles Ruud, *Fighting Words: Imperial Censorship and the Russian Press, 1804–1906* (Toronto: University of Toronto Press, 1982), pp. 97–137; G. V. Zhirkov, *Istoriiia tsenzury v Rossii XIX–XX vv.* (Moscow: Aspekt Press, 2001). For more on the division of roles between 'regular literary workers' [рядовые литературные работники] and 'literary generals' [литературные генералы], see V. E. Evgen'ev-Maksimov, *'Sovremennik' pri Chernyshevskom i Dobroliubove* (Leningrad: GIKHL, 1936), p. 5.
7. Barbara Heldt, 'Gender', in *The Cambridge Companion to the Classic Russian Novel*, ed. by Malcolm V. Jones and Robin Feuer Miller (Cambridge: Cambridge University Press, 1998), pp. 251–70 (p. 259); Beth Holmgren and Jehanne M. Gheith, 'Art and Prostokvasha: Avdot'ia Panaeva's Work', in *The Russian Memoir: History and Literature*, ed. by Beth Holmgren (Evanston, IL: Northwestern University Press, 2007), pp. 128–44 (pp. 130–31). For a recent contextualisation of *Semeistvo Tal'nikovykh* in the history of literary subjectivities in Russian literature, see Andrew Kahn, M. N. Lipovetskii, Irina Reyfman and Stephanie Sandler, *A History of Russian Literature* (Oxford: Oxford University Press, 2018), p. 399.
8. Panaeva, *Vospominaniia*, p. 171. In Heldt's opinion, the problem was not just the subversion of parental authority, but a subversion of parental authority from a female point of view. For more on her reading of *Semeistvo Tal'nikovykh* see Barbara Heldt, 'Gender', p. 259.
9. Evgen'ev-Maksimov, *'Sovremennik' v 40–50 gg.*, pp. 254–55.
10. Pisarev, 'Kukol'naia tragediia s buketom grazhdanskoi skorbi', p. 147.
11. On reception of Sand's works in Russia, see Lesley Herrmann, *'Jacques* in Russia: A Program of Domestic Reform for Husbands', *Studies in the Literary Imagination*, 12 (1979), 61–72; Carole Karp, 'George Sand and Turgenev: A Literary Relationship', *Studies in the Literary Imagination*, 12 (1979), 73–81; Ol'ga Demidova, 'Russian Women Writers of the Nineteenth Century', in *Gender and Russian Literature: New Perspectives*, ed. by Rosalind J. Marsh (Cambridge: Cambridge University Press, 1996), pp. 92–111 (pp. 96–100).
12. For canonical (if ideologically dated) view on George Sand's influence on Chernyshevskii see A. P. Skaftymov, 'Chernyshevskii i Zhorzh Sand', in *N. G. Chernyshevskii. Neizdannye teksty, materialy i stat'i*, ed. by S. Z. Katsenbogen (Saratov: n.p., 1928), pp. 223–43. Reprint in A. Skaftymov *Stat'i o russkoi literature* (Saratov: Saratovskoe knizhnoe izdatel'stvo, 1958), pp. 203–27. On Pisemskii and Sand, see Moser, *Pisemsky*, p. 197.

13. For more on the reception of Charlotte Brontë in Russia as well as on the general interest in women writers and women characters see O. R. Demidova, 'The Reception of Charlotte Brontë's Work in Nineteenth-Century Russia', *The Modern Language Review*, 89 (1994), 689–96.
14. After Panaev's death in 1862, the journal was handed over to Nekrasov. Even though his relationship with the censors examining *Sovremennik* was good, the journal was still excluded from several government subscription lists, such as those of the 'regimental libraries'. For a detailed account of the journal's struggles in 1861–62 see Evgen'ev-Maksimov, *'Sovremennik' pri Chernyshevskom i Dobroliubove*, pp. 485–507.
15. Joan Douglas Peters, *Feminist Metafiction and the Evolution of the British Novel* (Gainesville: University Press of Florida, 2002), p. 2.
16. N. Stanitskii [A. Ia. Panaeva], 'Zhenskaia dolia. Chast' pervaia', *Sovremennik*, 2 (1862), 51–176 (p. 52).
17. For more on this narrative practice, see Madeleine Kahn, *Narrative Transvestism*. In her study, Kahn explicitly states that she is concerned primarily with male writers adopting female narrative voices; nevertheless, the methodology she develops is universal and can be used to approach the cases of female writers' male narratorial voices.
18. Peters, *Feminist Metafiction and the Evolution of the British Novel*, p. 11.
19. Interestingly, Kelly analyses the same effect that Belinskii's criticism of contemporary women writers had on the future reception of their works. Catriona Kelly, *A History of Russian Women's Writing, 1820–1992*, pp. 25–26.
20. On Russian women writers' place in the Russian realist canon see Hilde Hoogenboom, *Noble Sentiments and the Rise of Russian Novels* (Toronto: Toronto University Press, 2021). In 2018, Moscow-based publisher *CommonPlace* launched a series of republications of texts by Russian women writers, edited by Maria Nesterenko. For more on the publisher's work, see Mariia Nesterenko, 'Zhenshchiny pishut o tom, chto volnuet imenno ikh', *Prochtenie.org* <https://prochtenie.org/texts/29447> [accessed 6 August 2019].
21. 'I picked up a pencil, and it took me only an hour to edit the whole book', <http://nekrasov.niv.ru/nekrasov/bio/panaeva/ocherk-chukovskogo.htm> [accessed 8 August 2019]. The memoirs were first published in instalments in *Istoricheskii vestnik* in 1889 and the first separate edition came out in 1890 under the title *Russkie pisateli i artisty*. (A. Ia. Panaeva, *Russkie pisateli i artisty. Vospominaniia A. Ia. Golovachevoi–Panaevoi* (St Petersburg: Izdatel'stvo V. I. Gubinskogo, 1890)).
22. K. I. Chukovskii, *Zhena Poeta (Avdot'ia Iakovlevna Panaeva)* (St Petersburg: Epokha, 1922).
23. K. I. Chukovskii, 'Panaeva i ee vospominaniia', in *Vospominaniia*, ed. by K. I. Chukovskii and N. L. Brodskii (Moscow: GIKHL, 1956), pp. 5–16 (p. 6).
24. As Holmgren and Gheith note, this reading was also in keeping with the nineteenth-century reception of women writers' work: 'Once again, a woman writer stands faulted for excessive details and emotion'. Holmgren and Gheith, 'Art and Prostokvasha', p. 134.
25. Chukovskii, 'Panaeva i ee vospominaniia', p. 9; 'K. I. Chukovskii, 'Panaeva' <http://nekrasov.niv.ru/nekrasov/bio/panaeva/ocherk-chukovskogo.htm> [accessed 10 August 2019]. An insightful examination of the discrepancies between the evocations of love in Nekrasov's lyrics and the actual historical circumstances of his relationships with women can be found in Richard Gregg's article, 'A Brackish Hippocrene: Nekrasov, Panaeva, and the "Prose in Love"', *Slavic Review*, 34 (1975), 731–51.
26. K. I. Chukovskii, 'Panaeva i Nekrasov', in *Semeistvo Tal'nikovykh: Povest'*, ed. by N. P. Nekrasov and K. I. Chukovskii (Leningrad: Academia, 1928), pp. 5–79 (p. 8).
27. Ibid., p. 6.
28. See, for example, entries on Panaeva in a Soviet literary encyclopaedia: P. I. Kaletskii, 'Panaeva A. Ia.', in *Literaturnaia entsiklopediia*, 11 vols (Moscow: OGIZ RSFSR, 1929–39), VIII (1934), p. 421. A similar attitude can be found in the other two major Soviet studies of Panaeva's work: U. M. Dolgikh, 'Zhizn' i literaturnoe tvorchestvo A. Ia. Panaevoi' (unpublished doctoral thesis, Leningradskii gosudarstvennyi pedogagicheskii institut im. A. I. Gertsena, 1977), p. 235; K. S. Kurova, 'Literaturnaia deiatel'nost' A. Ia. Panaevoi (Sotrudnichestvo pisatel'nitsy v "Sovremennike")' (unpublished doctoral thesis, Kazakhskii gosudarstvennyi universitet im. S. M. Kirova, 1950), p. 190.

29. I am talking here about research projects that led to the publication of 'Potsdam University Frauen Literatur Geschichte' series (*Russkie pisatel'nitsy i literaturnyi protsess v kontse XVIII–pervoi treti XX vv.: sbornik nauchnykh statei*, ed. by M. Sh. Fainshtein (Wilhelmshorst: F. K. Göpfert, 1995); *Russland aus der Feder seiner Frauen: Zum femininen Diskurs in der russischen Literatur: Materialien des am 21/22 Mai 1992 im Fachbereich Slavistik der Universität Potsdam durchgeführten Kolloquiums*, ed. by F. K. Göpfert (Munich: O. Sagner, 1992); *Vieldeutiges Nicht-zu-Ende-Sprechen: Thesen und Momentaufnahmen aus der Geschichte russischer Dichterinnen*, ed. by Arja Rosenholm and Frank Göpfert (Fichtenwalde: Göpfert, 2002)), as well as the joint publication of the University of Freiburg and the Tver' State University, *Zhenskii vyzov: russkie pisatel'nitsy XIX–nachala XX veka*, ed. by Elisabeth Cheauré and E. N. Stroganova (Tver': Liliia Print, 2006).
30. An exception to this rule, a 2006 study by S. Tatarkina, offered a historiographical reading of Panaeva's work and examined the poetics of space and subject organisation in her fiction, but it remains the sole Russian monograph on Panaeva in recent years. S. V. Tatarkina, 'Tvorchestvo A. Ia. Panaevoi v literaturnom kontekste epokhi: gendernyi aspekt' (unpublished doctoral thesis, Tomskii gosudarstvennyi universitet, 2006).
31. Ledkovsky, 'Avdotya Panaeva'.
32. Heldt, 'Gender', pp. 251–70.
33. Jane Costlow, 'Love, Work, and the Woman Question in Mid-Nineteenth-Century Women's Writing', in *Women Writers in Russian Literature*, ed. by Toby W. Clyman and Diana Greene (Westport: Greenwood Press, 1994), pp. 66–76. *Semeistvo Tal'nikovykh*, as well as *Zhenskaia dolia*, were further examined in the context of the women's liberation movement in Kelly, *A History of Russian Women's Writing, 1820–1992*, pp. 62–69.
34. As such, the novel was briefly discussed in Soviet scholarship of the period. See E. G. Bushkanets, 'N. G. Chernyshevskii i pisateli-demokraty', in N. G. Chernyshevskii. Stat'i, issledovaniia i materialy, ed. by E. I. Pokusaev (Saratov: Saratavskoe knizhnoe izdatel'stvo, 1958), pp. 105–54; K. S. Kurova, 'Tvorchestvo A. Ia. Panaevoi v 60-e gody', *Uchenye zapiski KGU: Iazyk i literatura*, 14 (1952), 39–58.
35. Catriona Kelly offers a good overview of this cross-pollination process in Kelly, 'The First-Person "Other": Sof'ia Soboleva's 1863 Story "Pros and Cons" (I Pro, i Contra)', *Slavonic and East European Review*, 73 (1995), 61–81 (p. 62).
36. 'But underneath this crude work — there is always conviction; this sketching is an inevitable consequence of a fiery desire to say everything, say it faster; in this abruptness there is always a lot of truth of everyday dramatism, picked up not in order to show off the author's style but to demonstrate a painful feeling of sympathy and anger, a feeling that is direct, brave and sincere.' (N. D. Khvoshchinskaia [V. Porechnikov], 'Provintsial'nye pis'ma o nashei literature. Pis'mo tret'e. "Zhenskaia dolia", roman Stanitskogo (Sovremennik, №3), "Otstalaia", povest' g-zhi Zhadovskoi (Vremia, №12)', *Otechestvennye zapiski*, 5 (1862), 37–38). For a very brief overview of the novel's reception see also O. A. Kuiantseva, 'Interpretatsiia romana A. Ia. Panaevoi "Zhenskaia dolia" v kritike i literaturovedenii', *Visnik LNU im. Tarasa Shevchenka*, 3.214 (2011), 148–52.
37. Pisarev, 'Kukol'naia tragediia s buketom grazhdanskoi skorbi', p. 147.
38. Ibid., pp. 147, 150.
39. Female critics had a slightly more nuanced view: see, for example, Maria Tsebrikova's 'Psevdo-novaia geroina (o romane I.A. Goncharova "Obryv")', *Otechestvennye zapiski*, 5 (1870), pp. 41–42.
40. Ibid., p. 176. For similar observations, see N. V. Shelgunov, 'Zhenskoe bezdushie: Po povodu sochinenii V. Krestovskogo-psevdonima', *Delo*, 9 (1870), 1–34. Pisarev also discussed 'the woman question' in D. I. Pisarev, *Sochineniia*, 10 vols (St Petersburg: Izdatel'stvo F. Pavlenkova, 1866–69), 1 (1866), pp. 80–125.
41. Pisarev, 'Kukol'naia tragediia s buketom grazhdanskoi skorbi', p. 184.
42. Costlow, 'Love, Work, and the Woman Question in Mid-Nineteenth Century Women's Writing', p. 64.
43. Ibid.
44. Catriona Kelly identifies two main varieties of Russian women's writing of the 1840s–1860s as 'the provincial tale' and 'the escape plot'. Kelly, *A History of Russian Women's Writing, 1820–1992*, pp. 59–79.

45. Mary Fleming Zirin, 'Women's Prose Fiction in the Age of Realism', in *Women Writers in Russian Literature*, ed. by Clyman and Greene, pp. 77–94 (p. 78).
46. Jehanne M. Gheith, *Finding the Middle Ground: Krestovskii, Tur, and the Power of Ambivalence in Nineteenth-Century Russian Women's Prose* (Evanston: Northwestern University Press, 2004), p. 17.
47. Arja Rosenholm, 'The "Woman Question" of the 1860s and the Ambiguity of the "Learned Woman"', in *Gender and Russian Literature*, ed. by Marsh, pp. 112–29 (p. 118). One major exception to this rule was Khvoshchinskaia's theory of realism, discussed in detail in Hilde Hoogenboom, '"Ya rab deistvitel'nosti": Nadezha Khvoschchinskaia, Realism, and the Detail', in *Vieldeutiges Nicht-zu-Ende-Sprechen*, ed. by Rosenholm and Göpfert, pp. 129–49. For more on the nineteenth-century women writers' constraints see Zirin, 'Women's Prose Fiction in the Age of Realism', p. 78. Zirin notes that Panaeva was 'a rare woman writer who lived in St. Petersburg, and her career was furthered by personal connections' (p. 78), as do Holmgren and Gheith, in 'Art and Prostokvasha', p. 129.
48. Joe Andrew, 'Telling Tales: Zhukova as Metaliterary Author', in *Vieldeutiges Nicht-zu-Ende-Sprechen*, ed. by Rosenholm and Göpfert, pp. 113–29. For more on metanarrative in Zhukova, see Svetlana Slavskaya Grenier, 'Becoming a Subject: Beyond the Objectifying Male Gaze (Zhukova's *The Locket* and *Self-Sacrifice*)', in Svetlana Slavskaya Grenier, *Representing the Marginal Woman in Nineteenth-Century Russian Literature: Personalism, Feminism, and Polyphony* (Westport: Greenwood Press, 2001), pp. 33–61.
49. Hilde Hoogenboom, 'The Society Tale as Pastiche: Maria Zhukova's Heroines Move to the Country', in *The Society Tale in Russian Literature: From Odoevskii to Tolstoi*, ed. by Neil Cornwell (Amsterdam: Rodopi, 1998), pp. 85–97 (p. 96).
50. The collection of articles *An Improper Profession: Women, Gender, and Journalism in Late Imperial Russia*, ed. by Barbara T. Norton and Jehanne M. Gheith (Durham, NC: Duke University Press, 2001), mentioned above, reports recent findings on the work not only of Evgeniia Tur and Panaeva, but also of less well-known figures such as Anna Volkova (Adele Lindenmeyer, 'Anna Volkova: From Merchant Wife to Feminist Journalist', in *An Improper Profession*, pp. 120–40), Maria Chekhova, Liubov' Gurevich, Maria Pokrovskaia (Linda Edmondson, 'Maria Pokrovskaia and *Zhenksii Vestnik*: Feminist Separatism in Theory and Practice', ibid., pp. 196–222), Ekaterina Kuskova (Barbara T. Norton, 'Journalism as a Means of Empowerment: The Early Career of Ekaterina Kuskova', ibid., pp. 222–49) and others. For a list of women journalists in Imperial Russia, see *An Improper Profession*, pp. 281–311.
51. Naomi Schor, 'Rereading in Detail: Or, Aesthetics, the Feminine, and Idealism', *Criticism*, 32.3 (1990), <http://digitalcommons.wayne.edu/criticism/vol32/iss3/3/> [accessed 12 August 2019]. For Schor's thoughts on theory of Realism in the writings of the French realist women writers see Naomi Schor, *Breaking the Chain: Women, Theory, and French Realist Fiction* (New York: Columbia University Press, 1985). In her article on Khvoshchinskaia's thoughts on Realism Hilde Hoogenboom briefly addressed this problem and identified Khvoshchinskaia's letters, fiction and literary criticism as an example of a corpus of texts suggested by Schor.
52. For more on Ivan Panaev's 'frequent and well-attended evening meetings', which brought together 'litterateurs and other people of their general acquaintance, claiming ties with literature', see *Literaturnye kruzhki i salony*, ed. by M. I. Aronson and S. A. Reiser (Leningrad: Priboi, 1929), pp. 235–37.
53. A thematic analysis of the conversations usually held at Panaeva's salon can be found in Ledkovsky, 'Avdotya Panaeva', pp. 426–27.
54. A small cache of remaining letters to Nekrasov has been discovered and published in *Literaturnoe nasledstvo*, 53–54 (1949), 117–30.
55. Margaret Cohen, *The Sentimental Education of the Novel* (Princeton: Princeton University Press, 1999), p. 195.
56. Other texts of a similar type included Nadezhda Khvoshchinskaia's *Pansionerka* (1861), Sof'ia Soboleva's *Bezvykhodnoe polozhenie* (1864), Marko Vovchok's *Sasha* (1859), *Zhivaia dusha* (1868) and others.
57. Hoogenboom, '"Ya rab deistvitel'nosti": Nadezha Khvoshchinskaia, Realism, and the Detail',

p. 134. Hoogenboom used Cohen's methodology in her exploration of Khvoshchinskaia's critical legacy on the theory of realism, whereas Gheith explored its uses for contextualising the aesthetic judgment of women's fiction in the mid-nineteenth-century literary establishment. Gheith, *Finding the Middle Ground*, p. 14.
58. Margaret Cohen, 'Preface: Reconfiguring Realism', in *Spectacles of Realism: Body, Gender, Genre*, ed. by Margaret Cohen and Christopher Prendergast (Minneapolis: University of Minnesota Press, 1995), pp. vii–xiii (p. x).
59. Margaret Cohen, 'In Lieu of a Chapter on Some French Women Realist Novelists', in *Spectacles of Realism*, ed. by Cohen and Prendergast, pp. 90–119 (p. 93).
60. Ibid., p. 90.
61. Ibid., p. 94.
62. Ibid., p. 113.
63. Stanitskii, 'Zhenskaia dolia. Chast' pervaia', p. 41.
64. Ibid.
65. Ibid.
66. Ibid., p. 42.
67. N. Stanitskii [A. Ia. Panaeva], 'Zhenskaia dolia. Chast' vtoraia. Okonchanie', *Sovremennik*, 5 (1862), 209–50 (p. 249).
68. For more on Gothic in late Russian realism, see Katherine Bowers, 'The Fall of the House: Gothic Narrative and the Decline of the Russian Family', in *Russian Writers and the Fin de Siècle*, ed. by Bowers and Kokobobo, pp. 145–62; Katherine Bowers, *Writing Fear: Russian Realism and the Gothic* (Toronto: University of Toronto Press, 2021).
69. For more on Panaeva's contemporaries' property and other legal rights, see Michelle Lamarche Marrese, *A Woman's Kingdom: Noblewomen and the Control of Property in Russia, 1700–1861* (Ithaca: Cornell University Press, 2002). Specifically on the intricacies of estate management, discussed in *Zhenskaia dolia*, see chapter 6, 'The Pomeshchitsa, Absent and Present: Women and Estate Management', pp. 171–205.
70. V. G. Belinskii, 'Letter to I. I. Panaev from 19 August 1839', in *Pis'ma*, 3 vols (St Petersburg: Tipografiia M. M. Stasiulevicha, 1914), I (1914), p. 331. First published in I. I. Panaev, 'Vospominanie o Belinskom', *Sovremennik*, 1 (1860), pp. 335–55.
71. For an analysis of this trope in Jane Eyre, see the by now classic chapter by Sandra M. Gilbert and Susan Gubar, 'A Dialogue of Self and Soul: Plain Jane's Progress', in *The Madwoman in the Attic* (New Haven and London: Yale University Press, 2000), pp. 336–72.
72. Stanitskii, 'Zhenskaia dolia. Chast' pervaia', p. 50.
73. Stanitskii, 'Zhenskaia dolia. Chast' vtoraia. Okonchanie', p. 232.
74. Cohen, 'In Lieu of a Chapter on Some French Women Realist Novelists', pp. 111–12.
75. Ibid.
76. Stanitskii, 'Zhenskaia dolia. Chast' pervaia', pp. 50–51.
77. Costlow, 'Love, Work, and the Woman Question in Mid-Nineteenth-Century Women's Writing', p. 64.
78. Cohen, 'In Lieu of a Chapter on Some French Women Realist Novelists', p. 94.
79. Ibid., p. 96.
80. Ibid., p. 97.
81. Ibid., p. 98.
82. Ibid., p. 97.
83. Stanitskii, 'Zhenskaia dolia. Chast' pervaia', p. 130.
84. Ibid., pp. 51–52, and later, N. Stanitskii [A. Ia. Panaeva], 'Zhenskaia dolia. Chast' vtoraia', *Sovremennik*, 4 (1862), 504–31 (p. 529).
85. Zirin, 'Women's Prose Fiction in the Age of Realism', p. 79.
86. Ibid., p. 78.
87. Kahn, *Narrative Transvestism*, p. 10.
88. Ibid., p. 8.
89. Holmgren and Gheith, 'Art and Prostokvasha', p. 132.
90. Stanitskii, 'Zhenskaia dolia. Chast' pervaia', p. 130.

91. Kahn, *Narrative Transvestism*, p. 2.
92. Zirin, 'Women's Prose Fiction in the Age of Realism', p. 79.
93. As Kahn points out, a defining feature of a narratorial transvestite self is its impermanence, as well as 'the transvestite's refusal to be defined by one gender or the other': the narratorial voice remains male and female at the same time. Kahn, *Narrative Transvestism*, pp. 10, 14.
94. *Vzbalamuchennoe more*, p. 549.
95. For an array of examples from the works by mid- and late nineteenth-century women writers see Dmitrii Ravinskii, 'Pisatel'nitsy o chitatel'nitsakh: zhenskoe chtenie na stranitsakh russkoi zhenskoi prozy XIX veka', in *Zhenskii vyzov*, ed. by Cheauré and Stroganova, pp. 51–61 (pp. 51–54).
96. Ibid., pp. 52–53.
97. 'Zhenskaia dolia. Chast' vtoraia', p. 526.
98. 'Zhenskaia dolia. Chast' pervaia', p. 102.
99. Ibid., p. 104.
100. Ibid., p. 104.
101. Ibid., p. 116.
102. Cohen, 'In Lieu of a Chapter on Some French Women Realist Novelists', pp. 112–16.
103. 'Zhenskaia dolia. Chast' pervaia', p. 61.
104. 'Zhenskaia dolia. Chast' vtoraia', p. 211.
105. 'Zhenskaia dolia. Chast' pervaia', p. 86.
106. Ibid.
107. Ibid., p. 89.
108. Peters, *Feminist Metafiction and the Evolution of the British Novel*, p. 2.
109. 'Zhenskaia dolia. Chast' pervaia', pp. 89–90.
110. 'Zhenskaia dolia. Chast' pervaia', p. 94.
111. For more on the performative and self-reflexive potential of satire, see Jean Weisgerber, 'Satire and Irony as Means of Communication', *Comparative Literature Studies*, 10 (1973), 152–71 (p. 163).
112. 'Zhenskaia dolia. Chast' vtoraia. Okonchanie', pp. 503–04.
113. Ibid., p. 504.
114. Ibid., p. 507.
115. Ibid., pp. 531–32.
116. 'Zhenskaia dolia. Chast' vtoraia', p. 211.
117. Ibid., p. 210.
118. Ibid., p. 249.
119. Kahn, *Narrative Transvestism*, p. 37.
120. Cohen, 'In Lieu of a Chapter on Some French Women Realist Novelists', p. 134.

CONCLUSION

In his widely read 2002 study *Consciousness and the Novel*, the literary critic David Lodge examined the multiple techniques by which consciousness is represented in — 'there, reader, take it quickly, if ye must!' — the novel. Guided by a similar fascination with the poetics of fiction, this book is a result of my own interest in finding out what exactly happens when narrative *self*-consciousness takes centre stage in the novel. And not in just any novel, but in the realist, ostensibly mimetic mid-nineteenth-century Russian novel, a genre that is itself responsible for the popular belief in the sanctity of the narratorial boundary to which Gérard Genette refers in his famous definition of metalepsis quoted as an epigraph to this book. Introducing the three writers whose relationship to the realist canon has been problematic, my study allows narratological studies to expand their usual scope of reference to include the Russian self-conscious realism of the 1860s.

My understanding of nineteenth-century Russian metafiction as 'self-conscious realism' is based on the twentieth-century theory of metafiction in its universal configuration, stripped of the specifics of national literary canons. Ever since a working definition of metafiction was formulated in the second half of the twentieth century, it has been possible to apply its interpretative framework to literary texts from any historical period, as long as they demonstrate narrative self-consciousness. Uniting different fields of study by the use of a similar methodology, it serves to illuminate ties between specific historical and social circumstances and their universal representation in narratives. Precisely such a synchronic approach has been practised in studies of metafiction in recent years, to which this study aims to serve as a useful addition.

Works by Patricia Waugh, Robert Alter, Dmitrii Segal and Mark Lipovetskii provide a starting point for my own methodological discussion, which aims to bridge a long-neglected gap between nineteenth-century Russian literary history and the most recent advances in narrative theory. I use literary texts, private documents and journal articles to argue that, with the advent of realism as the dominant literary aesthetic in the second half of the nineteenth century, self-consciousness did not go into eclipse in Russian fiction, but remained a constant presence. Moreover, an assumption to the contrary is based on a reductionist understanding of realism and a view of Russian novel-writing as purely imitative of its Western counterparts. In the preceding chapters, I have attempted to demonstrate the dissemination through mid-1860s Russian novels of this narrative technique, and to argue for its constitutive importance for Russian literature and the theory of realism.

In my approach to Chernyshevskii's novel, I aimed to offer a new answer to a pertinent question — how and why do certain books gain unparalleled political influence? Considered as an example of literary metafiction, Chernyshevskii's novel offers new insights into its own overanalysed poetics as well as into the Russian literary scene of the period. *Chto delat'?* was conceived as a vehicle for political ideas but in the end also became an example of a kind of fiction that Chernyshevskii himself promoted as a literary critic. Chernyshevskii's philosophical concern with the problem of the ontology of literary fiction was reflected in his choice of narrative strategies: the use of a highly self-conscious narrative voice, constantly exposing the artificial and constructed nature of the relayed narrative, and a purposefully maintained sense of ontological ambiguity, obvious in the undefined ontological status of the novel's characters, plot and the narrator himself. A careful reading of the novel's multiple metalepses allowed me to draw attention to the fundamental connection between Chernyshevskii's ideas on the ontology of literary fiction and his experiments with it in his novel. An exercise in close reading of the novel's metafictional passages, the analysis presented in this chapter exposed parallels between Chernyshevskii's narratorial voice in his articles and his literary fiction. Finally, a discussion of the metadiegetic aspects of the novel and its narrator, and a close reading of the novel's multiple metalepses, have exposed for the reader an underlying structure of metanarrative in *Chto delat'?*.

In the 1860s, the blurred boundaries between aesthetics and ideology meant that ideological and philosophic enquiries found their way into fiction through the use of narrative self-consciousness. Aiming to add Aleksei Pisemskii's theory of meta-realism and his perspective on literary aesthetics to a chorus of voices from which he had previously been excluded for political reasons, I have reconstructed Pisemskii's ideas based on a variety of sources: his correspondence, articles, literary criticism, fiction and views, reported by his contemporaries. In *Vzbalamuchennoe more*, Pisemskii's maverick narrator subverts an established literary tradition of omniscience and fashions an image of an author that would not seem out of place among self-consciously Romantic texts of decades earlier or among modernist meta-novels decades later. His appearance in an 1863 novel remains a curious phenomenon that challenges our assumptions about the predominantly mimetic nature of the Russian Realist tradition. This ontologically transgressive narrator occupies a fictional world presented to the reader in a series of frame-breaking and non-frame-breaking metalepses that define the overall structure of the novel.

Avdot'ia Panaeva's novel *Zhenskaia dolia*, as well as her other works of fiction, was published under a male pseudonym, Nikolai Stanitskii. Nonetheless, it featured a woman's perspective on the same issues of verisimilitude and didacticism in realist narratives that have occupied the other two writers whose texts are analysed in this book. The critical apparatus of feminist metafiction, rarely (or almost never) applied to nineteenth-century texts by Russian women writers, serves well to establish the specifics of Panaeva's narrative strategies. The issue of the masculinisation of the aesthetics of nineteenth-century literary realism is widely discussed in the scholarship on English and French novels but it remains a topic of marginal interest in Russian literary studies. Constrained by the social conventions that did not encourage women's participation in public debates, Panaeva put forward her thoughts on female emancipation, the power of imaginative literature, and the privileged point of view of traditional realist narratives, in a series of meta-observations or 'underarguments', integrated into the novel's narrative. A close reading of the passages in *Zhenskaia dolia* focused on the novel's transgressive narrator and his/her struggles against the boundaries of traditional gender roles. An analysis of *Zhenskaia dolia* as feminist metafiction and a feminine social novel allowed me to highlight the issues of narrative agenda and dominance that played out in the novel's plot and rhetoric.

Together, these three case studies challenge the reductionist understanding of Russian realism, showcasing the three writers who were consciously theorizing their own literary practice.

Metafiction often presents itself in the form of a novel because of that genre's tendency for introspection and dialogism. Literary works, as 'specific form[s] of philosophic thought in the broad sense',[1] have the capacity to explore — discursively — ideas that are of interest to philosophy. The literary origins of the problematisation of the ontology of fiction in Europe can be traced to the insights of Cervantes, whose 'critical-philosophical' awareness preceded Descartes's 'methodological skepticism'.[2] In a sense, the novel as a genre gained its unique introspective status through a critique of reality that was nevertheless expressed in a form that strove to achieve a recognisable mimetic representation.

It is therefore not surprising that metafiction as a narrative strategy tends to peak in the periods when the novel is rapidly developing, which is often mistaken for a crisis of the genre. In fact, these are the periods when novels are reinvented. Not every work of literature written in the mid-1860s contained metafictional elements (it would be equally fair to say that not every text produced in the 1970s and 1980s exemplified metafictional poetics), but my findings prove that the metafictional tradition in Russia remained strong throughout the nineteenth century and at times became dominant, as in the mid-1860s.

Naturally, the postmodernist (essentially poststructuralist) awareness of reality as a linguistic construct cannot be retrospectively imposed on any of the authors whose works are the object of this study. However, the peculiar fusion of ideological *Bildungsroman* and political *Künstlerroman*, for which the three novels analysed in this study can serve as representative examples, was a consequence of the specific intellectual atmosphere of the period. The abolition of serfdom, the wide-ranging social reforms, the final emergence of the intelligentsia as a distinct social group, and the prevalence of new forms of cultural production all contributed to the emergence of a heightened ideological self-awareness in this period.

Understanding the complex cultural processes of the long 1860s is of particular importance to contemporary Russian studies. The historical and social circumstances of the period did not only provide a conducive environment in which the inherently self-conscious nature of the Russian novel could be nurtured; they also forged a tradition in which any literary piece claiming to be truly literary had to be politically self-aware. As a result, modern Russian literature constantly questions its ontological status by measuring itself against the previous tradition of obligatory involvement with politics. The application of the theoretical framework of metafiction to the corpus of 1860s political novels challenges our assumptions about this most persistent of Russian literature's characteristic traits, re-examining its origins.

Notes to the Conclusion

1. Gary Saul Morson, *Narrative and Freedom: Shadows of Time* (New Haven: Yale University Press, 1994), p. 4. Morson further elaborates on Bakhtin's understanding that 'some of the greatest discoveries of world thought have taken place first, and sometimes, exclusively, in the visualisation of artistic form' (ibid., p. 87).
2. Alter, *Partial Magic*, p. x.

BIBLIOGRAPHY

Primary Texts

CHERNYSHEVSKII, N. G., *Polnoe sobranie sochinenii*, 15 vols (Moscow: GIKHL, 1939–53)
—— 'Moi svidaniia s F. M. Dostoevskim', in *F. M. Dostoevskii v vospominaniiakh sovremennikov*, ed. by A. S. Dolinin, 2 vols (Moscow: Khudozhestvennaia literatura, 1990), I, pp. 5–7
—— 'Russkii chelovek na rendez-vous. Razmyshleniia po prochtenii povesti g. Turgeneva "Asia"', *Atenei*, 18 (1858), 65–89
—— *Chto Delat'?*, ed. by T. I. Ornatskaia and S. A. Reiser (Leningrad: Nauka, 1975)
—— *What Is to Be Done?*, trans. by M. Katz (Ithaca: Cornell University Press, 1989)
FOWLES, JOHN, *The French Lieutenant's Woman* (London: Jonathan Cape, 1981)
GERTSEN, A. I., 'Vvoz nechistot v London', *Kolokol*, 15 December 1863, p. 1442
JAMES, HENRY, 'From the Preface to *The Tragic Muse*', in *The Portable Henry James*, ed. by John Auchard (London: Penguin, 2004), pp. 476–77
KHVOSHCHINSKAIA, N. D., 'Provintsial'nye pis'ma o nashei literature. Pis'mo tret'e. "Zhenskaia Dolia", roman Stanitskogo (Sovremennik, №3), "Otstalaia", povest' g-zhi Zhadovskoi (Vremia, №12)', *Otechestvennye zapiski*, 5 (1862), 37–38
PANAEV, I. I., 'Vospominanie o Belinskom', *Sovremennik*, 1 (1860), 335–55
PANAEVA, A. Ia., 'Zhenskaia dolia. Chast' pervaia', *Sovremennik*, 2 (1862), 51–176
—— 'Zhenskaia dolia. Chast' vtoraia', *Sovremennik*, 4 (1862), 504–31
—— 'Zhenskaia dolia. Chast' vtoraia. Okonchanie', *Sovremennik*, 5 (1862), 209–50
—— 'Kukol'naia tragediia s buketom grazhdanskoi skorbi', *Russkoe slovo*, 5 (1864), 1–58
—— *Russkie pisateli i artisty. Vospominaniia A. Ia. Golovachevoi–Panaevoi* (St Petersburg: Izdatel'stvo V. I. Gubinskogo, 1890)
—— *Vospominaniia* (Moscow: GIKHL, 1956)
PISAREV, D. I., *Literaturnaia kritika*, 3 vols (Leningrad: Khudozhestvennaia literatura, 1981)
—— *Sochineniia*, 10 vols (St Petersburg: Izdatel'stvo F. Pavlenkova, 1866–69)
—— *Polnoe sobranie sochinenii*, 6 vols (St Petersburg: Izdatel'stvo F. Pavlenkova, 1894–1907)
PISEMSKII, A. F., *Polnoe sobranie sochinenii*, 24 vols (St Petersburg: Vol'f, 1895)
—— *Polnoe sobranie sochinenii*, 8 vols (St Petersburg: Izdatel'stvo tovarishchestvo A. F. Marks, 1910–11)
—— *Pis'ma*, ed. by M. K. Kleman and A. P. Mogilianskii (Moscow: Izdatel'stvo Akademii nauk SSSR, 1936)
—— *Sobranie sochinenii*, 9 vols (Moscow: Pravda, 1959)
—— *Tysiacha dush* (Moscow: Komsomolskaia pravda, 2016)
PORECHNIKOV, V. see Khvoshchinskaia, N. D.
PUSHKIN, A. S., *Eugene Onéguine: A Romance of Russian Life in Verse*, trans. by Henry Spalding (London: Macmillan, 1881)
—— *Polnoe sobranie sochinenii*, 10 vols (Moscow and Leningrad: Izdatel'stvo Akademii nauk SSSR, 1949)
SALTYKOV, M. E., *Sobranie sochinenii*, 20 vols (Moscow: Khudozhestvennaia literatura, 1966–77)
STANITSKII, N. see Panaeva, A. Ia.

Secondary Literature

ABBOTT, H. PORTER, *The Cambridge Introduction to Narrative* (Cambridge: Cambridge University Press, 2002)
ALEKSANDROVA, I. V., 'A. S. Pushkin v tvorcheskom soznanii A. F. Pisemskogo', *II Krymskie pushkinskie chteniia: g. Kerch', 22–26 sentiabria 1992 g.: Materialy* (Simferopol': Krymskii komitet po pechati, 1993), 81–83
ALEKSEEV, V. A., *Istoriia russkoi zhurnalistiki, 1860–1880* (Leningrad: Leningradskii gosudarstvennyi universitet, 1963)
ALTER, ROBERT, *Partial Magic: The Novel as a Self-Conscious Genre* (Berkeley: University of California Press, 1975)
ANNENKOV, P. V., *Kriticheskie ocherki*, ed. by I. N. Sukhikh (St Petersburg: Izdatel'stvo RKhGI, 2000)
ANNINSKII, L. A., *Tri eretika, Pisateli o pisateliakh* (Moscow: Kniga, 1988)
ANTONOVA, G. N., 'N. N. Strakhov o romane "Chto delat'?"', in *N. G. Chernyshevskii: Stat'i, issledovaniia i materialy*, ed. by E. I. Pokusaev (Saratov: Izdatel'stvo Saratovskogo gosudarstvennogo universiteta, 1978), pp. 148–61
ARONSON, M. I., and S. A. REISER, eds, *Literaturnye kruzhki i salony* (Leningrad: Priboi, 1929)
ARUSTAMOVA, A. A., *Russko-amerikanskii dialog XIX veka: istoriko-literaturnyi aspekt* (Perm': Permskii gosudarstvennyi universitet, 2008)
BAL, MIEKE, *Narratology: Introduction to the Theory of Narrative* (Toronto: University of Toronto Press, 2009)
BARTH, JOHN, 'The Literature of Exhaustion', *The Atlantic Monthly*, 220.2 (1967), 29–34
BATESON, GREGORY, *Steps to Ecology of Mind* (Chicago: University of Chicago Press, 1972)
BEGLOV, V. L., 'Poisk "geroia vremeni" v romane A. F. Pisemskogo "Tysiacha dush"' in *Iz-za cherty*, ed. by I. E. Karpukhina (Sterlitamak: Sterlitamakskii gos. ped. in-t, 1999), pp. 38–52
BELOVA, N. M., *Roman N. G. Chernyshevskogo 'Chto delat'?' i prosvetitel'skaia literatura XVIII veka* (Saratov: Izdatel'stvo Saratovskogo universiteta, 1994)
BESSONOV, B. L., 'Ob avtorskoi prinadlezhnosti romana "Tri strany sveta"', *Nekrasovskii sbornik*, 6 (1978), 111–30
BETHEA, DAVID M., ed., *The Pushkin Handbook* (Madison: University of Wisconsin Press, 2005)
BOBORYKIN, P. D., 'Pamiati Pisemskogo', in *Literatura i zhizn'* <http://dugward.ru/library/pisemskiy/boborykin_pamyati_pisemsk.html> [accessed 7 August 2019]
—— *Za polveka: Vospominaniia* (Moscow: Zakharov, 2003)
BOGRAD, V. E., *Zhurnal 'Sovremennik', 1847–1866: Ukazatel' soderzhaniia* (Moscow: GIKHL, 1959)
BOOTH, WAYNE C., *The Rhetoric of Fiction* (Harmondsworth: Penguin, 1987)
BORISOV, I., 'Alekseevskii ravelin v 1862–65 gg. (Iz moikh vospominanii)', *Russkaia starina*, 12 (1901), 573–78
BOWERS, KATHERINE, 'The Fall of the House: Gothic Narrative and the Decline of the Russian Family', in *Russian Writers and Fin de Siècle: The Twilight of Realism*, ed. Katherine Bowers and Ani Kokobobo (Cambridge: Cambridge University Press, 2015), pp. 145–62
BOWERS, KATHERINE, and A. KOKOBOBO, eds, *Russian Writers and the* Fin de Siècle*: The Twilight of Realism* (Cambridge University Press, 2015)
BOWERS, KATHERINE, *Writing Fear: Russian Realism and the Gothic* (Toronto: University of Toronto Press, 2021)
BRODSKII, N. L. and N. P. SIDOROV, *Kommentarii k romanu N. G. Chernyshevskogo 'Chto delat'?'* (Moscow: Mir, 1933)

BROOKS, PETER, *The Melodramatic Imagination: Balzac, Henry James, Melodrama, and the Mode of Excess* (New Haven: Yale University Press, 1976)

BRUNSON, MOLLY, *Russian Realisms: Literature and Painting, 1840–1890* (DeKalb: Northern Illinois University Press, 2016)

BUKHSHTAB, B. IA., *Bibliograficheskie razyskaniia po russkoi literature XIX veka* (Moscow: Kniga, 1966)

BUSHKANETS, E. G., 'N. G. Chernyshevskii i pisateli-demokraty', in *N. G. Chernyshevskii. Stat'i, issledovaniia i materialy*, ed. by E. I. Pokusaev (Saratov: Saratavskoe knizhnoe izdatel'stvo, 1958), pp. 105–54

BYKOV, D. L., and M. O. EFREMOV, *Grazhdanin Poet. 31 nomer khudozhestvennoii samodeiatelnosti. Grazhdane besy* (Moscow: KoLibri, 2012)

CHEAURÉ, ELISABETH and E. N. STROGANOVA, eds, *Zhenskii vyzov: russkie pisatel'nitsy XIX– nachala XX veka* (Tver': Liliia Print, 2006)

CHERNYSHEVSKAIA, N. M., and I. V. POROKH, eds, *Delo Chernyshevskogo: sbornik dokumentov* (Saratov: Privolzhskoe knizhnoe izdatel'stvo, 1968)

CHESHIKHIN-VETRINSKII, V. E., 'Aleksei Feofilaktovich Pisemskii', in *Istoriia russkoi literatury*, ed. by D. N. Ovsianiko-Kulikovskii (Moscow: Mir, 1909), pp. 232–52

CHRISTENSEN, INGER, *The Meaning of Metafiction: A Critical Study of Sterne, Nabokov, Barth and Beckett* (Bergen: Universitetsforlagen, 1981)

CHUKOVSKII, K. I., 'Panaeva i ee vospominaniia', in *Vospominaniia*, ed. by K. I. Chukovskii and N. L. Brodskii (Moscow: GIKHL, 1956)

—— 'Panaeva i Nekrasov', in *Semeistvo Tal'nikovykh: Povest'*, ed. by N. P. Nekrasov and K. I. Chukovskii (Leningrad: Academia, 1928), pp. 5–79

—— *Zhena Poeta (Avdot'ia Iakovlevna Panaeva)* (St Petersburg: Epokha, 1922)

CLARK, KATERINA, *The Soviet Novel: History as Ritual* (Bloomington: Indiana University Press, 2000)

CLYMAN, TOBY W., and DIANA GREENE, eds, *Women Writers in Russian Literature* (Westport: Greenwood Press, 1994)

COHEN, MARGARET, and CHRISTOPHER PRENDERGAST, eds, *Spectacles of Realism: Body, Gender, Genre* (Minneapolis: University of Minnesota Press, 1995)

COHEN, MARGARET, *The Sentimental Education of the Novel* (Princeton: Princeton University Press, 1999)

CORNWELL, NEIL, ed., *The Society Tale in Russian Literature: From Odoevskii to Tolstoi* (Amsterdam: Rodopi, 1998)

CURRIE, MARK, ed., *Metafiction* (London: Longman, 2001)

DEMCHENKO, A. A., 'Nikolai Chernyshevskii: k 180-letiiu so dnia rozhdeniia', *Izvestiia Saratovskogo universiteta*, 9.1 (2009), 36–44

—— 'Pamiati M. I. Perper', *Novoe literaturnoe obozrenie*, 53 (2002), 258–60

DEMCHENKO, A. A., ed., *N. G. Chernyshevskii: pro et contra* (St Petersburg: RKhGA, 2008)

DEMCHENKO, A. A., and E. I. POKUSAEV, *N. G. Chernyshevskii: nauchnaia biografiia* (Saratov: Izdatel'stvo Saratovskogo universiteta, 1992)

DEMIDOVA, O. R., 'The Reception of Charlotte Brontë's Work in Nineteenth-Century Russia', *The Modern Language Review*, 89 (1994), 689–96

DOBRENKO, EVGENII, and GALIN TIHANOV, eds, *A History of Russian Literary Theory and Criticism: The Soviet Age and Beyond* (Pittsburgh: University of Pittsburgh Press, 2011)

DOLGIKH, U. M., 'Zhizn' i literaturnoe tvorchestvo A. Ia. Panaevoi' (unpublished doctoral thesis, Leningradskii gosudarstvennyi pedogagicheskii institut im. A. I. Gertsena, 1977)

DROZD, ANDREW M., *Chernyshevskii's 'What Is to Be Done?': A Reevaluation* (Evanston: Northwestern University Press, 2001)

ECO, UMBERTO, *The Role of the Reader: Explorations in the Semiotics of Text* (Bloomington: Indiana University Press, 1984)

Egorov, B. F., *Izbrannoe, Esteticheskie idei v Rossii XIX veka* (St Petersburg: Letnii sad, 2009)
Eremin, M. P., *A. F. Pisemskii* (Moscow: Znanie, 1956)
Etkind, A. M., *Tolkovanie Puteshestvii: Rossiia i Amerika v travelogakh i intertekstakh* (Moscow: Novoe literaturnoe obozrenie, 2001)
Evgen'ev-Maksimov, V. E., *'Sovremennik' pri Chernyshevskom i Dobroliubove* (Leningrad: GIKHL, 1936)
—— *'Sovremennik' v 40–50 gg.: ot Belinskogo do Chernyshevskogo* (Leningrad: Izdatel'stvo pisatelia, 1934)
—— *Poslednie gody 'Sovremennika': 1863–1866* (Leningrad: GIKHL, 1939)
Fainshtein, M. Sh., ed., *Russkie pisatel'nitsy i literaturnyi protsess v kontse XVIII–pervoi treti XX vv.: sbornik nauchnykh statei* (Wilhelmshorst: F. K. Göpfert, 1995)
Fanger, Donald, *Dostoevsky and Romantic Realism* (Chicago: University of Chicago Press, 1974)
Finke, Michael C., *Metapoesis: The Russian Tradition from Pushkin to Chekhov* (Durham, NC: Duke University Press, 1995)
Freeborn, Richard, *The Rise of the Russian Novel: Studies in the Russian Novel from 'Eugene Onegin' to 'War and Peace'* (Cambridge: Cambridge University Press, 1973)
Frolova, Iu. Iu., 'Poetika romana A. F. Pisemskogo "Tysiacha dush": khudozhestvennyi sintez realizma i sentimentalizma' (unpublished doctoral thesis, Voronezhskii gosudarstvennyi pedagogocheskii universitet, 2009)
—— 'Roman A. F. Pisemskogo "Tysiacha dush" i literaturnaia traditsiia' in *Eikhenbaumovskie chteniia-6: materialy iubileinoi nauchnoi konferentsii* (Voronezh: Voronezhskii gosudarstvennyi pedagogocheskii universitet, 2007), pp. 60–66
Fusso, Susan, *Editing Turgenev, Dostoevsky and Tolstoy: Mikhail Katkov and the Great Russian Novel* (DeKalb: Northern Illinois University Press, 2017)
Gasperetti, David, *The Rise of the Russian Novel: Carnival, Stylization, and Mockery of the West* (DeKalb: Northern Illinois University Press, 1998)
Gass, William H., *Fiction and the Figures of Life* (New York: Knopf, 1970)
Genette, Gérard, *Narrative Discourse: An Essay in Method*, trans. by Jane E. Lewin (Ithaca, NY: Cornell University Press, 1980)
Gheith, Jehanne M., *Finding the Middle Ground: Krestovskii, Tur, and the Power of Ambivalence in Nineteenth-Century Russian Women's Prose* (Evanston: Northwestern University Press, 2004)
Ginzburg, L. Ia., *O literaturnom geroe* (Leningrad: Sovetskii pisatel', 1979)
—— *O psikhologicheskoi proze* (Moscow: Intrada, 1999)
Gippius, Vassilii, 'Pushkin v bor'be s Bulgarinym v 1830–1831 gg.', *Pushkin: Vremennik Pushkinskoi komissii*, 6 (1941), 235–55
Goffman, Erving, *Frame Analysis: An Essay on the Organization of Experience* (Harmondsworth: Penguin, 1975)
Göpfert, F. K., ed., *Russland aus der Feder seiner Frauen: Zum femininen Diskurs in der russischen Literatur: Materialien des am 21/22 Mai 1992 im Fachbereich Slavistik der Universität Potsdam durchgeführten Kolloquiums* (Munich: O. Sagner, 1992)
Gregg, Richard, 'A Brackish Hippocrene: Nekrasov, Panaeva, and the "Prose in Love"', *Slavic Review*, 34 (1975), 731–51
Grenier, Svetlana Slavskaya, *Representing the Marginal Woman in Nineteenth-Century Russian Literature: Personalism, Feminism, and Polyphony* (Westport: Greenwood Press, 2001)
Gromova, L. D., V. N. Anoshkina, V. B. Kataev, eds, *Istoriia russkoi literatury XIX veka. 70–90-e gody* (Moscow: Izdatel'stvo MGU, 2001)
Gural'nik, U. A., *Nasledie N. G. Chernyshevskogo-pisatelia i sovetskoe literaturovedenie: itogi, zadachi, perspektivy izucheniia* (Moscow: Nauka, 1980)

HERRMANN, LESLEY, 'Jacques in Russia: A Program of Domestic Reform for Husbands', *Studies in the Literary Imagination*, 12 (1979), 61–72

HODKINSON, OWEN, *Metafiction in Classical Literature: The Invention of Self-Conscious Fiction* (London and New York: Routledge, 2016)

HOLMGREN, BETH, ed., *The Russian Memoir: History and Literature* (Evanston: Northwestern University Press, 2007)

HOOGENBOOM, HILDE, *Noble Sentiments and the Rise of Russian Novels* (Toronto: University of Toronto Press, 2021)

HUTCHEON, LINDA, *Narcissistic Narrative: The Metafictional Paradox* (Waterloo, Ont.: Wilfrid Laurier University Press, 1980)

—— *Narcissistic Narrative: The Metafictional Paradox*, 2nd edn (Waterloo, Ont.: Wilfried Laurier University Press, 2013)

IMHOF, RUDIGER, *Contemporary Metafiction: A Poetological Study of Metafiction in English since 1939* (Heidelberg: Winter, 1986)

ISER, WOLFGANG, *The Implied Reader: Patterns of Communication in Prose Fiction from Bunyan to Beckett* (Baltimore, MD: Johns Hopkins University Press, 1974)

JABLON, MADELYN, *Black Metafiction: Self-Consciousness in African American Literature* (Iowa City: University of Iowa Press, 1997)

JEFFERSON, ANN, *Reading Realism in Stendhal* (Cambridge: Cambridge University Press, 1988)

JENKINS, MAYA, 'A Study of A. F. Pisemsky and his Fate in Russian Literature' (unpublished doctoral thesis, University of London, University College, 1977)

JONES, MALCOLM V., and ROBIN FEUER MILLER, eds, *The Cambridge Companion to the Classic Russian Novel* (Cambridge: Cambridge University Press, 1998)

KAHN, ANDREW, M. N. LIPOVETSKII, IRINA REYFMAN, and STEPHANIE SANDLER, *A History of Russian Literature* (Oxford: Oxford University Press, 2018)

KAHN, MADELEINE, *Narrative Transvestism: Rhetoric and Gender in the Eighteenth-Century English Novel* (Ithaca, NY: Cornell University Press, 1991)

KALETSKII, P. I., 'Panaeva A. Ia.', in *Literaturnaia entsiklopediia*, 11 vols (Moscow: OGIZ RSFSR, 1929–39), VIII (1934), p. 421

KANDEL, B. L., 'Bibliografiia perevodov romana "Chto delat'?" na iazyki narodov SSSR i na inostrannye iazyki', in *Chto delat'?* (Leningrad: Nauka, 1975), pp. 862–69

KANTOR, V. K., 'Srublennoe derevo zhizni. Mozhno li segodnia razmyshliat' o Chernyshevskom?', *Oktiabr'*, 2 (2000), 157–80

KARAMZIN, N. M., *Izbrannye sochineniia*, 2 vols (Moscow: Khudozhestvennaia literatura, 1964)

KARP, CAROLE, 'George Sand and Turgenev: A Literary Relationship', *Studies in the Literary Imagination*, 12 (1979), 73–81

KATKOV, M. N., 'K kakoi my prinadlezhim partii', *Russkii vestnik*, 37 (1862), 832–44

—— 'Neskol'ko slov po povodu odnogo ironicheskogo slova', *Russkii vestnik*, 38 (1862), 463–81

—— 'Roman Turgeneva i ego kritiki', *Russkii vestnik*, 39 (1862), 393–424

—— 'Zametka dlia izdatelia Kolokola', *Russkii vestnik*, 39 (1862), 834–52

—— 'O nashem nigilizme (po povodu romana Turgeneva)', *Russkii vestnik*, 40 (1862), 402–26

—— 'Po povodu stat'i "Rokovoi vopros"', *Russkii vestnik*, 45 (1862), 398–418

KATZ, MICHAEL R., 'The Conclusion of *What Is to Be Done?*', *Russian Review*, 41 (1982), 181–96

KELLY, CATRIONA, 'The First-Person "Other": Sof'ia Soboleva's 1863 Story "Pros and Cons" (I Pro, i Contra)', *The Slavonic and East European Review*, 73 (1995), 61–81

—— *A History of Russian Women's Writing, 1820–1992* (Oxford: Clarendon Press, 1994)

KHATIAMOVA, M. A., *Formy literaturnoii samorefleksii v russkoi proze pervoi treti XX veka* (Moscow: Iazyki slavyanskoi kultury, 2008)

KOKOBOBO, ANI, *Russian Grotesque Realism* (Athens, OH: Ohio State University Press, 2018)

KOLESNIKOFF, NINA, *Russian Postmodernist Metafiction* (New York: Peter Lang, 2011)

KONDAKOV, I. V., 'Ot istorii literatury — k poetike kul'tury', *Voprosy literatury*, 2 (1997), 49–59

KOZ'MIN, B. L., *Zhurnalistika 60-kh godov XIX veka* (Moscow: Vysshaia partiinaia shkola, 1948)

KRUGLOVA, E. N., 'Khudozhestvennaia pozitsiia A. F. Pisemskogo v literaturnom protsesse 1840–60-kh godov' (unpublished doctoral thesis, Ivanovskii gosudarstvennyi universitet, 2008)

——*Khudozhestvennaia pozitsiia A. F. Pisemskogo v literaturnom protsesse 1840–60-kh godov: Avtoreferat dissertatsii na soiskanie uchenoi stepeni kandidata filologicheskikh nauk* (Kostroma: Ivanovskii gosudarstvennyi universitet, 2008)

KUIANTSEVA, A. O., 'Interpretatsiia romana A. Ia. Panaevoi "Zhenskaia Dolia" v kritike i literaturovedenii', *Visnik LNU im. Tarasa Shevchenka*, 3.214 (2011), 148–52

KUROCHKIN, V. S. [ZNAMENSKII], 'Pronitsatel'nye chitateli. (Iz rasskazov o starykh liudiakh)', *Iskra*, 32 (1863), 421–29

KUROVA, K. S., 'Tvorchestvo A. Ia. Panaevoi v 60-e gody', *Uchenye zapiski KGU: Iazyk i literatura*, 14 (1952), 39–58

——'Literaturnaia deiatel'nost' A. Ia. Panaevoi (Sotrudnichestvo pisatel'nitsy v "Sovremennike")' (unpublished doctoral thesis, Kazakhskii gosudarstvennyi universitet im. S. M. Kirova, 1950)

LAMARCHE MARRESE, MICHELLE, *A Woman's Kingdom: Noblewomen and the Control of Property in Russia, 1700–1861* (Ithaca: Cornell University Press, 2002)

LAZERSON, B. I., 'Ironiia v publitsistike N. G. Chernyshevskogo', in *N. G. Chernyshevskii: Stat'i, issledovaniia i materialy*, ed. by E. I. Pokusaev (Saratov: Izdatel'stvo Saratovskogo universiteta, 1958), pp. 272–335

LEDKOVSKY, MARINA, 'Avdotya Panaeva: Her Salon and Her Life', *Russian Literature Triquarterly*, 9 (1974), 426–32

LEMKE, M. K., *Epokha tsenzurnykh reform 1859–1865 godov* (St Petersburg: Gerold, 1904)

——*Politicheskie protsessy M. I. Mikhailova, D. I. Pisareva i N. G. Chernyshevskago: po neizdannym dokumentam* (St Petersburg: Izdatel'stvo O. N. Popovoi, 1907)

LENIN, V. I., *Chto delat'? Nabolevshie voprosy nashego dvizheniia* (Stuttgart: Verlag von J. H. W. Dietz, 1902)

——*Lenin o literature i iskusstve* (Moscow: Khudozhestvennaia literatura, 1976)

LIPOVETSKII, M. N., *Russkii postmodernizm: ocherki istoricheskoi poetiki* (Ekaterinburg: Ural'skii gosudarstvennyi pedagogicheskii universitet, 1997)

LIPOVETSKII, MARK, *Russian Postmodernist Fiction: Dialogue with Chaos* (New York: M. E. Sharpe, 1999)

LISTRATOVA, A. V., 'O literaturno-obschestvennoi positsii A. F. Pisemskogo 60-kh godov', *Uchenye zapiski Ivanovskogo gosudarstvennogo pedagogicheskogo instituta*, 38 (1967), 48–49

LOMUNOV, K. N., ed., *'Chto delat'?' N. G. Chernyshevskogo: istoriko-funktsional'noe issledovanie* (Moscow: Nauka, 1990)

LORENZ, SARAH RUTH, 'Visionary Mimesis: Imitation and Transformation in the German Enlightenment and Russian Realism' (unpublished doctoral thesis, University of California, Berkeley, 2012)

LOSEFF, LEV, *On the Beneficence of Censorship: Aesopian Language in Modern Russian Literature* (Munich: Otto Sagner, 1984)

LOTMAN, IU. M., *Roman A. S. Pushkina 'Evgenii Onegin': Kommentarii. Posobie dlia uchitelia* (Leningrad: Prosveshenie, 1983)

LOTMAN, L. M., 'A. F. Pisemskii', in *Istoriia russkoi literatury* (Leningrad: Nauka, 1982), pp. 203–31
LOVELL, TERRY, *Pictures of Reality: Aesthetics, Politics and Pleasure* (London: BFI Publishing, 1980)
LUNACHARSKII, A. V., *Stat'i o literature* (Moscow: Khudozhestvennaia literatura, 1988)
MANCHESTER, LAURIE, *Holy Fathers, Secular Sons: Clergy, Intelligentsia, and the Modern Self in Revolutionary Russia* (DeKalb: Northern Illinois University Press, 2008)
MARKOVICH, V. M., and G. E. POTAPOVA, eds, *Pushkin: Pro et contra*, 2 vols (St Petersburg: Izdatel'stvo Russkogo khristianskogo gumanitarnogo instituta, 2000)
MARSH, ROSALIND J., ed., *Gender and Russian Literature: New Perspectives* (Cambridge: Cambridge University Press, 1996)
MARTINSEN, DEBORAH A., ed., *Literary Journals in Imperial Russia* (Cambridge: Cambridge University Press, 1997)
MARUSENKO, M. A., 'Atributsiia romanov "Tri strany sveta" i "Mertvoe ozero"', *Vestnik SPbGU*, 1 (1997), 37–52
MASHINSKII, S. I., ed., *N. V. Gogol' v vospominaniiakh sovremennikov* (Moscow: GIKHL, 1952)
MEL'GUNOV, B. V., 'O novykh atributsiiakh romanov "Tri strany sveta" i "Mertvoe ozero"', *Russkaia literatura*, 3 (1998), 98–103
METLASOVA, T. M., *Intertekstual'nost', reministsentsii i avtorskie maski v romane N. G. Chernyshevskogo 'Povesti v povesti'. Avtoreferat dissertatsii na soiskanie uchenoi stepeni kandidata filologicheskikh nauk* (Saratov: Saratovskii gosudarstvennyi universitet, 2006)
MILIUKOV, A. P., *Otgoloski na literaturnye i obshhestvennye iavleniia* (St Petersburg: Tipografia F. S. Sushchinskago, 1875)
MILLER, O. F., *Russkie pisateli posle Gogolia: chteniia, rechi i stat'i*, 3 vols (St Petersburg: Izdatel'stvo tovarishchestva M. O. Vol'f, 1890–1906)
MORSON, GARY SAUL, 'Reading Between the Genres: Dostoevsky's *Diary of a Writer* as Metafiction', *Yale Review*, 68 (1978), 224–34
—— *The Boundaries of Genre: Dostoevsky's Diary of a Writer and the Traditions of Literary Utopia* (Austin: University of Texas Press, 1981)
—— *Narrative and Freedom: The Shadows of Time* (New Haven: Yale University Press, 1994)
MOSER, CHARLES A., 'Pisemskii's Literary Protest: An Episode from the Polemics of the 1860s in Russia', *Études slaves et est-européennes*, 8.1–2 (1963), 60–72
—— *Pisemsky: A Provincial Realist* (Cambridge, MA: Harvard University Press, 1969)
—— *Esthetics as Nightmare: Russian Literary Theory, 1855–1870* (Princeton: Princeton University Press, 1989)
NABOKOV, VLADIMIR, *Eugene Onegin: A Novel in Verse by Aleksandr Pushkin*, trans. and comm. by Vladimir Nabokov, 4 vols (New York: Bollingen Foundation, 1964)
NIKULICHEV, Iu. V., 'Bog, mamona i obyknovennye novye liudi: ot "Kto vinovat?" k "Chto delat'?"', *Voprosy literatury*, 2 (2014), 142–75
NORTON, BARBARA T., and JEHANNE M. GHEITH, eds, *An Improper Profession: Women, Gender, and Journalism in Late Imperial Russia* (Durham, NC: Duke University Press, 2001)
NOVIKOVA, N. N., and B. M. KLOSS, *N. G. Chernyshevskii vo glave revoliutsionerov 1861 goda* (Moscow: Nauka, 1981)
ORWIN, DONNA TUSSING, *Consequences of Consciousness: Turgenev, Dostoevsky, and Tolstoy* (Stanford, CA: Stanford University Press, 2007)
PAPERNO, IRINA, *Chernyshevsky and the Age of Realism: A Study in the Semiotics of Behavior* (Stanford, CA: Stanford University Press, 1988)
—— 'Russkie kritiki 1830–1860-kh godov v bor'be za vlast'', *Novoe literaturnoe obozrenie*, 6 (2011), 403–07

―――*Semiotika povedeniia: N. G. Chernyshevskii: Chelovek epokhi realizma* (Moscow: Novoe literaturnoe obozrenie, 1996)
PAVLOVA, E. V., *Belletristika A. F. Pisemskogo 1840–1850-kh gg. i problema khudozhestvennogo metoda: Avtoreferat dissertatsii na soiskanie uchenoi stepeni kandidata filologicheskikh nauk* (Cherepovets: Pskovskii gosudarstvennyi universitet, 2007)
―――'Belletristika A. F. Pisemskogo 1840–1850-kh gg. i problema khudozhestvennogo metoda' (unpublished doctoral thesis, Pskovskii gosudarstvennyi universitet, 2007)
PETERS, JOAN DOUGLAS, *Feminist Metafiction and the Evolution of the British Novel* (Gainesville: University Press of Florida, 2002)
PLEKHANOV, S. N., *Pisemskii* (Moscow: Molodaia gvardiia, 1986)
POKUSAEV, E. I., 'N. G. Chernyshevskii i M. E. Saltykov-Shchedrin', *Uchenye zapiski Saratovskogo gosudarstvennogo universiteta im. N. G. Chernyshevskogo*, 19 (1948), 35–101
PRINCE, GERALD, *Narratology: The Form and Functioning of Narrative* (Berlin: Mouton, 1982)
PROKOF'EV, V. A. and OTHERS, eds, *Spodvizhniki Chernyshevskogo* (Moscow: Molodaia gvardiia, 1961)
PUSTARNAKOV, V. F., *Filosofiia prosveshcheniia v Rossii i vo Frantsii: opyt sravnitel'nogo analiza* (Moscow: Rossiiskaia akademiia nauk, Institut filosofii, 2002)
PUSTOVOIT, P. G., *A. F. Pisemskii v istorii russkogo romana* (Moscow: Izdatel'stvo Moskovskogo universiteta, 1969)
REIFMAN, P. S., 'Shchedrin i Chernyshevskii (po materialam khronik "Nasha obshchestvennaia zhizn"')', *Uchenye zapiski Tartuskogo gosudarstvennogo universiteta. Trudy po russkoi i slavianskoi filologii. XI. Literaturovedenie*, 209 (1968), 109–12
REISER, S. A., 'Nekotorye problemy izucheniia romana "Chto delat'?"', in *Chto delat'?* (Leningrad: Nauka, 1975), pp. 782–834
REITBLAT, A. I., *Faddei Venediktovich Bulgarin: ideolog, zhurnalist, konsul'tant sekretnoi politsii: Stat'i i materialy* (Moscow: Novoe literaturnoe obozrenie, 2016)
RIFFATERRE, MICHAEL, *Fictional Truth* (Baltimore: Johns Hopkins University Press, 1989)
RIMMON-KENAN, SHLOMITH, *Narrative Fiction: Contemporary Poetics* (London: Methuen, 1983)
ROSE, MARGARET A., *Parody//meta-fiction: An Analysis of Parody as a Critical Mirror to the Writing and Reception of Fiction* (London: Croom Helm, 1979)
ROSENHOLM, ARJA, and FRANK GÖPFERT, eds, *Vieldeutiges Nicht-zu-Ende-Sprechen: Thesen und Momentaufnahmen aus der Geschichte russischer Dichterinnen* (Fichtenwalde: Göpfert, 2002)
ROSHAL', A. A., *Pisemskii i revoliutsionnaia demokratiia* (Baku: Azerbaidzhanskoe gosudarstvennoe izdatel'stvo, 1971)
RUDENKO, IU. K., *Chernyshevskii-romanist i literaturnye traditsii* (Leningrad: Izdatel'stvo Leningradskogo universiteta, 1989)
―――*Chernyshevskii-romanist i literaturnye traditsii. Avtoreferat dissertatsii na soiskanie uchenoi stepeni doktora filologicheskikh nauk* (Leningrad: Leningradskii gosudarstvennyi universitet, 1990)
―――*Roman N. G. Chernyshevskogo 'Chto delat'?': Esteticheskoe svoeobrazie i khudozhestvennyi metod* (Leningrad: Izdatel'stvo LGU, 1979)
RUUD, CHARLES, *Fighting Words: Imperial Censorship and the Russian Press, 1804–1906* (Toronto: University of Toronto Press, 1982)
SCANLAN, JAMES P., 'Chernyshevskii and Rousseau', in *Western Philosophical Systems in Russian Literature: A Collection of Critical Studies*, ed. by Anthony M. Mlikotin (Los Angeles: University of Southern California Press, 1979), pp. 103–19
SCHOLES, ROBERT, *Fabulation and Metafiction* (Urbana: University of Illinois Press, 1979)
SCHOR, NAOMI, *Breaking the Chain: Women, Theory, and French Realist Fiction* (New York: Columbia University Press, 1985)

SEGAL, D. M., *Literatura kak okhrannaia gramota* (Moscow: Vodolei, 2006)
SHELGUNOV, N. V., 'Zhenskoe bezdushie: Po povodu sochinenii V. Krestovskogo-psevdonima', *Delo*, 9 (1870), 1–34
—— *Literaturnaia kritika* (Leningrad: Khudozhestvennaia literatura, 1974)
SHEPHERD, DAVID, *Beyond Metafiction: Self-Consciousness in Soviet Literature* (Oxford: Clarendon Press, 1992)
SINIAKOVA, L. N., *Kontseptsiia cheloveka v romanakh A. F. Pisemskogo 1860–1870-kh gg.* (Novosibirsk: Novosibirskii gosudarstvennyi universitet, 2007)
SKABICHEVSKII, A. M., *A. F. Pisemskii, ego zhizn' i literaturnaia deiatel'nost* (St Petersburg: Tipografiia tovarishchestva 'Obshchestvennaia pol'za', 1894)
—— *Ocherkii istorii russkoi tsenzury, 1700–1863 gg.* (St Petersburg: Tipografiia tovarishchestva 'Obshchestvennaia pol'za', 1892)
SKAFTYMOV, A. P., *Stat'i o russkoi literature* (Saratov: Saratovskoe knizhnoe izdatel'stvo, 1958)
SOBOLEVA, OLGA, 'Ostrovskii v sovremennoi shkole', *Literaturnaia gazeta*, 36 (2014), p. 4
SOLOV'EV, N. S., 'Teoriia bezobraziia', *Epokha*, 7 (1864), 1–16
SOMOFF, VICTORIA, *The Imperative of Reliability: Russian Prose on the Eve of the Novel 1820–1850* (Evanston: Northwestern University Press, 2015)
SPIRES, ROBERT, *Beyond the Metafictional Mode: Directions in the Modern Spanish Novel* (Lexington: University Press of Kentucky, 1984)
STEPANOV, N. L., and U. R. FOKHT, eds, *Problemy tipologii russkogo realizma* (Moscow: Nauka, 1969)
TAMARCHENKO, G. E., '"Chto delat'?" i russkii roman shestidesiatykh godov', in *Chto delat'?* (Leningrad: Nauka, 1975), pp. 747–82
—— *Chernyshevskii-romanist* (Leningrad: Khudozhestvennaia literatura, 1976)
—— *Romany N. G. Chernyshevskogo* (Saratov: Saratovskoe knizhnoe izdatel'stvo, 1954)
TATARKINA, S. V., 'Tvorchestvo A. Ia. Panaevoi v literaturnom kontekste epokhi: gendernyi aspekt' (unpublished doctoral thesis, Tomskii gosudarstvennyi universitet, 2006)
TEPLINSKII, M. V., 'Avtor-povestvovatel'' v romane N. G. Chernyshevskogo "Chto delat'?"', *N. G. Chernyshevskii: stat'i, issledovaniia i materialy*, 8 (1978), 127–37
TERRAS, VICTOR, *Handbook of Russian Literature* (New Haven: Yale University Press, 1985)
TODD, WILLIAM MILLS III, *Fiction and Society in the Age of Pushkin: Ideology, Institutions, and Narrative* (Cambridge, MA: Harvard University Press, 1986)
TOLSTOI, F. M. [ROSTISLAV], 'Lzhemudrost'' gerocv g. Chernyshevskogo', *Severnaia pchela*, 27 May 1863, pp. 551–53
TSEBRIKOVA, MARIA, 'Psevdonovaia geroina (o romane I.A. Goncharova "Obryv")', *Otechestvennye zapiski*, 5 (1870), 41–42
TSEITLIN, A. G., 'Siuzhetika antinigilisticheskogo romana', *Literatura i marksizm*, 2 (1929), 33–74
TYNIANOV, IU. N., *Poetika, istoriia literatury, kino* (Moscow: Nauka, 1977)
USPENSKII, B. M., 'Iazykovaia programma N. M. Karamzina i ego storonnikov', in *Kratkii ocherk istorii russkogo literaturnogo iazyka (XI–XIX vv.)* (Moscow: Gnozis, 1994), pp. 150–56
VAIL', P., and A. GENIS, *Rodnaia rech'* (Moscow: Nezavisimaia gazeta, 1994)
VAKHRUSHEV, V. S., '"Chto delat'?" i "Avtobiografia" N. G. Chernyshevskogo: igrovye khody avtorskoi mysli', *N. G. Chernyshevskii: stat'i, issledovania, materialy*, 13 (1999), 14–30
VALENTINOV, N. G., *Nedorisovannyi portret* (Moscow: Terra, 1993)
M. I. VAYSMAN, 'Melodramaticheskaia i ideologicheskaia modal'nost'' v romane N.G. Chernyshevskogo "Chto delat'?"', *Vestnik Piatigorskogo gosudarstvennogo lingvisticheskogo universiteta*, 3.2 (2009), 193–96
—— *Melodramaticheskaia modal'nost v romane N. G. Chernyshevskogo 'Chto delat'?': Avtoreferat dissertatsii na soiskanie uchenoi stepeni kandidata filologicheskikh nauk* (Perm': Permskii gosudarstvennyi natsional'nyi issledovatel'skii universitet, 2011)

—— 'Problemy osveshcheniia romana N. G. Chernyshevskogo "Chto delat'?" v nauchnoi i kriticheskoi literature (1863–2011)', *Vestnik Permskogo universiteta. Rossiiskaia i zarubezhnaia filologiia*, 1 (2011), 130–39

—— '"Unnecessary Melodrama": Ideology and Narrative Legacy in Nikolai Chernyshevskii's *What Is to Be Done?* (1863) and William Godwin's *Caleb Williams* (1794)', *Modern Language Review*, 112.1 (2017), 1–19

VDOVIN, A. V., 'Chernyshevskii vs. Feierbakh: (psevdo)istochniki dissertatsii "Esteticheskie otnosheniia iskusstva k deistvitel'nosti"', *Zeitschrift für Slavische Philologie*, 68.1 (2011), 39–66

VDOVIN, A. V., K. YU. ZUBKOV, and A. S. FEDOTOV, eds, *Sovremennik protiv Moskvitianina: literaturno-kriticheskaia polemika 1850-kh gg.* (St Petersburg: Nestor-Istoriia, 2015)

VENGEROV, S. A., *Aleksei Feofilaktovich Pisemskii: Kritiko-biograficheskii ocherk* (Moscow: Tovarishchestvo M. O. Vol'f, 1884)

VERDEREVSKAIA, N. A., *Russkii roman 40–60-kh godov XIX veka: tipologiia zhanrovykh form* (Kazan': Izdatel'stvo Kazanskogo universiteta, 1980)

WAUGH, PATRICIA, *Metafiction: The Theory and Practice of Self-Conscious Fiction* (London: Routledge, 1984)

WEISGERBER, JEAN, 'Satire and Irony as Means of Communication', *Comparative Literature Studies*, 10 (1973), 152–71

WELLEK, RENÉ, 'Auerbach's Special Realism', *The Kenyon Review*, 16 (1954), 299–307

—— *Concepts of Criticism*, ed. by Stephen G. Nichols, Jr. (New Haven: Yale University Press, 1973)

WOODHOUSE, JENNY, 'A Realist in a Changing Reality: A. F. Pisemsky and "Vzbalamuchennoye More"', *The Slavonic and East European Review*, 64 (1986), 489–505

ZAITSEV, V. A., 'Vzbalamuchennyi romanist', *Russkoe slovo*, 10 (1863), 23–44

—— 'Glupovtsy, popavshie v "Sovremennik"', *Russkoe slovo*, 2 (1864), 34–42

ZAITSEVA, E. L., 'Poetika psikhologizma v romanakh A. F. Pisemskogo' (unpublished doctoral thesis, Rossiiskii Universitet Druzhby Narodov, 2008)

ZELINSKII, V. V., 'Aleksei Feofilaktovich Pisemskii, ego zhizn', literaturnaia deiatel'nost' i znachenie ego v istorii russkoi pis'mennosti: kritiko-biograficheskii ocherk', in A. F. Pisemskii, *Polnoe sobranie sochinenii*, 24 vols (St Petersburg: Tovarishchestvo M. O. Vol'f, 1885), I, pp. 15–107

ZHAO, Y. H., 'The Rise of Metafiction in China', *Bulletin of the School of Oriental and African Studies, University of London*, 55.1 (1992), 90–99

ZHIRKOV, G. V., *Istoriia tsenzury v Rossii XIX–XX vv.* (Moscow: Aspekt Press, 2001)

ZHULEV, G. N., 'Gor'kaia sud'bina kota, ili legkaia boinia. Vzbalamuchennaia opera v neskol'kikh aktakh', *Iskra*, 4 (1863), 583

ZUBKOV, K. IU., 'Antinigilisticheskii roman kak polemicheskii konstrukt radikal'noi kritiki', *Vestnik MGU. Seriia 9. Filologiia*, 4 (2005), 122–40

—— 'Roman A. F. Pisemskogo "Vzbalamuchennoe more": vospriiatie sovremennikov i istoriia teksta', in *Ozernaia tekstologiia: trudy IV letnei shkoly na karel'skom peresheike po tekstologii i istochnikovedeniiu russkoi literatury* (Poselok Poliany (Uusikirko) Leningradskoi oblasti: St. Peterburgskii institut iudaiki, 2007), pp. 97–109

—— 'Povesti i romany A. F. Pisemskogo 1850-kh godov: povestvovanie, kontekst, traditsiia' (unpublished doctoral thesis, SPbGU, 2011)

—— 'Ekspertnyi korpus Uvarovskoi premii dlia dramaturgov: sostav i evoliutsiia', *Karabikha: Istoriko-literaturnyi sbornik*, 10 (2018), 92–118

Online Resources

BOBORYKIN, P. D., 'Pamiati Pisemskogo', in *Literatura i zhizn*' <http://dugward.ru/library/pisemskiy/boborykin_pamyati_pisemsk.html> [accessed 7 August 2019]

CHUKOVSKII, K. I., 'Panaeva' <http://nekrasov.niv.ru/nekrasov/bio/panaeva/ocherk-chukovskogo.html> [accessed 10 August 2019]

NESTERENKO, MARIIA, 'Zhenshchiny pishut o tom, chto volnuet imenno ikh', *Prochtenie.org* <https://prochtenie.org/texts/29447> [accessed 6 August 2019]

PIER, JOHN, 'Metalepsis', in *The Living Handbook of Narratology* <http://wikis.sub.uni-hamburg.de/lhn/index.php/Metalepsis> [accessed 13 August 2019]

SCHMID, WOLF, 'Implied Author', in *The Living Handbook of Narratology* <hup.sub.uni-hamburg.de/lhn/index.php ?title=Implied Author &oldid=2068> [accessed 9 August 2019]

SCHOR, NAOMI, 'Rereading in Detail: Or, Aesthetics, the Feminine, and Idealism', *Criticism*, 32.3 (1990) <http://digitalcommons.wayne.edu/criticism/vol32/iss3/3/> [accessed 12 August 2019]

Slovar'Ozhegova: tolkovyi slovar' russkogo iazyka <http://www.ozhegov.com/words/11435.shtml> [accessed 18 August 2019]

Tolkovyi slovar' Dalia onlain <http://slovardalja.net/word.php?wordid=12229> [accessed 18 August 2019]

INDEX

aesopian language 35
Akhmatova, Anna 5
Amis, Martin 4
Anennkov, Pavel 83
Antonovich, Maksim 21
Askochenskii, Viktor 27
Auerbach, Erich 91
Avenarius, Vasilii 27

Bart, John 4
Beckett, Samuel 5
Belinskii, Vissarion 9, 10, 24, 37, 50, 88, 90–92, 123
Bellow, Saul 4
Bestuzhev-Marlinskii, Aleksandr 23
Biblioteka dlia chteniia 81, 84, 87, 89
Boborykin, Petr 79, 89
Borges, Jorge Luis 4
Botkin, Vasilii 40
Bradbury, Malcolm 4
Brontë, Charlotte 113
Bulgakov, Mikhail 5
Bulgarin, Faddei 23
Burgess, Anthony 4
Buslaev, Fedor 89

censorship 112–13
Cervantes 5, 7, 89, 145
Chekhov, Anton 5, 6
Chernyshevskii, Nikolai:
  life:
    at university 31
    family 56
    at *Sovremennik* 20, 21, 24, 25, 32, 81, 118, 199
    arrest and exile 34, 39, 42
    trial 57
    in scholarship and criticism 26, 35–37, 39–40, 89
  works:
    Antropologicheskii printsip v filosofii 37
    Chto delat? 2, 6, 10, 12, 13, 21, 25–27, 31–67, 94, 97, 105, 111, 113, 117, 125, 130, 143–44
    Esteticheskie otnosheniia iskusstva k deistvitel'nosti 31
    Istoriia material'noi i umstvennoi deiatel'nosti chelovechestva 42
    Kriticheskii slovar' idei i faktov 42
    Ne nachalo li peremeny? 37
    Povesti v povesti 34
    Prolog 34

journal articles 49
  aesthetic theory 67
Chukovskii, Kornei 114–16
Cortázar, Julio 4

Diderot, Denis 5, 26
Dobroliubov, Nikolai 21, 38, 92, 118
Dostoevskii, Fedor 3, 5, 6, 9, 20, 36, 79, 86
  Besy 86
  Dnevnik pisatelia 5
Druzhinin, Aleksandr 80–81, 91

Egorov, Boris 21
Eliot, George 6, 91
  Adam Bede 6
Enlightenment 26, 50

Fet, Afanasii 40
Fielding, Henry 6, 45, 66, 91
Fowles, John 4

Gass, William H. 4
Gertsen, Aleksandr 46, 81, 82
Gide, André 5
Ginzburg, Lidiia 8, 38
Gogol, Nikolai 3, 5, 6, 8, 9, 23, 36, 88, 89, 90, 91, 93, 113, 132
  Mertvye dushi 5, 23, 90
  Revizor 132
Goncharov, Ivan 20, 46, 79, 82, 83
Grass, Günter 5

Hegel, Georg Wilhelm Friedrich 37

Jakobson, Roman 3, 5, 11

Karamzin, Nikolai 49
Katkov, Mikhail 22, 25, 81, 84–86, 97, 98
Khvoshchinskaia, Nadezhda 20, 131
Kraevskii, Andrei 32, 80, 92

Lenin, Vladimir 34, 86
Leont'ev, Konstantin 21, 27
Lermontov, Mikhail 3, 89
Leskov, Nikolai 20, 40, 82

Mandel'shtam, Osip 5

metalepsis 11–12, 35–37, 54–55, 58–59, 65–66, 104–05, 143
Miliukov, Pavel 85, 87
Moser, Charles A. 21–22, 24, 36, 82
Moskvitianin 80

Nabokov, Vladimir 1, 4–6
narrative transvestism 11–12, 114, 128
Nekrasov, Nikolai 25, 32, 34, 37, 42, 81, 84, 111, 112, 115
nihilism 84, 86

Odoevskii, Vladimir 23
ontology 26–27, 35, 37–38, 57, 64, 66–67, 94, 144–45
Ostrovskii, Nikolai 79, 80–81, 105
Otechestvennye zapiski 32, 81, 90

Panaev, Ivan 32, 111, 119
Panaeva, Avdot'ia:
  life:
    at *Sovremennik* 20, 25, 32, 111–12
    in scholarship and criticism 26, 114–16
  works:
    Bezobraznyi muzh 120
    Domashnii ad 120
    Mertvoe ozero 112
    Neobdumannyi shag 120
    Neostorozhnoe slovo 112
    Sashka 120
    Semeistvo Tal'nikovykh 112
    Stepnaya baryshnia 120
    Tri strany sveta 112
    Vospominaniia 114, 116
    Zhenskaia dolia 2, 11–13, 21, 25–27, 97, 111–35, 144–45
parody 1, 9, 22, 36, 81, 113, 119, 132
Peterburgskie vedomosti 84, 102
Pisarev, Dmitrii 10, 21, 26, 38, 40, 80, 82, 87, 112, 116, 117, 118, 128
Pisemskii, Aleksei:
  life:
    as editor and journalist 20, 25, 81–82, 84, 117, 119, 125
    in criticism and scholarship 26, 79, 80
  works:
    Bogatyi zhenikh 81
    Gor'kaia sud'bina 81
    Liudi sorokovykh godov 87
    Ob izdanii zhurnala "Biblioteka dlia Chteniia" v 1861 godu 81
    Russkie lguny 90
    Staraia barynia 81
    Starcheskii grekh 26, 93, 101–02

Tiufiak 80
Tysiacha dush 81
Vzbalamuchennoe more 12–13, 21, 25, 27, 36, 46, 80–104, 111, 113, 128, 130, 144
  aesthetic theory 10, 27, 88–92, 144
Pletnev, Petr 32
Pogodin, Mikhail 80
Pomialovskii, Nikolai 45
prolepsis 43–45
Pushkin, Aleksandr 1, 3, 4, 6, 8, 31, 36, 89
  Evgenii Onegin 1, 5, 9, 23, 98

Rozanov, Vladimir 5
Russkii vestnik 25, 38, 40, 81, 84–86, 97, 102
Russkoe slovo 41, 116–17

Saltykov-Shchedrin, Mikhail 41, 80
  Gospoda Golovlevy 123
Sand, George 89, 112
Scott, Walter 89
Sentimentalism 120
Severnaia pchela 39, 40
Shelgunov, Nikolai 80–81, 88, 117–18
Shklovskii, Viktor 1, 39
Smollett, Tobias 89
Sovremennik 10, 21, 25, 31–34, 37, 39, 42, 81, 83–84, 102, 111–19
Stendhal 7, 8, 20, 120
Sterne, Laurence 5, 31, 45, 60, 66
Strakhov, Nikolai 39–40
Sue, Eugène 96

Tolstoi, Lev 3, 6, 8, 20, 36, 79, 86, 91, 94
  Sevastopol'skie rasskazy 111
translation 31, 34, 42
Tur, Evgeniia 20, 114, 116, 118
Turgenev, Ivan 20, 22, 46, 79, 82–84, 87, 90
  Ottsy i deti 21, 86
  Zapiski okhotnika 111

unreliable narrator 39, 41, 48, 66
Uspenskii, Nikolai 45

Vaginov, Konstantin 5
Valuev, Petr 83
Vel'tman, Aleksandr 23
Viazemskii, Petr 32
Vonnegut, Kurt 4

Wellek, René 91
woman question 25, 49, 113, 116–18, 120, 130, 134–35

Zhukova, Mariia 114, 119